The Transformation of the Classical Heritage

Peter Brown, General Editor

The Memory of the Eyes

The Memory of the Eyes

Pilgrims to Living Saints in Christian Late Antiquity

Georgia Frank

UNIVERSITY OF CALIFORNIA PRESS

Berkeley   Los Angeles   London

University of California Press
Berkeley and Los Angeles, California

University of California Press, Ltd.
London, England

Library of Congress Cataloging-in-Publication Data
Frank, Georgia, 1963–
    The memory of the eyes : pilgrims to living saints in
    Christian late antiquity / Georgia Frank.
       p.   cm. — (The Transformation of the classical
    heritage ; 30)
    Includes bibliographical references and index.
    ISBN 0-520-22205-9 (alk. paper)
    1. Historia monachorum in Aegypto. 2. Palladius,
Bishop of Aspuna, d. ca. 430. Lausiac history. 3. Christian
pilgrims and pilgrimages—History. 4. Monasticism and
religious orders—Egypt—History. I. Title. II. Series.
BR190.H573 F73   2000
270.2—dc21

                                        99-056845

Manufactured in the United States of America

09 08 07 06 05 04 03 02 01 00   10 9
8 7 6 5 4 3 2 1

Portions of chapter 2 have appeared in "The *Historia Monachorum* and Ancient Travel Writing," *Studia Patristica* 30
(1997): 191–95, and in "Miracles, Monks, and Monuments:
The *Historia Monachorum in Aegypto* as Pilgrims' Tales," in
Pilgrimage and Holy Space in Late Antique Egypt, edited by
David Frankfurter (Leiden: Brill, 1998), 483–505. Reprinted
with permission.

Chapter 4 of this book is a revised and expanded version of
my chapter "The Pilgrim's Gaze in the Age before Icons," in
*Other Ways of Seeing: Visuality before and beyond the Renais-
sance*, edited by Robert S. Nelson (Cambridge University
Press, forthcoming). Reprinted with the permission of Cambridge University Press.

For my parents

CONTENTS

ACKNOWLEDGMENTS

Many teachers, friends, and colleagues have given generously of themselves to support and encourage me during this project. It is a great pleasure to thank them here. Michael E. Stone first introduced me to the richness of pilgrims' stories in a graduate research course at Harvard University in 1988. The ensuing doctoral dissertation took shape under the expert guidance of Susan Ashbrook Harvey and Margaret R. Miles. I count myself fortunate to have had such trusting, generous, and, above all, inspiring teachers.

Derek Krueger deserves special thanks for reading and commenting on various drafts of every chapter. An astute reader of saints' lives, he deepened my own appreciation for the power of Christian storytelling. I am also grateful to Peter Brown, Elizabeth A. Clark, James Goehring, Patricia Cox Miller, and an anonymous reader for UC Press, who, at various stages, graciously read the entire manuscript and offered valuable suggestions for improvement.

Many other colleagues provided expert comments on individual chapters. Several of them also shared their own research prior to publication. In particular, I thank David Brakke, Virginia Burrus, Douglas Burton-Christie, Susan Calef, Amy DeRogatis, David Frankfurter, Helmut Koester, Blake Leyerle, Pierre Maraval, Robert S. Nelson, Claudia

Rapp, Ian Rutherford, Elizabeth Ann Schechter, Teresa Shaw, Gary Vikan, James Wetzel, Robert L. Wilken, and Lawrence Wills. Our conversations over the years have been an endless source of insight and delight. Even with the benefit of these expert readers, I bear full responsibility for any errors. At Colgate, I received talented research assistance from Alisa Herrin, Rachel Lutwick, and Sarah Murkett. I am also indebted to several librarians, for whom geographical distance and tight schedules present no obstacle. In particular, I thank Allan Janik and Laura Whitney at Harvard Divinity School, as well as Anne Ackerson, Emily Hutton, and Faith Stivers at Colgate. For shepherding this project from manuscript to book, I am grateful to Kate Toll and Cindy Fulton at UC Press. Erika Büky deserves special thanks for copyediting with such a keen eye, as does Barbara Cohen for preparing the index. I am also glad to thank various organizations for the financial assistance needed to complete this project, including a dissertation fellowship from the Mellon Foundation, a summer fellowship from the National Endowment for the Humanities, and several grants from Colgate's Faculty Research Council.

My most profound debt, however, is to my family: my husband, Jeffrey McArn, whose laughter and patience are gifts beyond measure; our daughters, Madlyn and Halley, irrepressible wonders to our eyes; and my parents, Joseph Allan Frank and Brigitte Paquet Frank, who first taught me to follow the heart and to whom I dedicate this work as a token of my love and gratitude.

Hamilton, New York
January 6, 1999

ABBREVIATIONS

I refer to ancient works by their standard English titles in the text of the book. Titles of ancient works follow abbreviations from the *Oxford Classical Dictionary* (2d ed., edited by N. G. L. Hammond and H. H. Scullard [Oxford: Clarendon, 1970], ix–xxii), or Quasten (3:556–62; 4:613–27), with occasional modification. Where I have quoted from modern translations, I also cite the translator's name or series abbreviation and page number(s). For series or multivolume works, volume number is also provided as needed. In the notes, however, I have preserved the scholarly convention of Latin abbreviations for these works. For abbreviations set in boldface below, full bibliographical citations to critical editions and modern translations can be found in the primary sources section of the bibliography.

ACW	Ancient Christian Writers
ANF	Select Library of the Ante-Nicene Fathers
Apophth.	*Apophthegmata patrum*, Greek alphabetical collection
CCSL	Corpus Christianorum, Series Latina
CS	Cistercian Studies

CSCO	Corpus Scriptorum Christianorum Orientalium
CSEL	Corpus Scriptorum Ecclesiasticorum Latinorum
CWS	Classics of Western Spirituality
DOP	*Dumbarton Oaks Papers*
DS	*Dictionnaire de spiritualité, ascétique et mystique, doctrine et histoire*
Ep.	*Epistula*
FC	Fathers of the Church
GCS	Die Griechischen christlichen Schriftsteller der ersten drei Jahrhunderte
HL	Palladius, *Historia lausiaca*
HM	*Historia monachorum in Aegypto* (Greek text)
Hom.	*Homilia, Homiliae*
HR	Theodoret, *Historia religiosa*
HTR	*Harvard Theological Review*
It. Eg.	Egeria, *Itinerarium Egeriae*
JAAR	*Journal of the American Academy of Religion*
JAC Suppl. 20	Akten des XII. internationalen Kongresses für christliche Archäologie. Bonn, 1991. 2 vols. *Jahrbuch für Antike und Christentum, Ergänzungsband* 20 (1995): Münster: Aschendorf
JECS	*Journal of Early Christian Studies*
JRS	*Journal of Roman Studies*
JTS	*Journal of Theological Studies*
Lampe, *PGL*	G. W. H. Lampe, *Patristic Greek Lexicon* (Oxford: Clarendon, 1961)
LCL	Loeb Classical Library

LVJer	Athanasius, *Lettre à des vierges qui étaient allées prier à Jérusalem*
NewDocs	G. H. R. Horsely, ed., *New Documents Illustrating Early Christianity* (Macquarie University: Ancient History Documentary Research Centre, 1981)
NPNF	Select Library of the Nicene and Post-Nicene Fathers
PG	*Patrologia Graeca*, ed. J. P. Migne
PL	*Patrologia Latina*, ed. J. P. Migne
PTS	*Patristische Texte und Studien*
Quasten	Johannes Quasten, *Patrology*, 4 vols. Repr. Westminster, Md.: Christian Classics, 1983–1986
Regnault, no.	Lucien Regnault, ed. *Les sentences des pères du désert: Série des anonymes* (Spiritualité Orientale, 43; Sablé-sur-Sarthe/Bégrolles-en-Mauges: Solesmes-Bellefontaine, 1985)
RSR	*Recherches de science religieuse*
SC	Sources chrétiennes
SH	Subsidia Hagiographica
SP	*Studia Patristica*
TU	Texte und Untersuchungen zur Geschichte des altchristlichen Literatur
V.	*Vita*
V. Ant.	Athanasius, *Vita Antonii*
V. Mel.	Gerontius, *Vita Melaniae*
VC	*Vigiliae Christianae*

ONE

Pilgrims to the Living in Context

The first step for any pilgrim lands not on the road, but somewhere in the imagination. Long before Jerome set out on his own journey to the Egyptian desert in the fourth century, he wrote stories of pilgrims traveling to Egyptian holy men, as in the *Life of Saint Paul, the First Hermit*.[1] When friends made actual journeys, Jerome could barely withhold his vicarious delight. He wrote to Rufinus in 374: "I hear you are penetrating the secret recesses of Egypt, visiting the companies of monks and paying a round of visits to the heavenly family upon earth."[2] Having created the ideal pilgrim, Jerome's next step was to imitate him. Thus in 386 he repeated Rufinus's journey, seeking out for himself the "secret recesses" and "heavenly families" he had imagined.

In the years preceding that journey, Jerome, like many Christians of his day, fed his fascination by reading the lives of these saints.[3] Such

---

1. On the dating, see J. N. D. Kelly, *Jerome: His Life, Writings, and Controversies* (New York: Harper & Row, 1975), 60–61. For an insightful analysis of the *Life of Paul* as it reflects Jerome's ambivalence toward the desert, see now Patricia Cox Miller, "Jerome's Centaur: A Hyper-icon of the Desert," *JECS* 4 (1996): 209–33, esp. 214–16, nn. 31–32.

2. Jerome, *Ep.* 3.1 [to Rufinus, 374] (Labourt, 1.11).

3. For example, Jerome, *Ep.* 127.5. On the visits of eastern ascetics to the

tales recounted the wonder-working and wisdom of distant monastics, for whom the desert became a stage for biblical spectacles. Christian audiences were drawn by these stories into another world, one shaped (and authenticated) by unceasing prayer, prophecy, healing, and exorcism. Some men and women became so deeply attracted to this world that they set out to see the living saints for themselves. Such visitors did not escape hagiographers' attention: just as converts to monasticism made "the desert a city," as Athanasius famously remarked, so pilgrims who flocked to the living saints left "every road resembling a river."[4] Such panoramic language points to the popularity of this practice but tells us little about pilgrims' religious experiences.

This book sets out to fill that gap by exploring the religious sensibilities of pilgrims who journeyed to visit living saints. Two works are central to this investigation: *The History of the Monks in Egypt*, an anonymous description by a Jerusalem monk written in the final years of the fourth century, and the *Lausiac History* (ca. 420) by Palladius, bishop of Helenopolis. These travelogues provide the most extensive firsthand accounts we have of pilgrims' journeys. Through collections of vignettes describing their encounters, pilgrims offered a distinctive window on this world. To be sure, it is hardly a *transparent* window: we cannot rely on these pilgrims for a detailed or accurate account of monastic life in Egypt.[5] But that is not my main object. I examine the literary sensibilities of these pilgrim-authors as a way of gaining deeper insight into their

---

West, see Philip Rousseau, *Ascetics, Authority and the Church in the Age of Jerome and Cassian* (Oxford: Oxford University Press, 1978), 79–83, 93–95.

4. Theodoret, *HR* 26.11 (Price, 165). Cf. *V. Ant.* 14 (Gregg. 42–43); *V. Chariton*, 16 (DiSegni, 406); *V. Daniel Styl.* 16 (Dawes/Baynes, p. 16); *Syr. V. Sym.*, 106 (Doran, 174–75). On pilgrimage to Simeon's pillar, see André-Jean Festugière, *Antioche païenne et chrétienne: Libanius, Chrysostome et les moines de Syrie* (Paris: Boccard, 1959), 351–52.

5. On the development of Egyptian monasticism, see Rousseau, *Ascetics*, 9–55; Ewa Wipszycka, "Le monachisme égyptien et les villes," *Travaux et mémoires* 12 (1994): 1–44.

religious sensibilities. As literary works, these travelogues provide a window that is framed, textured, and tinted by pilgrims' own desires and delights. The poetics of pilgrims' writings can afford a more nuanced understanding of their perceptions and religious aspirations. Through these stories from the desert, one discovers the literary worlds pilgrims roamed long before they set out into the desert.

TALES OF THE MONKS

The appetite for monastic lore was especially keen in the final decades of the fourth century. As young monks in Bethlehem, John Cassian and his friend Germanus hung on every word of an Egyptian cellmate, who was later exposed as a fugitive abbot seeking to escape the burdens of leadership. Although the abbot's time with the young monks was cut short, he nevertheless inspired them "to travel around quickly to the holy men and monasteries" of Egypt.[6] Modern readers of the *Institutes* and *Conferences* can lose sight of this younger Cassian, whose writings on Egypt were intended to serve emerging monastic establishments in Gaul. Still, one catches glimpses of the youthful monk, infatuated by the exotic appeal of distant sages.[7] A similar exoticism inspired another Gallic writer, Sulpicius Severus, to record the travels of his friend Postumianus.[8] From these snippets, lay audiences pieced together an alluring image of holy people in distant lands.

One figure in particular, a virgin known as Litia of Thessalonica, captures well these intersecting interests between tales of the monks and

6. *Conl.* 17.2 (Ramsey, 587); cf. 17.5. On Pinufius, see Cassian, *Conl.* 20.1–2; *Inst.* 4.31.

7. On this monastic agenda in Cassian's writings, see Rousseau, *Ascetics*, 177–85, and now Columba Stewart, *Cassian the Monk* (New York: Oxford University Press, 1998), 15–19.

8. *Dial.* 1.1 (NPNF 2.11.24). On the *Dialogues'* affinities with other travel writing, see Clare Stancliffe, *St. Martin and His Hagiographer* (Oxford: Clarendon, 1983), 102–7.

ascetic travel. A Coptic version of the *Lausiac History* mentions that she was a "scribe writing books" who set out to visit Macarius the Egyptian after hearing a report about him.[9] As a scribe, she might have transcribed the very tales of the monks that kindled her desire to travel. Her story conveys the elision between geographical distance and tales of remote monks.

Along with actual pilgrims there were armchair pilgrims, those who demanded and consumed stories of travels to the saints without ever making such journeys themselves. Thus although both the *Lausiac History* and the *History of the Monks of Egypt* were composed by actual pilgrims, the impetus to record their memories came from audiences who probably never made the journey. Sadly, those armchair pilgrims rarely figure in scholarly investigations into pilgrimages to the living. Part of the problem is that most of these studies have drawn primarily from saints' lives, or, to put it in pilgrims' terms, from the perspective of the destination (or the saint) and not the pilgrim. As saints' lives would have us see the phenomenon, pilgrims had concrete needs that the holy persons met.[10] Pilgrims needed a cure; the holy man healed. Pilgrims requested a prophecy; the holy man delivered. Pilgrims sought wisdom; the holy man imparted it. This supply-and-demand model distorts our picture of the pilgrims. The pilgrim is cast either as worthy supplicant or as intrusive nuisance.[11] Such studies neglect how pilgrims expressed

9. Butler, *The Lausiac History*, part 1, 149–50, citing Amélineau, *Monuments pour servir . . . Monastères de la Basse Egypte*, 240–41.

10. Derwas J. Chitty, *The Desert a City* (Crestwood, N.Y.: Saint Vladimir's Seminary Press, 1966), 46–53. Bernhard Kötting, "Wallfahrten zu lebenden Personen im Altertum," in *Wallfahrt kennt keine Grenzen*, ed. L. Kriss-Rettenbeck and G. Mohler (Munich/Zurich: Schell & Steiner, 1984), 226–34. Briefly discussed in Pierre Maraval, *Lieux saints et pèlerinages d'Orient: Histoire et géographie des origines à la conquête arabe* (Paris: Cerf, 1985), 50, and Élisabeth Malamut, *Sur la route des saints byzantins* (Paris: CNRS, 1993), 199–208. A noteworthy exception is Rousseau, *Ascetics*, esp. 79–83, 93–95.

11. Evagrius of Pontus regarded visitors as far worse than a nuisance: their persistent knocking at the door and urges to touch holy men's clothes made

their own sense of displacement, their expectations, and their spiritual progress. In short, the supply-and-demand model of previous studies has failed to offer what I call, for lack of a better term, pilgrims' *spirituality*.

Recovering the experiences of pilgrims in a distant time and place is a task fraught with obstacles, particularly because they apparently felt little need to record introspective moments, moods, or reflections. Yet their aspirations and religious imagination are not lost to us. The narrative features of pilgrims' stories can reveal a great deal about their cognitive states, perceptions, and rituals.[12] The tales of late antique pilgrims amount to more than a serial catalog of monks and localities. More storytellers than census-takers, these pilgrims used language that, on closer inspection, reveals their religious sensibilities and expectations. Thus I approach the *History of the Monks in Egypt* and the *Lausiac History* more as literary creations than as historical chronicles. When pilgrims describe the wonders and terrors of monasticism, I do not discount incredible details or attempt to judge the plausibility of such reports. If the aim is to understand the totality of pilgrims' experiences as represented through their stories, we should regard these tales as meaningful fictions through which pilgrims generated an image of monastics with which their audience could interact.[13] To accommodate their audience's expectations they borrowed familiar tropes and vocabu-

---

them none other than agents of the demon vainglory (*Praktikos* 13; trans. Bamberger, 19).

12. Most instructive is Candace Slater's comparison of pilgrims' and residents' stories about Padre Cícero, *Trail of Miracles: Stories from a Pilgrimage in Northeast Brazil* (Berkeley: University of California Press, 1986), 117–48, esp. 130, 146–47. I thank Peter Brown for this reference.

13. My thinking here is shaped by Averil Cameron's groundbreaking study, *Christianity and the Rhetoric of Empire: The Development of Christian Discourse* (Berkeley: University of California Press, 1991), esp. 89–119, 141–52. Also important is Candace Slater's work on the affinities between narrative form and ritual behavior in pilgrims' narratives (*Trail of Miracles*, esp. 130, 228).

lary from other types of travel tales, including accounts of otherworldly and exotic voyages.

My task, then, is to identify these literary "traces" and understand their role in shaping pilgrims' perceptions of holy people. Through a literary analysis of pilgrims' writings, one discovers a religious imagination that borrows from travel writing, the Bible, saints' lives, and visionary literature, all of which shaped the ways pilgrims described journeying to see sacred persons.

HOLY PLACES, HOLY PEOPLE, AND THE BIBLICAL PAST

In addition to broadening the literary context for pilgrimages to the living, I also consider a broader ritual context: pilgrimages to the biblical holy places. Many pilgrims to the Holy Land reported visiting holy people in the course of their tours of the holy places. Many such tours took place as early as the 380s. Jerome, accompanied by the Roman widow Paula and her daughter, Eustochium, toured the holy places in Palestine as well as the monastic settlements around Alexandria and Nitria.[14] At this time another pilgrim from the West, known as Egeria, visited monks in Nitria, the Thebaid, and eventually in Syria. No doubt her interest was piqued by the various monastics who served as hosts and guides during her journey.[15] Some pilgrims began their tours of the holy places with visits to monastics, as Melania the Younger did in 417 when she toured cells around Alexandria on her way to Jerusalem, to "worship (προσκυνέω) at the Holy Places."[16] Such combined tours to

14. Jerome, *Ep.* 108.9–14.

15. *It. Eg.* 9.1, 6; 7.1. Cf. Hagith Sivan, "Pilgrimage, Monasticism, and the Emergence of Christian Palestine in the Fourth Century," in *The Blessings of Pilgrimage*, ed. Robert Ousterhout (Urbana: University of Illinois Press, 1990), 54–65.

16. *V. Mel.* 34–40, esp. 34, cf. 37 (Clark, 50–52). On the date of her departure for Jerusalem, see Clark, *Life of Melania the Younger*, 219 n. 58. Palladius

holy places and holy people remained common well into the seventh century.[17]

The connection between holy places and holy people seemed natural to these Christians. Cassian and Germanus were standing in the Cave of the Nativity at Bethlehem when they vowed to set out for the monasteries of Egypt.[18] That so many pilgrims to the holy places also made visits to holy people suggests that journeying to holy destinations, whether people or places, reflects a coextensive piety. Unfortunately, pilgrims' vocabulary does not allow us to push this claim further, since there was no single word in either Greek or Latin for travel to a holy destination, or "pilgrimage," as moderns tend to use (and overuse) the term.[19] A single paragraph from the *Life of Melania the Younger* (chapter

---

(*HL* 46.2, 5) mentions a similar path undertaken by Melania's grandmother, Melania the Elder, who toured Nitria for six months and then settled in Jerusalem, though under different circumstances. Cf. Jerome, *Ep.* 4.2; Nicole Moine, "Melaniana," *Revue des études augustiniennes* 15 (1980): 3–79, esp. 13–19.

17. For example, Leontius of Neapolis, *Life of Symeon the Holy Fool*, 1 (Ryden, 124; Krueger, 134), the life of a sixth-century figure that reflects seventh-century practices (Krueger, 134 n. 7); Cyril of Scythopolis, *V. Sab.* 63 (Schwartz, 164.14–15; Price, 174); id., *V. Euth.* 6 (Schwartz, 14.5–9; Price, 9). See Yizhar Hirschfeld, *The Judean Desert Monasteries in the Byzantine Period* (New Haven: Yale University Press, 1992), 16. Bernard Flusin, *Miracle et histoire dans l'œuvre de Cyrille de Scythopolis* (Paris: Études Augustiniennes, 1983), 116–17. Bernard Flusin and J. Paramelle, eds., "De Syncletica in deserto Iordanis," *Analecta Bollandiana* 100 (1982): 305–17. On the close ties between Judaean desert monasticism and holy land pilgrimage, see Yizhar Hirschfeld, "Life of Chariton: In Light of Archaeological Research," in *Ascetic Behavior in Greco-Roman Antiquity*, ed. Vincent Wimbush (Minneapolis: Fortress, 1990), 425–47, esp. 428.

18. Cassian, *Conl.* 17.5; on their itinerary, see Stewart, *Cassian the Monk*, 8–12.

19. For terms referring to holy land pilgrimage, see Maraval, *Lieux saints et pèlerinages*, 137–38. Matthew Dillon's list of classical Greek terms for cults and festivals (*Pilgrims and Pilgrimage in Ancient Greece* [New York: Routledge, 1997], xv–xvi) suggests a similar emphasis on the activity performed at the destination,

37) illustrates the problem: her visits to famous monks are described in terms of "visit[ing] the saints" (ἱστορήσομεν τοὺς ἁγίους), "tour[ing]" (περιῆγον) the cells, and setting forth for "spiritual *emporia*" (τὴν πνευματικὴν ἐμπορίαν)—a shopping expedition.[20] Without an umbrella term for what we might consider pilgrim behaviors and dispositions, it is important not to exaggerate differences between the two types of journeys.

To be sure, there are real differences between journeying to holy places and to holy people; not least among them, holy places do not react to the pilgrim's presence, do not walk away or look one in the eye. Whether those differences are significant to pilgrims' experiences requires more careful consideration. Too narrow a focus on the destinations runs the risk of obscuring other elements, including the pilgrim. It is more helpful to take into consideration the type of pilgrimage or, specifically, the *shape* of a journey. As the Hinduist David Haberman has observed, some pilgrimages are linear, leading the pilgrim toward a single, fixed destination, whereas others, which he calls "circular" or "goalless" pilgrimages, have no ultimate object. The presence or absence of a goal, he claims, determines pilgrims' behaviors, attitudes, and experiences.[21] Christian pilgrimages in late antiquity might also be classified along these lines, with pilgrimage to holy places fitting the model of

rather than on the journey as the defining activity. On *theoria* as the defining activity, see Ian Rutherford, "Theoric Crisis: The Dangers of Pilgrimage in Greek Religion and Society," *Studi e materiali di storia delle religioni* n.s. 19 (1995): 275–92.

20. *V. Mel.* 37 (Gorce, 196; Clark, 52; emended). Both Gorce and Clark miss the mercantile overtones by translating *emporia* simply as "expedition." I thank Peter Brown for calling to my attention the mercantile dimension of *emporia*. Cf. Eusebius, *Dem. Evang.* 5 (proem); see Lampe, *PGL*, s.v. "ἐμπορία," 457a.

21. On this typological distinction, see David L. Haberman, *Journey through the Twelve Forests: An Encounter with Krishna* (New York: Oxford, 1994), esp. 71–76 (I thank one of the Press's anonymous readers for recommending

"linear" pilgrimage, and journeys to holy people coming closer to the type of open-ended, circular journey that Haberman studies.[22]

Although typologies such as Haberman's allow us to recognize the distinctiveness of pilgrimages to the living, both types of journeys also share important affinities. Given the emphasis on inversion, opposition, and otherness in current theories of pilgrimage,[23] it is easy to overlook significant circumstances common to both types of pilgrimage. Pilgrims to holy places often relied on monastics for guidance, lodging, and access to sacred places.[24] Such frequent contacts also provided occasions

---

this work). In a different context (rural Brazilian pilgrimage), Candace Slater calls attention to the linearity and circularity of narrative forms pertaining to a single destination (*Trail of Miracles*, 146–47). On the irrelevance of current theories of "sacred center" for interpreting circular pilgrimages such as the Krishnaite circumambulation of Braj, see Haberman, *Journey through the Twelve Forests*, 69–72; cf. Mircea Eliade, *The Myth of the Eternal Return* (New York: Bollingen, 1954).

22. Even if Haberman's distinction between the dispositions of pilgrims and ascetics does not apply to late antique Christians (*Journey through the Twelve Forests*, 107).

23. For example, Victor Turner, "The Center Out There: Pilgrim's Goal," *History of Religions* 12 (1973): 191–230. More rewarding than the application of anthropological models has been the use of literary and semiotic theory for interpreting ancient pilgrims' narratives, as in Blake Leyerle, "Landscape as Cartography in Early Christian Pilgrimage Narratives," *JAAR* 64 (1996): 119–43.

24. On contacts between pilgrims to the holy places and Palestinian monks, see Hirschfeld, *Judean Desert Monasteries*, 55–56; Joseph Patrich, *Sabas: Leader of Palestinian Monasticism* (Washington, D.C.: Dumbarton Oaks, 1995), 8–9; Christine Saulnier, "La vie monastique en Terre Sainte auprès des lieux de pèlerinages (IVe siècle)," in *Miscellanea Historiae Ecclesiasticae* 6, section 1: *Les transformations dans la société chrétienne au IVe siècle* (Bibliothèque de la revue d'histoire ecclésiastique 67; Brussels, 1983), 223–48, esp. 240–43.

On the archaeology of pilgrimage, see esp. Elzbieta Makowiecka, "Monastic Pilgrimage Centre at Kellia in Egypt," *JAC Suppl.* 20, 2:1002–15; Philippe Bridel, "La dialectique de l'isolement et de l'ouverture dans les monastères kelliotes: Espaces réservés—espaces d'accueil," in *Le site monastique copte des Kellia:*

for sharing stories about more illustrious monks, as we know from Egeria, who describes these conversations in her diary.[25]

> [The bishop at Haran] was kind enough to tell us much else besides, as indeed did the other holy bishops and holy monks, always about God's Scriptures, or the deeds of holy monks, whether it was miracles done by those who had already passed away, or the deeds done today by those "still in the body," especially the ascetics. For I want you to realize, loving sisters, that the monks' conversation is always either about God's Scriptures or the deeds of the great monks.[26]

Egeria's stress on the two sole topics of conversation, scripture and the deeds of the monks, reminds us how closely pilgrims associated the Bible with the holy places and people. In fact, although routes to holy people were far less systematized than circuits of holy places,[27] the desire to experience the Bible more vividly lay behind both types of travel.

The most interesting continuity between pilgrimage to living saints and to holy places rests in the reading habits of the pilgrims themselves. The Bible was the touchstone against which the holiness of people or places was measured, as Melania's studies prior to travel illustrate.

Sources historiques et explorations archéologiques (Geneva: Mission suisse d'archéologie copte, 1986). On the hospice, see Hirschfeld, *Judean Desert Monasteries*, 196–200; for Egypt, J. Maspero and E. Drioton, *Fouilles exécutées à Baouît* (Cairo: Institut français d'archéologie orientale, 1931), vi–viii. For literary evidence of guesthouses, see Malamut, *Sur la route des saints byzantins*, 207. On possible ceramic evidence for pilgrims' presence, see Ewa Wipszycka, "Aspects économiques de la vie aux Kellia," in *Le site monastique copte des Kellia*, 117–44; reprinted in id., *Études sur le christianisme dans l'Égypte de l'Antiquité* (Studia Ephemeridis Augustinianum 52; Rome: Institutum Patristicum Augustinianum, 1996), 332–62, esp. 355–56.

25. *It. Eg.* 21.3 (Wilkinson, 120–21).

26. *It. Eg.* 20.13 (Wilkinson, 120).

27. Pierre Maraval, "Les itinéraires de pèlerinage en Orient (entre le 4e et le 7e S.)," *JAC Suppl.* 20, 1:291–300.

According to her biographer, she was an avid reader of both the Bible and saints' lives. In fact, we are told, she read the entire Bible three or four times in a given year and also copied, interpreted, and distributed it for others. Even though "the Bible never left her holy hands,"[28] she also managed to devote considerable energies to reading biographies of famous ascetics, "as if she were eating dessert."[29] This assiduity suggests that for Melania, reading the deeds and words of famous ascetics was, in effect, an extension of her biblical studies.[30]

That continuity between scripture and hagiography plays itself out in her itinerary.[31] Had the scriptures and lives been disconnected in her mind, she would probably have gone directly to Jerusalem rather than start the journey in Egypt. That she chose to visit the Egyptian monks before she set sail for Jerusalem suggests that in Egypt she was already effectively, if not, actually, engaged in an uninterrupted meditation on the scriptures. Like that of Paula, who visualized Christ in the flesh both at Golgotha and before monks in Egypt,[32] Melania's journey provided the occasion for immediate perception of the biblical figures themselves. For these two women, to gaze at holy people or holy places was to gaze at the scriptures.

A more concrete expression of the desire to gaze on the biblical past is found in the souvenirs pilgrims brought home almost two centuries later. The images decorating pilgrims' flasks often created anachronisms by combining iconographic details from a biblical story with con-

28. *V. Mel.* 21 (Clark, 44).

29. *V. Mel.* 23 (Clark, 45).

30. Melania's reading habits illustrate well Marc Van Uytfanghe's notion of the "Bible 'actualisée' " ("L'empreinte biblique sur la plus ancienne hagiographie occidentale," in *Le monde latin antique et la Bible*, ed. Jacques Fontaine and Charles Pietri [Paris: Beauchesne, 1985], 565–610, esp. 572); cf. Lynda Coon, *Sacred Fictions: Holy Women and Hagiography in Late Antiquity* (Philadelphia: University of Pennsylvania Press, 1997), esp. 1–27.

31. *V. Mel.* 37 (Clark, 52).

32. Jerome, *Ep.* 108.10, 14.

temporary architectural or liturgical details from the holy site. For example, on one souvenir, the women who discovered Jesus' empty tomb are depicted carrying a liturgical implement (a censer), rather than the spices and ointments described in the Gospel accounts. And the empty tomb shows the grillwork that enclosed the fifth-century shrine.[33]

These flasks, though dating from a later period, provide an iconographic analogy to the experiences fourth-century pilgrims describe. The image on the flask represents an event that occurs both in the biblical past and in the pilgrim's present. When Jerome spoke of entering biblical time, he signaled those transcendent moments to his readers by invoking a mode of perception he called the "eye of faith."[34] Sometimes he left the *oculis fidei* out altogether and spoke literally of seeing Christ in his burial shroud.[35] This idea that the human eye can see beyond

33. Gary Vikan, "Pilgrims in Magi's Clothing: The Impact of Mimesis on Early Byzantine Pilgrimage Art," in Ousterhout, *The Blessings of Pilgrimage*, 97–107, esp. 101–2. See also Gary Vikan, "Art, Medicine and Magic in Early Byzantium," *DOP* 38 (1984): 65–86. Both Vikan and J. Z. Smith (*To Take Place: Toward Theory in Ritual* [Chicago: University of Chicago Press, 1987], 86–94) draw special attention to this ritual convergence of biblical time and pilgrim's time. See also E. D. Hunt, *Holy Land Pilgrimage in the Later Roman Empire, A.D. 312–460* (Oxford: Clarendon, 1984), esp. 83–127; Charles Renoux, "The Reading of the Bible in the Ancient Liturgy of Jerusalem," in *The Bible in Greek Christian Antiquity*, ed. and trans. Paul M. Blowers (Notre Dame: University of Notre Dame Press, 1997): 389–414, esp. 402–4; Jean-Daniel Dubois, "Un pèlerinage Bible en main: L'itinéraire d'Égérie (381–384)," in *Moïse géographe: Recherches sur les représentations juives et chrétiennes de l'espace*, ed. Alain Desreumaux and Francis Schmidt (Paris: Vrin, 1988), 55–77, esp. 62–74. On an emerging Christian theology of the holy places during the fourth century, see Robert Wilken, *The Land Called Holy: Palestine in Christian History and Thought* (New Haven: Yale University Press, 1992), 108–25; and P. W. L. Walker, *Holy City, Holy Places? Christian Attitudes to Jerusalem and the Holy Land in the Fourth Century* (Oxford: Clarendon, 1990), 35–130.

34. Jerome, *Ep.* 108.10 (NPNF 2.6.199).

35. Jerome, *Ep.* 46.5 (NPNF 2.6.62).

physical appearances to gain a fuller perception of biblical events or figures is important for understanding the spirituality of pilgrims to the living.

PILGRIMS AND SENSORY PIETY

Although pilgrims to the living rarely mentioned using their own "eye of faith" or "spiritual vision,"[36] their reports suggest that they attached great importance to seeing a holy person. Lives of the saints had instilled that expectation in them; in the widely read *Life of Anthony*, for example, pilgrims would have been struck by the profound visual impression he made on visitors.[37] In his climactic description of Anthony's first appearance after twenty years' seclusion, Athanasius provides a liturgical tone to the *epiphaneia* of the holy man, who "came forth as though from some shrine. . . . This was the first time he appeared from the fortress for those who came out to see him. And when they beheld him, they were amazed to see that his body had maintained its former condition . . . just as they had known him prior to his withdrawal."[38] Significant here are the theatrical overtones, with the star who feels "elated" when he sees his followers. The details of this open-air theater supplied the cues by which the literary audience could identify itself with the spectators in the desert.

Two letters to the holy man Paphnutius also reflect this keen interest in seeing the holy man. In a badly damaged papyrus from the mid-fourth century,[39] a woman named Valeria wrote to Paphnutius to ask

36. Paula's experience comes closest to this idea: Jerome, *Ep.* 108.14.

37. Athanasius, *V. Ant.* 14, 88; cf. 62.

38. *V. Ant.* 14 (Gregg, 42).

39. *P. Lond.* 6 (1924) 1926 in *Jews and Christians in Egypt*, ed. and trans. H. Idris Bell (London: British Museum, 1924), 108–10; reprinted with commentary in *NewDocs* 4, no. 123, 245–50. Translations are taken from *NewDocs* edition. The practice of sending letters in lieu of making pilgrimages is reported by Callinicos in the *V. Hypatii*, 36.7, ed. G. J. M. Bartelink, SC 177 (1971). On the

that he pray for her breathing disorder. More striking is the way she put the request: "Even though in body I have not come to your feet, yet in spirit I have come to your feet." These words simulate a journey: her letter becomes the vehicle by which she "approaches" the holy man. And with that imagined approach comes a visual perception of Paphnutius: "By those who are ascetics and devotees," she explains, "religious revelations are exhibited."[40] Her request, then, suggests a surrogate pilgrim, approaching the feet of a body that displays the divine "revelations."

One finds a similar emphasis on visual experience in another letter to Paphnutius, this time from a supplicant requesting a prayer for the pilgrim who is delivering the letter.[41] His request is: "[May] the man who is setting out to your piety be found worthy to embrace [Paphnutius] also with [his] very eyes."[42] To "embrace" with the eyes signals not just the assumption that virtue is visible but also the belief that seeing the holy provides an active, tactile encounter with it. Thus even when describing the vicarious experience of meeting a holy man, Christians showed what they came to expect of such encounters: a visual access to the divine.

These sensory expectations, at a time when Christians pondered the meanings of the Incarnation, are not difficult to understand. One important implication of the idea that God assumed a body in the person of Jesus was that God now infused the entire material world, including places, bodies, and objects. How to perceive that divine presence became an important question for theologians. As more Christians claimed to taste, see, and touch divine presence in their devotions, it

---

letter as an instrument of visual presence, see Evagrius, *Ep. ad Melaniam*, 1 (Parmentier, 8).

40. *P. Lond.* 6 (1924) 1926, lines 9–11 (Bell, 108–9): τῶν γὰρ ἀσκούντων καὶ θρησκευόντων ἀποκαλύματα δικνέοντε.

41. *P. Lond.* 1925, mid-fourth century C.E. (Bell, 106–7).

42. *P. Lond.* 1925, lines 6–7.

became increasingly difficult to uphold the apologists' stance that "in order to know God, we need no body at all," as Origen once said.[43]

Within a century of Origen's protest, Ephrem the Syrian valorized the senses when he described the Incarnation in the following terms: "For it was not simply a body that our Lord put on; He likewise arrayed Himself with limbs and clothes so that by reason of his limbs and clothes, the afflicted would be encouraged to approach Him."[44] Significant here is Ephrem's insistence that incarnation meant more than simply having a body. Even the clothes on that body fulfilled a divine purpose, providing more points of sensory access to the divine. Ephrem explains the importance of the clothed body: "Those who were encouraged by His tenderness would approach his body, while those who were apprehensive for fear of Him would approach His clothing."[45] By insisting on various ways to "approach" that body,

43. Origen, *C. Cels.* 7.33 (Chadwick, 421). See also Robert J. Hauck, "'They Saw What They Said They Saw': Sense Knowledge in Early Christian Polemic," *HTR* 81 (1988): 239–49. On the implications of incarnational thinking, see Athanasius, *De incarnatione* 8, text in *Contra Gentes and De Incarnatione*, ed. and trans. R. W. Thomson (Oxford: Oxford University Press, 1971); Evagrius, *Ep. ad Melaniam*, 3 (Parmentier, 10); Susan Ashbrook Harvey, "St. Ephrem on the Scent of Salvation," *JTS* n.s. 49 (1998): 109–28. For a discussion of the doctrine's implications for holy places, see Walker, *Holy City, Holy Places?* 80–92, 118–20; Robert A. Markus, *The End of Ancient Christianity* (Cambridge: Cambridge University Press, 1990), 139–55; id., "How on Earth Could Places Become Holy? Origins of the Christian Idea of Holy Places," *JECS* 2 (1994): 257–71. For an overview of the political and social conditions behind that new investment in the material world, see Peter Brown, *The Rise of Western Christendom: Triumph and Diversity, A.D. 200–1000* (Oxford: Blackwell, 1996), 34–44.

44. Ephrem, *Sermo de Domino nostro*, 13.2 (FC 91: 288–89).

45. Ibid., cf. 48.1 ("Glory to the Hidden One who put on visibility so that sinners could approach him" [FC 91: 323]); additional examples are discussed in Sebastian Brock, "Clothing Metaphors as a Means of Theological Expression in Syriac Tradition," in *Typus, Symbol, Allegorie bei den österlichen Vätern und ihren Parallelen im Mittelalter*, ed. M. Schmidt (Regensburg: Friedrich Pustet, 1982), 11–40, esp. 15–18.

Ephrem created the conditions for a sensory awareness through proximity.

Christian pilgrims described how sanctity smelled and how it sounded; most of all, they testified to how it looked.[46] The spectacle of desert asceticism was conveyed through physical descriptions of holy people and in comments that stress the importance of face-to-face encounters. As one pilgrim explained, he came to a holy man because "the memory of what we have seen is not easily erased."[47] Thus, even if readers were not given a clear idea of exactly what was meant by "we have seen," they knew that the visual encounter had had a permanent effect. By these and other literary flags, the reader learned to scrutinize the narrative for visual cues—in short, to expect visible sanctity. In these sensory cues, audiences marked a path by which to "approach" holiness, even if only in the imagination.[48]

The sensory dimensions of this literature call our attention to a larger concern among late antique Christians: how the physical senses might recognize, know, and respond to the presence of the sacred.[49] This question plays itself out in the pilgrims' tales, which generate vicarious sensory experiences for the audience.

THE CULTURE OF VISIBILITY

To appreciate how Christian narratives created visual access to the divine, it is worth considering similar techniques in Greco-Roman liter-

46. For example, Jerome, *V. Pauli*, 9 (Harvey, 365); *HM* 1.4–9; *HR* 3.22. For a highly self-conscious study of Hindu pilgrimage as a sensory drama, see E. Valentine Daniel, *Fluid Signs: Being a Person the Tamil Way* (Berkeley: University of California Press, 1984), 245–87.

47. *HM* 1.19 (Russell, 54–55).

48. Patricia Cox Miller refers to these cues as "perceptual constructs," that is to say, rhetorical framing devices for representing sensory experience ("Desert Asceticism and the 'Body from Nowhere,'" *JECS* 2 [1994]: 137–53).

49. Wilken, *Land Called Holy*, 85–91.

ature. Christian writers shared with the larger Greco-Roman culture an impulse to render the unseen visible. Roman rituals used words, gestures, and images to conjure gods and venerable ancestors for the beholder.[50] From panegyrics at the imperial processions to the magical formulas for making the god appear, words generated visible presence.[51] Even in a culture whose gods claimed the ultimate control over visibility,[52] the conviction persisted that the proper use of language can bring unseen realities before the eyes. Thus, while it remained a divine prerogative to make the unseen gods visible, Greco-Roman writers claimed for themselves the power to render all other unseen realities visible. Orators, historians, and novelists took up this challenge in ingenious ways.

50. As in the use of *imagines*, "wax models of faces" prominently displayed in homes of the Roman elite, which were worn by actors at funeral processions so that the deceased would be accompanied by "the entire company of his house that had ever existed." Pliny, *Nat. hist.* 35.2.6 (LCL 9:265). For an in-depth study of the use of *imagines*, see now Harriet Flower, *Ancestor Masks and Aristocratic Power in Roman Culture* (Oxford: Clarendon, 1996), esp. 32–47, 97–106, 281–305. The literature on Roman spectacles and ceremonies is vast. Significant for their integration of image, ritual, and visual perception are S. R. F. Price, *Rituals and Power: The Roman Imperial Cult in Asia Minor* (Cambridge: Cambridge University Press, 1984), esp. 188–206; Sabine G. MacCormack, *Art and Ceremony in Late Antiquity* (Berkeley: University of California Press, 1981), esp. 1–89; Andrew Feldherr, *Spectacle and Society in Livy's* History (Berkeley: University of California Press, 1998); Carlin Barton, *The Sorrows of the Ancient Romans: The Gladiator and the Monster* (Princeton: Princeton University Press, 1993), esp. 85–91.

51. On magic spells conjuring visibility, see esp. *PGM* III.166; IV.475–829 ("Mithras Liturgy"), IV.3221–26; *PDM* xiv.290–94. On formulas for invisibility, *PGM* I.222–31, 247–62; VII.619–27. On the application of various ointments to the eyes to prepare for a "god's arrival," see *PDM* xiv.140–44, xiv.820–23. References are to *The Greek Magical Papyri in Translation, including the Demotic Spells*, ed. Hans Dieter Betz, 2d ed. (Chicago: University of Chicago Press, 1992).

52. For a general treatment of divine epiphany, see Robin Lane Fox, *Pagans and Christians* (New York: Knopf, 1987), 102–67.

The ability to evoke the unseen was taught at a very young age. School exercises, or *progymnasmata*, and rhetorical handbooks instructed students to strive for descriptions so vivid that images would come to the mind. This type of rhetorical device came under many names: *descriptio, ekphrasis, enargeia, hypotyposis, diatyposis, evidentia, repraesentio, illustratio, demonstratio.* Common to all of them was the idea that abundant detail would awaken the audience's mental senses and ultimately visualize the event, person, or place being described.[53] The rhetorician Quintilian, for instance, took visibility to be the hallmark of fine oratory, advising orators to aim "not so much to narrate as to exhibit," so that their speeches would appeal more to the eye than to the ear.[54] And Lysias was lauded for his magisterial use of *enargeia*, which Dionysius of Halicarnassus described as "a certain power he has of conveying the things he is describing to the senses of his audience, and it arises out of his grasp of circumstantial detail."[55] There was no such thing as too much detail, for in details the orators could "bring before the eyes all the circumstances," as Quintilian advised.[56] Only in amassing details of the parts, a rhetorical strategy advocated by Quintilian as well as later orators, might the audience visualize the whole.[57]

53. On the importance of visualization for these descriptive techniques, see Ann Vasaly, *Representations: Images of the World in Ciceronian Oratory* (Berkeley: University of California Press, 1993), 20, 89–102; Liz James and Ruth Webb, "'To Understand Ultimate Things and Enter Secret Places': Ekphrasis and Art in Byzantium," *Art History* 14 (1991): 1–17, esp. 3. For a useful checklist of rhetorical treatises, see George A. Kennedy, "Historical Survey of Rhetoric," in *Handbook of Classical Rhetoric in the Hellenistic Period, 330 B.C.–A.D. 400*, ed. Stanley E. Porter (Leiden: Brill, 1997), 3–41, esp. 19–41.

54. Quintilian, *Inst. orat.* 6.2.32 (LCL 2:435); 8.3.62; 9.2.40. Cf. Hermogenes, *Progymnasmata*, 23.11 (Patillon, 148).

55. Dionysius of Halicarnassus, *Lys.* 7 (trans. S. Usher; LCL I:33).

56. Quintilian, *Inst. orat.* 6.2.31 (LCL 2:435).

57. "It is less effective to tell the whole news at once than to recount it detail by detail" (Quintilian, *Inst. orat.* 8.3.69; LCL 3:247). The third-century Aquila Romanus referred to this technique as *leptologia*, a serial description of many

Vivid description, or *enargeia*, relied on the audience's capacity not just to receive these mental images but also to expand them. In *On the Sublime*, a first-century C.E. treatise attributed to Longinus, the author recommended choosing images, or *phantasiai*, with sufficient emotional and visual power to allow the audience to join in this conjuring.[58] It is ironic that only through an excess of detail might the listener become inspired to conjure further, "imagin[ing] to himself other details that the orator does not describe."[59] Quintilian underscored this distinction between mere seeing and directly engaging these mental pictures: "Vivid illustration *(evidentia)* . . . is something more than mere clearness, since the latter merely lets itself be seen, whereas the former thrusts itself *(ostendit)* upon our notice."[60] At the heart of this subtle distinction between images that are seen and images that make themselves seen is a distinction between a passive and an active audience. Only if the image was "thrust" on them would an audience engage in the visualization Quintilian had in mind. The intent was to "make our audience feel as if they were actual eyewitnesses to the scene [described]."[61] Here Quintilian links the pictorializing function of language with the idea of presence *(in rem praesentem)*. As "eyewitnesses" the audience was invited not simply to watch the spectacle but rather to use their eyes to trigger a range of sense perceptions and emotions. Only through visualizing

---

details (*De figuris sententiarum et elocutionis* 2, ed. Halm, 23.16–17, cited in Michael Roberts, *The Jeweled Style: Poetry and Poetics in Late Antiquity* [Ithaca: Cornell University Press, 1989], 38–44, esp. 40–41). The aim, in Roberts's apt phrase, is to "create the impression of exhaustivity" (41).

58. Longinus, *De subl.* 15.1–2 (LCL 214–17).

59. Quintilian, *Inst. orat.* 8.3.64 (LCL 3:245); cf. 6.2.29–32, 10.7.15–16; Vasaly, *Representations*, 95–96.

60. Quintilian, *Inst. orat.* 8.3.61 (LCL 4:245); cf. 4.2.63–64.

61. Quintilian, *Inst. orat.* 4.2.123 (LCL 2:117); on *enargeia*, see also G. Zanker, "*Enargeia* in the Ancient Criticism of Poetry," *Rheinisches Museum für Philologie* 124 (1981): 297–311; Alessandra Manieri, *L'immagine poetica nella teoria degli antichi:* Phantasia *ed* enargeia (Pisa: Istituti editoriali e poligrafici internazionali, 1998).

language could this emotional and synesthetic effect be achieved.[62] Moreover, visibility, as a rhetorical effect, was believed to have profound moral implications and consequences. Unless the orator could make members of the audience see—and thereby feel—a distant event, any moral lessons inherent in the story would be lost.[63]

The connection between visibility and morality is even more pronounced in late ancient novels, which communicated the moral status of characters through moments of visual perception. Beyond indulging a penchant for pictorial description, novelists used visual language as a code for both heroes and villains, humans and gods. Two novels in particular, Achilles Tatius's *Leucippe and Clitophon* and Apuleius's *Metamorphoses* (or *The Golden Ass*, as the work is better known), established a set of visual cues by which readers could judge character and divinity. It is worth examining some of these literary "moments of perception" in greater detail.[64]

Achilles Tatius's *Leucippe and Clitophon* was composed in the late second century and continued to be copied into the fourth century.[65] From the moment the work opens, the reader is deluged with descriptions of

62. A point underscored by G. Zanker, who notes the close connection between *enargeia* and the sense of sight ("*Enargeia,*" 297–301, 309–10). On the multisensory dimensions of *enargeia*, see Mary Carruthers, *The Craft of Thought: Meditation, Rhetoric, and the Making of Images, 400–1200* (Cambridge: Cambridge University Press, 1998), 130–33, 148. Recent work on Roman historiography has examined the function of rhetorical tropes of visibility; see, for example, Gary B. Miles, *Livy: Reconstructing Early Rome* (Ithaca: Cornell University Press, 1995), 10–11; Feldherr, *Spectacle and Society*, esp. 1–19; J. Davidson, "The Gaze in Polybius's Histories," *JRS* 81 (1991): 10–24; Matthew Leigh, *Lucan: Spectacle and Engagement* (Oxford: Clarendon, 1997), 10–15.

63. On Livy's use of visualization to serve his ethical aims, see Feldherr, *Spectacle and Society*, 9 and n. 26.

64. A term borrowed from Sarah Stanbury's study of the poetics of visual experience in the *Gawain*-poet (*Seeing the* Gawain-*Poet: Description and the Act of Perception* [Philadelphia: University of Pennsylvania Press, 1991], esp. 2–8).

65. John J. Winkler, in *Collected Ancient Greek Novels*, ed. B. P. Reardon

paintings, landscapes, and the beloved.[66] All this visibility overwhelms the young hero, Clitophon, whose "eyes were filled to the brim with pleasure" on arriving in Alexandria. The reader follows Clitophon's eyes as they try "to travel along every street" but fail.[67] In a moment of exhilaration and exhaustion, Clitophon concedes his happy defeat: "Turning round and round to face all the streets, I grew faint at the sight and at last exclaimed, like a luckless lover, 'Eyes, we have met our match!' "[68] His readers could surely appreciate the sentiment.

In this context it is worth pausing to consider vision within a larger set of sensory cues. Most striking about Achilles Tatius's novel is the way in which the use and misuse of the eyes distinguish the good characters from the bad (who include a cast of unsavory interlopers). The good lovers, Leucippe and Clitophon, make right use of their eyes. In this typology, the gaze that is returned is the mark of authentic love. Thus, Clitophon's confidant, Clinias, deems him to be "lucky in love" precisely because the young lovers have endless opportunities to exchange glances, "a kind of copulation at a distance," according to Clinias.[69]

(Berkeley: University of California Press, 1989), 170. I follow Winkler's translation and paragraph divisions.

66. Paintings: see, for example, 1.1; 3.6–8; 5.3; places: 1.1 (Sidon); 4.12 (Nile); 5.1 (Alexandria); lover's gaze: 1.4–6, 19; 2.1–5. On the role of pictorial description and spectacles in Achilles Tatius, see Shadi Bartsch, *Decoding the Ancient Novel: The Reader and the Role of Pictorial Description in Heliodorus and Achilles Tatius* (Princeton: Princeton University Press, 1989), 7–79.

67. Achilles Tatius, 5.1 (Winkler, 233).

68. Achilles Tatius, 5.1 (Winkler, 233); on other landscapes, cf. 4.12, 18. The allusions are to Plato's description of the lover's gaze (*Phaedrus* 251 b, c). This "flow of beauty" into the eye is echoed in several places, as in, 1.4, 9; 5.13. For a useful list of citations to the "flow of beauty" topos in other ancient novels, see M. B. Trapp, "Plato's *Phaedrus* in Second-Century Greek Literature," in *Antonine Literature*, ed. D. A. Russell (Oxford: Clarendon, 1990), 141–73, esp. 155; cf. 172, esp. 6.iv.

69. Achilles Tatius, 1.9 (Winkler, 182–83); Clitophon's relentless gaze is mentioned again when he describes two episodes of visualization, one as Leu-

The weeping eye is another device by which Achilles Tatius exposes both the true lover's wisdom and the false suitor's ignorance. In one episode, Clitophon notes the irony in the fact that profound despair *prevents* the eye from weeping.[70] The teardrop is a key signifier in this tale of mistaken appearances and false identities. One of the most poetic moments in the novel comes when Clitophon, as narrator, observes how the eyes of the beloved radiate when a suspended tear fills the eye.[71] And when Clitophon, the true lover, is finally brought to tears, he describes in detail their intimate connection to the soul.[72] The villain, in contrast, weeps crocodile tears, as in Thersandros's comic and grotesque display of tears. When he cries at the sight of Leucippe's genuine tears, he "believes . . . he is in love."[73] Yet Thersandros finds neither catharsis nor redemption in his tears; they only delude him further. Only the true lover knows the eye and its ties to the true, inner self. And, as Thersandros's tears confirm, those who abuse the eyes will never have the object of their desire.

Failure to use the eyes is also a mark of villainy. In this scheme, the unrequited lover is one who fails to love with the eyes. Callisthenes, we are told, is a "hearsay suitor," the type who "fall[s] in love with a rumor and suffer[s] with . . . [his] ears the agonies usually experienced by the soul from love's wound in the eye."[74] As these false lovers demonstrate, unless love begins in the eye, it is doomed. It comes as no surprise to the

---

cippe sings (2.1) and the other when he reads her letter (5.15), as well as one when the lovers are reunited (8.12). Cf. Charmides, the smitten general, who stages a spectacle of his "Nile horse" for the sole purpose of finding a way to stare at Leucippe (4.3). It is hardly a coincidence that as he describes its insatiable appetite, she gazes at the animal, while he (animalistically) gazes at her.

70. Achilles Tatius, 3.11.

71. Achilles Tatius, 6.7.

72. Achilles Tatius, 7.4; cf. 5.15.

73. Achilles Tatius, 6.7 (Winkler, 253).

74. Achilles Tatius, 2.13 (Winkler, 195); cf. Thersandros, who becomes enamored with Leucippe solely from a verbal description of her beauty (6.4).

reader that false lovers, such as Melite (Clitophon's new "betrothed") and Thersandros are those most frustrated by an unrequited gaze. Melite complains to Clitophon that she would have been content "just to look at [him], which is all [he has] been good for."[75] Likewise, Thersandros pleads with Leucippe to look him in the eye rather than "let the loveliness of [her] eyes spill onto the earth." If she would only return his gaze, he begs, her beauty might "flow into these eyes of mine."[76] Exasperated, he uses his hands to achieve what her eyes refuse to do: he jerks her head back by the hair and pulls up her chin to make her meet his gaze.[77] That Thersandros has to resort to physical force to obtain Leucippe's gaze is itself an indictment of the false lover who manipulates vision.

The right use of vision is exemplified by Clitophon, the lover who receives and gives the gaze effortlessly. Clinias remarks on Clitophon's good fortune to have this reciprocated gaze. And even when the lovers are separated, Clitophon recalls how he has managed to conjure Leucippe's image in his mind while reading a letter from her. Like a theurgist disclosing his methods, Clitophon teaches the reader to make those who are absent present once again: "I scrutinized each word," he says, "as if seeing her through the letters . . . ma[king] the visible tangible (τὰ ὁρώμενα ὡς δρώμενα)."[78] More than a simple descriptive device, then, in Achilles Tatius's novel the eye functions as a moral marker, a tool by which the author villainizes his villains and authenticates the true lovers.

Apuleius of Madauros, too, uses sensory language to shape both the characters and the plot of his narrative. Indeed, the entire plot of *The Golden Ass* can be understood as Lucius's meanderings through the realms of "blind Fortune" and "seeing Fortune."[79] Within this over-

75. Achilles Tatius, 5.25.4 (Winkler, 247).
76. Achilles Tatius, 6.6 (Winkler, 252).
77. Achilles Tatius, 6.18.
78. Achilles Tatius, 5.19 (Winkler, 243).
79. Apuleius, *Met.* 5.9; 11.15. Here I follow P. G. Walsh's translation, *Apuleius: The Golden Ass* (Oxford: Clarendon, 1994).

arching visual paradigm, however, the dangers of visual experience are equally pronounced: his insatiable voyeurism initiates and prolongs his miserable odyssey as an ass.[80] Yet his moments of greatest humiliation and greatest joy come when he himself becomes a public spectacle.[81] This visual drama about voyeurs and spectacles draws to a close when "seeing Fortune" looks on him and he, in turn, sees Isis,[82] as if to suggest that the reciprocated gaze is the assurance of his deliverance.

Apuleius's most instructive commentary on the senses, however, is found in the Cupid and Psyche tale, a story within the story. To be sure, many elements in the tale, about a mortal girl's abduction to the enchanted realm of a divine husband who "was invisible to her, but she could touch and hear him,"[83] mirror Lucius's own plight, not least of which is the theme of *curiositas*. Yet the tale can also be read independently of the larger novel as a self-contained sensory drama, revolving around competing worlds where sensory experience is differently organized.

The contrast in sensory orders is marked from the outset of the story. The reader soon learns that Psyche is virtually divinized by human gazes: "People gazed on that girl's human countenance when appeasing the divine will of the mighty goddess."[84] That she also fell under the

---

80. A proclivity he comes to enjoy, even as an ass: "I refreshed my inquisitive eyes by gazing through the open gate at the highly pleasing spectacle afforded by the show" (10.29; Walsh, 212). The fact that the ass is occasionally blindfolded accentuates his role as voyeur (e.g., 9.15–22). The centrality of visual experience is also borne out by various characters' names, such as Lucius and Photis, which are derived from Latin and Greek words for light (*lux* and φῶς). And, as John J. Winkler perceptively remarks, the name Lucius is used strictly for the man and not for the ass, lending further significance to the "light-less" plight of the ass (*Auctor & Actor: A Narratological Reading of Apuleius's* Golden Ass [Berkeley: University of California Press, 1985], 149–51).

81. Apuleius, *Met.* 3.9–10, 12, 22; 10.29; 11.16, 24.

82. Apuleius, *Met.* 11.19, 24–25.

83. Apuleius, *Met.* 5.5 (Walsh, 82).

84. Apuleius, *Met.* 4.29 (Walsh, 75).

divine gaze of Venus is significant. Here is a goddess accustomed to having a mirror continuously held before her face by dutiful attendants.[85] Yet as a never-ending spectacle, the object of "all eyes" and of an "admiration [that] is accorded to an exquisitely carved statue," Psyche is miserable.[86] Her exile to the divine realm is a liberation from this gaze. The reader can sense the transformation in Apuleius's description of her new setting: "You would know as soon as you entered that you were viewing the bright and attractive retreat of some god."[87] In this place she finds repose, and, above all, recovers the ability to look; the spectacle has become the spectator.

Even as Apuleius serves up some of the lushest sensory descriptions of the entire novel, the unseen remains equally important. The reader soon discovers an alternative world where the senses operate and interact differently. As Psyche gazes with delight upon her new surroundings, she encounters a disembodied voice,; the otherness of this sensory order is clear.[88] Amid the visual splendors of this place, Psyche must adjust to the continuous presence of disembodied voices and sounds. As Apuleius describes the scene, "She could see no living soul, and merely heard words emerging from thin air: her serving-maids were merely voices. When she had enjoyed the rich feast, a singer entered and performed unseen, while another musician strummed a lyre which was likewise invisible. Then the harmonious voices of a tuneful choir struck her ears, so that it was clear that a choral group was in attendance, though no person could be seen."[89] While layering voice on voice, servant by

85. Apuleius, *Met.* 4.31.

86. Apuleius, *Met.* 4.32 (Walsh, 77).

87. Apuleius, *Met.* 5.1 (Walsh, 80).

88. "Haec ei summa cum voluptate visenti offert sese vox quaedam corporis nuda" (5.2). Even in this brief sentence, Apuleius holds two modes of sensory awareness in tension by contrasting an embodied seeing, qualified by the term *voluptas*, connoting sensory pleasure, with an aural experience of a disembodied voice *(vox corporis nuda)*.

89. Apuleius, *Met.* 5.3 (Walsh, 81); her sisters also enjoy the invisible hospi-

servant, he crowds the space with "invisible" and "unseen" presences. Sight, however, is not eliminated. After all, Psyche is not struck blind (an accident commonly associated with epiphany in the ancient imagination).[90] Instead, every sense is engaged, while sight alone is redirected and thereby redefined.

Psyche is permitted to see her surroundings but never the presence of those who share them with her. We are told how her eye delighted in the opulent stones and gems on which she stood, and the luminous doors, colonnade, and rooms that glimmered even when "the sun refused to shine."[91] It is hard to miss the irony of her situation: she may look in every corner of the mansion, but the closest she comes to meeting the eye of another being is when she sees silver wall reliefs of "beasts and wild cattle [who] met the gaze of those who entered there."[92] Even more ironic is the fact that the invisible beings demand absolute control of her eyes. Thus the disembodied voice asks, "Why . . . do you gaze open-mouthed?"[93] And, more than once, her husband enjoins her "not . . . even to set eyes" on her distraught sisters or "catch a glimpse of them."[94]

---

tality: "All this music soothed their spirits, with the sweetest tunes as they listened, though no human person stood before them" (5.15; Walsh, 88).

90. As in Athena's blinding of Tiresias after he saw her bathing: "Whosoever shall behold any of the immortals, when the god himself chooses not, at a heavy price shall he behold" (Callimachus, *Hymn* 5.100–102 [LCL; A. W. Mair, trans., pp. 119–21]). For an insightful discussion of this hymn and the problem of divine visibility, see Nicole Loraux, "What Tiresias Saw," in *The Experiences of Tiresias: The Feminine and the Greek Man*, trans. Paula Wissing (Princeton: Princeton University Press, 1995), 211–26. Christian preachers and commentators also commented on blindness as proof of epiphany, as in Ephrem the Syrian's interpretation of Saul's blinding (*Sermo de Domino nostro*, 30.4 = FC 308–9; cf. Acts of the Apostles 9:1–19).

91. Apuleius, *Met.* 5.1 (Walsh, 81).

92. Apuleius, *Met.* 5.1 (Walsh, 81).

93. Apuleius, *Met.* 5.2 (Walsh, 81).

94. Apuleius, *Met.* 5.5 (Walsh, 82); cf. 5.12.

As restrictive as the divine bridegroom's injunctions may be, Psyche enjoys a more intense experience of all her other senses, finding beauty through smell and touch. Psyche's aesthetic reorientation is most pronounced as she interacts with her invisible (and nameless) bridegroom: "I beg you by these locks of yours, which with their scent of cinnamon dangle all around your head, by your cheeks as soft and smooth as my own, by your breast which diffuses hidden heat."[95] Yet without vision and visibility her world remains a "blessed prison."[96]

Even if visibility is not inherent to beauty, it is necessary to Psyche's ability to remain embodied. The nostalgia for visibility is most pronounced when Psyche shines the lamp on her husband as he sleeps: "Even the lamplight was cheered and brightened on seeing him." And once again, Psyche is "awe-struck at this wonderful vision," and "gazed repeatedly on the beauty of that divine countenance" and the "flashing brilliance . . . of dewy wings."[97] It is significant that until he becomes visible, the husband is nameless. Only at this luminous moment in the tale is the name Cupid first mentioned.

The aftermath of this encounter offers further sensory twists. For only at his betrayal, after Psyche sees his body, does Cupid fly away, leaving Psyche to "watch . . . her husband's flight as far as her eyes allowed."[98] Having wreaked their damage, her eyes gaze helplessly on a vanishing body. One is left to wonder if visibility causes her to gain the divine body or to lose it.

In grieving the loss of Cupid, Psyche then joins another sensory order, a world where the inanimate, yet visible, bursts into speech. Reeds prophesy; waters speak; and even a tower consoles her.[99] Still, the body she has lost is ultimately her own, as Apuleius understands the

95. Apuleius, *Met.* 5.13 (Walsh, 87).

96. Apuleius, *Met.* 5.5 (Walsh, 82).

97. Apuleius, *Met.* 5.22 (Walsh, 92–93).

98. Apuleius, *Met.* 5.25 (Walsh, 94).

99. Apuleius, *Met.* 6.12, 14, 17.

flight of the sensory body: "The hopelessness of the situation turned Psyche to stone. She was physically present, but her senses deserted her."[100] Once again Psyche becomes the statue she had been when humans worshipped her as Venus. This time, however, she is the object not of many gazes but of a single divine gaze, the "steady gaze of benevolent Providence."[101]

When Cupid and Psyche are eventually reconciled, the marriage feast marks Psyche's reembodiment. The musicians who serenade the couple are visible, as are the Graces who fill the room with sweet aromas. Vision, which threatened to undermine the union, in fact solidifies it. To mark the reunion, Cupid and Psyche eventually welcome their firstborn, appropriately named Voluptas, or "Pleasure," a name reminiscent of the embodied gaze *(cum voluptate visenti)* with which Psyche inspected her divine surroundings at the opening of the tale.[102]

The visual cues in *Leucippe and Clitophon* and *The Golden Ass* suggest the power of narrative to enhance the interpretive possibilities of the human body as a sensory body. Attuned to what characters perceive and how they use their eyes, the reader becomes fluent in the language of the eyes. Through this literature the audience becomes "all eyes," capable of detecting false lovers, vindicating genuine ones, and even discovering how the recovery of the sensory body can unite the human and the divine. These two novels exemplify the double impulse not only to visualize but also to render judgments based on those visual cues. More than the rhetorical handbooks, the novels demonstrate the power of visual detail as vivid description. By this *enargeia*, the reader is primed to

---

100. Apuleius, *Met.* 6.14 (Walsh, 108).

101. Apuleius, *Met.* 6.15 (Walsh, 108).

102. Apuleius, *Met.* 6.24; cf. 5.1. In a separate context, Michel Foucault offers this gloss on the term: *voluptas* is the sort of pleasure "whose origin is to be placed outside us and in objects whose presence we cannot be sure of: a pleasure, therefore, which is precarious in itself, undermined by the fear of loss, and to which we are drawn by the force of a desire that may or may not find satisfaction . . . [a] kind of violent, uncertain, and conditional pleasure" (*The Care of*

pierce thin appearances and probe the sensory dramas that enliven and expose the characters. Such attentiveness, cultivated through novels, rhetoric, and history, suggests how keenly Christian pilgrims might have read the characters they encountered in pilgrims' testimonies.

SENSING THE BIBLICAL PAST

I focus on three tendencies or impulses that shaped the spirituality of pilgrims to the living: *exoticism*, by which I mean the desire to know the marvels of distant lands; *sensory engagement*, the conviction that the physical senses, and particularly vision, could perceive divine presence; and *biblical realism*, a desire to participate in sacred moments from the biblical past. All three impulses are found in both the *History of the Monks in Egypt* and the *Lausiac History*. Both travelogues can be understood as hybrid works, a combination of travelers' tales and biography that blend monastic anecdotes and miracle accounts. This nexus is crucial for discerning pilgrims' expectations as well as for understanding the affinities between pilgrimage and other devotional practices.

The impulse to exoticize monasticism had roots in ancient travel writing. Chapter 2 is concerned with tracing the affinities between the Christian travelogues and pagan descriptions of distant lands. Pilgrims borrowed and adapted narrative devices found in exotic travel writing to represent their experiences to their reading and listening audiences. They did not seek to represent all the varieties of monastic organizations; rather, they constructed monasticism as a thoroughly biblical undertaking.[103] In depicting the monastic world as a charmed biblical land, these writers developed various ways to engage their readers. It

---

the Self, vol. 3 of *The History of Sexuality*, trans. Robert Hurley [New York: Vintage, 1986], 66). All this strikes me as an apt, if unwitting, summary of Psyche's ordeal. Cf. s.v. "voluptās" in *Oxford Latin Dictionary*, ed. P. G. W. Glare (Oxford: Clarendon, 1982), 2102b.

103. James Goehring, "The Encroaching Desert: Literary Production and Ascetic Space in Early Christian Egypt," *JECS* 1 (1993): 281–96. See esp. 291–93

was not enough to spice their works with biblical allusions; their narratives were crafted to allow pilgrims to engage the biblical world.

Christians developed their own poetics of travel writing, that is to say, the tropes, conventions, and structures through which to report their experiences. Three tropes, in particular, gave expression to pilgrims' experiences: distance, marvel, and the sacred past. I examine how the authors of the Christian travelogues positioned Egyptian monasticism both spatially and temporally at a comfortable distance from the reader's world. By these displacements, pilgrim-authors assumed the license to portray monastics as "living monuments" of the biblical past.

The effect of these tropes, however, extends far beyond their stylistic, descriptive, or retrospective dimensions. Closer examination of these descriptive tools reveals the perceptual force to shape an audience's expectations. The travelogues simultaneously express and generate pilgrims' experiences, rather than simply transcribe the places and people visited. Far from stenographic, their reports are, rather, literary creations, in the sense that they are selective representations of experience.[104] Whenever a traveler encounters something strange or unfamiliar, she cannot help but domesticate it into familiar categories. In the act of describing experience, then, travel writing invariably *constructs* realities.[105] To reach a deeper understanding of pilgrims' reports as *prospective* devices, the investigator must pay careful attention to the language, arrangement, and the telling omissions that make up a pilgrim's report. Attention to the literary texture of these works yields a richer under-

---

for a discussion of what Goehring refers to as the "desertification" of Egypt. Id., "Withdrawing from the Desert: Pachomius and the Development of Village Monasticism in Upper Egypt," *HTR* 89 (1996): 267–85. Goehring highlights a literary polarization of desert and city.

104. See Mary B. Campbell, *The Witness and the Other World: Exotic European Travel Writing, 400–1600* (Ithaca: Cornell University Press, 1988), 2–4.

105. François Hartog demonstrates this for ancient Greek travel writing in *The Mirror of Herodotus: The Representation of the Other in the Writing of History*, trans. Janet Lloyd (Berkeley: University of California Press, 1988).

standing of pilgrims' narrative patterns. Those patterns, in turn, allow the interpreter to detect the religious sensibilities behind pilgrimage to the living.

Yet, as the analysis of the pagan novels and rhetorical handbooks suggests, some of the most instructive uses of those visualizing tropes appear outside the corpus of pilgrims' testimonies that have survived. Rather than limit the investigation to hagiographic, monastic, and epistolary writings that explicitly mention pilgrims to the living, my study also examines narratives that had the potential to shape pilgrims' perceptions of their sacred destinations.

Looking beyond pilgrims' reports, then, chapter 3 focuses on Christian works describing travel to a divine and somewhat embodied presence. In particular, I analyze the traveler's perspective in otherworldly journeys, apocalypses, and spiritual treatises on the soul's journey toward God: that is to say, stories with the potential to affect how pilgrims perceived the holy men and women they encountered. The resonances between the "real" journeys that pilgrims describe and the "imagined" journeys recounted in otherworldly and fictionalized accounts are striking in their portrayal of the holy body.

This analysis expands the literary resources by which to interpret and reconstruct pilgrims' behaviors and dispositions. When other types of religious and imaginative literature enter the discussion, the pilgrims' spirituality comes into sharper focus. Such connections are easier to establish for pilgrims like Jerome, who both created an idealized pilgrim and left a record of his own travels.[106] It stands to reason, then, that other types of travel narratives shaped pilgrims' renderings of their own experiences. Thus fabulous journeys provide an important tool for interpreting the experiential dimensions of any pilgrims' account.

From allegorical journeys, I return to Christian descriptions of physical pilgrimage. Chapter 4 focuses on pilgrims to the holy places and

---

106. The same might also be said for Palladius, who found his ur-pilgrim in the letters of the Apostle Paul, a mimetic relation I discuss in chapter 2.

how they construed their sensory engagement with the holy sites. Significant here is their understanding of the "eye of faith," an expression that stood for a broad range of visual and visionary experiences, including instances of conjuring and participating in events from the biblical past. Beyond demonstrating the primacy of sight at the holy places, this chapter also asks what qualities of seeing constitute the "eye of faith." Why fourth-century pilgrims associated their most transformative moments with vision becomes a more complex problem when one considers the increasing use of touch in accounts from later centuries. What at first appears as a rupture or shift in the use of the senses at the holy places turns out to be a radical realization of cultural assumptions about the materiality of vision in late antiquity, a notion with profound implications for pilgrims' relation to the past.

Chapter 5 continues this investigation of pilgrims' visuality with a detailed examination of their renditions of the physical appearance of holy people, in particular their detailed descriptions of facial appearance. In keeping with the earlier discussion of monuments, this discussion nuances that analogy by examining the ascetic face, in isolation from the body, as the real monument. Much like the ancient novelists, who clued their readers to the interpretive possibilities in the eyes, pilgrims to the living reveal the interpretive possibilities of the ascetic face. In particular, these pilgrims appropriated and adapted the larger culture's assumptions about the intimate relation between visible features of the face and inner states, a set of assumptions that, independently of Christianity, gave rise to techniques of face-reading, or physiognomy. The remainder of the chapter probes the significance of the ascetic face in the broader context of ancient fascination with reading bodies. Against this background of ancient physiognomic theory, pilgrims' rather formulaic descriptions of the ascetic face take on a new meaning.

As a sensory analysis of these travelogues demonstrates, pilgrims forged a Christian visual piety that drew on ancient physiognomy and optical theories as a way to articulate a mode of biblical realism that could be experienced away from the holy places. In their Christianized, and, specifically, biblicized physiognomy, pilgrims devised ways of "reading" the ascetic face for access to the biblical past. By expressing religious experience through facial language, pilgrims communicated to their audiences that seeing holy people was an opportunity to participate in the biblical past.

Those intersecting themes of pilgrimage, the biblical past, and the power of vision converge most succinctly in a brief episode reported in the *Life of Symeon the Holy Fool.* After completing their pilgrimage to Jerusalem, Symeon and his companion, John, spotted monasteries in the Judean desert. They paused to consider what lay in the distance. As Leontius reports their conversation, "John saw the monasteries all around the holy Jordan, and said . . . to Symeon, 'Do you know the ones who dwell in these houses which are before us?' The other said to him, 'Who are they?' And John said, 'Angels of God.' Symeon said to him in wonder, 'Can we see them?' 'If we will become like them, yes,' said the other."[107] Although this seventh-century tale postdates the pilgrims I discuss here, it communicates the powerful notion that to become was to see. What exactly they wanted to see, monks or angels, however, remains ambiguous. Even the reader does not find out, for John and Symeon's immediate impulse was to remount their horses and continue their journey home. Their response is telling. As tantalizing as it was to see the monks/angels and thereby continue to see the biblical past they had just experienced in Jerusalem, that transformation was premature, suggesting that only as Symeon's ascetic career unfolded might he truly see and become.

In addition to conveying the transformative power of vision, this story serves as a useful reminder that pilgrims' experiences were learned experiences, patterned on the biblical stories, pilgrims' reports, imaginative literature, and monastic hagiography that late antique Christians encountered. The final chapter explores the implications of those sensibilities for interpreting other aspects of Christian piety, and specifically

---

107. *Life of Symeon the Holy Fool,* 1 (Ryden, 124; Krueger, 134).

the veneration of relics and icons. I focus on the intersection of visual and visionary experience in these practices, suggesting an affective engagement similar to that claimed by pilgrims. All this serves to open up new ways of understanding the intensity of visual experience that shaped late antique piety, and not just pilgrimage. These later developments suggest a broader context for understanding Christian attitudes to the beholder. In a time when moral teachers also feared the eye, warning Christians that to see is to have,[108] pilgrims opened up new possibilities for this precious sense, showing instead that to see was to be.

108. For example, "What the eye sees it appropriates" (Pseudo-Shenoute, *On Christian Behaviour,* 40.6–7, ed. K. H. Kuhn [CSCO, 206–7/Scriptores Coptici, 29–30; Louvain: CSCO, 1960], 30:23).

TWO

Desert Ascetics
and Distant Marvels
The Historia as Travelogue

What lies beyond is full of marvels and unreality,
the land of poets and fabulists, of doubt and obscurity.
Plutarch, V. Thes. 1 (LCL, 1:3)

To those accustomed to the thick descriptions that enliven modern travel writing, both the *History of the Monks* and the *Lausiac History* may appear rather thin. Their authors took little interest in mapping the strange lands they encountered or writing guidebooks for future pilgrims. As the vexing silences suggest, that job was left to the cartographers, gazetteers, liturgical specialists, and travel guides of the day. In these pilgrims' accounts one finds little information about the landscape or any travel companions.[1] And although written in the first person,

1. On the interpretive implications of "scenic" or "social" emptiness, see Mary B. Campbell, " 'The Object of One's Gaze': Landscape, Writing, and Early Medieval Pilgrimage," in *Discovering New Worlds: Essays on Medieval Exploration and Imagination*, ed. Scott D. Westrem (New York: Garland, 1991), 3–15, esp. 4–5; and Blake Leyerle, "Landscape as Cartography in Early Christian Pilgrimage Narratives," *JAAR* 64 (1996): 119–43, esp. 125–26.

neither work could be called introspective or personal. There are no "interior castles" to speak of. Both works face outward, to the surfaces of Egyptian monasticism, from the vast, desert landscape to the furrows of a monk's brow.

The "surfaces" of monasticism, however, are puzzling. As with other pilgrims' reports, one finds place-names, a few geographical coordinates, and names of holy men and women visited. Yet there are also some enigmatic details—monks with angelic faces and a reputation for miracles so strong that, at times, the author cuts short an eyewitness account in order to record hearsay about miracles a particular ascetic once performed.[2]

What can these odd figures of speech and narrative choices tell us about pilgrims' experiences? To recent literary historians, these puzzling expressions are not empty tropes but symptoms of an author's efforts to grapple with the otherness of Egyptian monastic culture. A better understanding of the nature and function of travel writing can lend insight into pilgrims' perceptions and offer the modern interpreter access to their representations of their experiences, that is to say the stylized and symbolic language through which they simultaneously recorded and interpreted their memories.[3] If taken as literary creations

2. *HM* 6.1; 8.24, 26.

3. Recent studies of medieval pilgrims' reports offer fresh perspectives on the poetics of travel writing: Mary B. Campbell, *The Witness and the Other World: Exotic European Travel Writing, 400–1600* (Ithaca: Cornell University Press, 1988); and Donald R. Howard, *Writers and Pilgrims: Medieval Pilgrimage Narratives and Their Posterity* (Berkeley: University of California Press, 1980). On rhetorical analysis, see Ruth Morse, *Truth and Convention in the Middle Ages: Rhetoric, Representation, and Reality* (Cambridge: Cambridge University Press, 1991), esp. 15–84. On the value of a literary approach for uncovering pilgrims' experiences, see Barbara Nimri Aziz, "Personal Dimensions of the Sacred Journey: What Pilgrims Say," *Religious Studies* 23 (1987): 247–61, esp. 247–48. For literary patterns in late antique pilgrims' descriptions of the Holy Land, see Leyerle, "Landscape as Cartography"; Laurie Douglass, "A New Look at the *Itinerarium Burdigalense*," *JECS* 4 (1996): 313–34; Campbell, *Witness*, 15–45.

and not factual records, such as a census or tax report, pilgrims' writings can reveal the world as it was imagined and experienced.[4] Those sensibilities emerge when one pays close attention to the narrative patterns, repetitions, and omissions in pilgrim narratives. As the medievalist Donald Howard once put it, "Travel itself is 'imaginative': travels are fictions to the extent that the traveler sees what he wants or expects to see, which is often what he has read."[5]

Closer attention to the literary texture of pilgrims' writings reveals their worldview. One questions less the veracity of these accounts and exposes more how travel writing becomes an act of cultural translation whereby travelers use the language they already know to describe what they struggle to know. In this groping representation, pilgrims may draw on familiar stories and prior expectations, many of which are derived from other texts. Indeed, the consequences of that re-presentation and misrepresentation are quite complex. As Edward Said and others have demonstrated of the modern period, travel writing often perpetuates political and ideological programs.[6] The importance of these studies notwithstanding, pilgrims' writings also reflect shifting religious sensibilities. Thus, even the most plot-poor and stilted accounts can reveal pilgrims' perceptions of space, of time, and of the transcendent possibilities of pilgrimage. With a better understanding of how travel writers

4. Campbell, *Witness*, 4–6.

5. Howard, *Writers and Pilgrims*, 10.

6. Edward Said, *Orientalism* (New York: Vintage, 1978), esp. 54–73. On Pausanias's *Guide to Greece* as a response to Roman imperial power in the second century C.E., see Jaś Elsner, *Art and the Roman Viewer: The Transformation of Art from the Pagan World to Christianity* (Cambridge: Cambridge University Press, 1995), 125–55. For the colonialist dynamics of modern travel writing, see, for instance, Mary W. Helm, *Ulysses' Sail: An Ethnographic Odyssey of Power, Knowledge, and Geographical Distance* (Princeton: Princeton University Press, 1988), esp. 22–33; Peter Bishop, *The Myth of Shangri-La: Tibet, Travel Writing and the Western Creation of Sacred Landscape* (Berkeley: University of California Press, 1989), esp. 1–24; Mary Louise Pratt, *Imperial Eyes: Travel Writing and Transculturation* (New York: Routledge, 1992), esp. 6–9.

chose to tell their stories, we gain insight into the workings of the pilgrims' imagination.

Literary approaches to travel writing also illumine how ancient pilgrims and their audiences perceived holy people. The *History of the Monks in Egypt* and *the Lausiac History* employ familiar conventions of exotic travel writing as a means to portray monasticism to monks and lay people in different regions. If read as pilgrims' writings, rather than as monastic chronicle, both works reveal the fascination that the ascetic movement held for outsiders. What pilgrims' texts show us—in a way that sayings collections, rules, and monastic biography do not—are the ideals and idealizations that drew many pilgrims to seek out desert ascetics. Since few interpreters have identified the *historia* as a type of pilgrim's narrative, the first part of my discussion focuses on the affinities shared by these early fifth-century anthologies and travel writing. The remainder of the discussion explores how particular narrative techniques both exoticized and domesticated foreign monasticism for distant readers.

THE *HISTORIAI* AS TRAVEL WRITING

In a recent study of ancient historiography, Glen Bowersock warns, "With works of imaginative literature there is nothing more ruinous for historical understanding than genre theory or a mindless search for antecedents, origins, and distant parallels."[7] Indeed, the *historiai* can be understood as works of imaginative literature, presenting a distant and charmed world to their audiences. And yet, without falling victim to the paralysis Bowersock describes, questions of genre are worth revisiting precisely because they reveal the shared assumptions between authors and audiences.[8]

7. G. W. Bowersock, *Fiction as History: Nero to Julian* (Berkeley: University of California Press, 1994), 14.

8. For a clear overview of theories of literary genre and their heuristic import, see Richard A. Burridge, *What Are the Gospels? A Comparison with*

Like most travel writing, the *historia* is "the beggar of literary forms."[9] The hybrid character of these reports is already apparent in the *History of the Monks in Egypt*. This work, from the opening years of the fifth century, combines biographical vignettes, novellas, anecdotes, and travel impressions to create a regional panorama of monastic culture. Within a half-century, two other writers borrowed this format, using a series of brief sketches to describe individual holy people or various monastic communities they encountered in other regions. In 420, Palladius, bishop of Helenopolis, recounted his visits among Palestinian and Egyptian ascetics in a work known as the *Lausiac History*. And in the 440s, Theodoret, bishop of Cyrrhus, transposed the genre to another region, finding in the brief notice a convenient venue for parading the heroes and heroines of Syrian asceticism. Despite their regional focus, all three works appealed to a larger, international audience. And their relatively rapid translation into Latin expanded their readership considerably.[10]

Although most readers today recognize the presence of travel tales in the *historiai*, few have regarded them as pilgrims' texts, for several possible reasons. First, to many moderns, pilgrimage is exclusively about physical holy places, an assumption that eliminates other types of destinations, such as people or otherworldly places. Yet even if one adopts a

---

Graeco-Roman Biography (Cambridge: Cambridge University Press, 1991), esp. 26–81, 109–27; Mary Gerhart, "Generic Studies: Their Renewed Importance in Religious and Literary Interpretation," *JAAR* 45 (1977): 309–25.

9. The phrase is from a modern editor, Bill Buford, quoted in Jim Miller, "Literature's New Nomads," *Newsweek*, August 18, 1989, 50.

10. The *historia*, as a genre, invited numerous translations, conflations, expansions, and abridgements. On the intersecting textual history of the *Lausiac History* and the *History of the Monks*, see Cuthbert Butler, *The Lausiac History of Palladius* (Texts and Studies, 6, parts 1–2; Cambridge: Cambridge University Press, 1904) 1:6–22. The relation between the Greek and Latin versions of the *HM* is discussed in André-Jean Festugière, "Le problème littéraire de l'*Historia monachorum*," *Hermes* 83 (1955): 257–84; cf. Philip Rousseau, *Ascetics, Author-*

more inclusive definition of pilgrimage,[11] the biographical emphasis in the *historiai* is undeniable. As the goals of these journeys, holy people can indeed eclipse the journey itself. In surveys of patristic literature the *historiai* are usually mentioned in discussions of ascetic literature and described as "tales of the monks."[12] The fact that they were composed by pilgrims is noted but rarely enters into a consideration of the text's genre. To these modern interpreters, travel appears incidental to the biographical purpose of the works.

The *historiai* indeed bear a strong resemblance to ancient biographical anthologies, most notably pagan collections about famous philosophers, such as the anthologies by Philostratus or Eunapius.[13] An even closer parallel can be found in Christian writings, such as monastic collections of sayings, or *apophthegmata*, some of which are arranged according to their attribution to famous monastic teachers. Topography and biography come even closer in a Christianized work known as the *Lives of the Prophets*. If one accepts David Satran's persuasive analysis, the work suited early Byzantine Christian efforts to connect Bible, place, and holy person.[14]

What sets the *historiai* apart from these other collections is the presence of a traveler whose first-person narrative all but dissolves intellec-

---

ity, and the Church in the Age of Jerome and Cassian (Oxford: Oxford University Press, 1978), 16 n. 27; and more recently, C. P. Bammel, "Problems of the *Historia Monachorum*," *JTS* 47 (1996): 92–104. For a useful summary of the debates, see Frances Young, *From Nicaea to Chalcedon* (Philadelphia: Fortress, 1983), 38–39.

11. For example, "a journey undertaken by a person in quest of a place or a state that he or she believes to embody a valued ideal" (Alan Morinis, "Introduction," in *Sacred Journey: The Anthropology of Pilgrimage*, ed. Alan Morinis [Westport, Conn.: Greenwood, 1992], 4).

12. Young, *From Nicaea to Chalcedon*, 38–44.

13. Pierre Canivet, *Le monachisme syrien selon Théodoret de Cyr* (Théologie historique 42; Paris: Beauchesne, 1977), 65–66, 68–69, 79–82.

14. David Satran, *Biblical Prophets in Byzantine Palestine* (Leiden: Brill, 1995), 60–63, 101–10, esp. 107.

tual genealogies and institutional concerns, locating the holy person squarely in traveled space. Whereas the philosophical anthologies traced a lineage of intellectual traditions, the *historiai* followed a traveled route.[15] As extra-monastic, itinerant observers, the authors of the early *historiai* took little interest in the more localized master-disciple relationships found in *apophthegmata.*[16] The narrator of a *historia* remains a present voice, more self-conscious than the hagiographer or disciple writing in the self-effacing third person. Although he occasionally disappears from view as he recounts tales and journeys by others, the author's "rhetorical presence" as a traveler is central to the shape of the narrative.[17]

To appreciate the *historia*'s roots in travel writing, one can look to later anthologies that omitted the traveler's presence altogether in favor of a thoroughly biographical genre. With the appearance of the *Historia religiosa* in the 440s, Theodoret departed from the geographical plan of earlier works and arranged his regional work chronologically, beginning with reminiscences of deceased ascetics, then proceeding to his contemporaries, a scheme that undercuts the possibility of any continuous travel report.[18] Although he mentions his own travel experiences intermittently, they have no effect on the shape of the work. The difference of emphases between the *History of the Monks* and Theodoret's work are most apparent in the opening lines of any notice. Whereas a place-name provides the author of the *History of the Monks* with an opportunity to describe his journey, Theodoret appears more

15. Eunapius, for instance, connects his lives by means of teacher-disciple relations, as in *Vitae Sophistarum* (LCL, 377).

16. Canivet, *Monachisme syrien*, 79–82. Pierre Canivet and Alice Leroy-Molinghen, *Théodoret de Cyr* (SC 234 [1977]), 13.

17. On this term see Campbell, *Witness*, 15.

18. Theodoret mentions three organizing principles at key transitions: chronology (dead saints, then "those still living" [*HR* 21.1]); setting (desert saints, then ascetics in "inhabited lands" [*HR* 4.1; Canivet, *Monachisme syrien*, 83–86, 147–52]); and gender (male saints, then female saints [*HR* 29.1]).

interested in the political history of a place.[19] Yet, as in the earlier anthologies, Theodoret retains a regional focus, grounding famous ascetics in the religious landscape.[20]

The sixth century marks several important changes in the shape of the *historia*. With a growing interest in hagiographic anthologies for monastic use, the travel-based *historia* soon disappeared. Later anthologies severed all ties to travel writing, a shift in focus found in the *Lives of the Eastern Saints* by John of Ephesus (507–589) and the *Spiritual Meadow* by John Moschus (ca. 550–619), both of which are primarily hagiographic in structure and emphasis.[21] By the tenth century, collec-

---

19. For example, *HR* 1.2; 2.1; 5.1; cf. 21.2, on Theodoret's decision to place James first among the living saints.

20. For example, Theodosius (*HR* 10.1–2), whose manual labors (plowing, sowing, building docks) transformed the larger physical surroundings well beyond his small cell; cf. James of Cyrrhestica (*HR* 21.4–5; Price, 134), whose residency on the mountain "made it distinguished and revered, although formerly it was totally undistinguished and sterile. So great is the blessing it is confidently believed to have now received that the soil on it has been exhausted by those coming from all sides to carry it off for their benefit. Living in this place, he is observed by all comers." Cf. the role of narrative in "recharging" the holy dirt following the death of Saint Symeon the Younger, as suggested by V. Déroche's analysis of the *Life*, "Quelques interrogations à propos de la *Vie de Saint Syméon le Jeune*," *Eranos* 94 (1996): 63–83, esp. 78–82.

21. John Moschus, *Pratum spirituale*. Text: *PG* 87, cols. 2851–3112. Translated by John Wortley, *The Spiritual Meadow of John Moschos*, CS 139 (Kalamazoo: Cistercian, 1992). See H. Chadwick, "John Moschus and his Friend Sophronius the Sophist," *JTS* n.s. 25 (1974): 41–74, esp. 41–49. John of Ephesus, *Lives of the Eastern Saints*, ed. and trans. E. W. Brooks, *Patrologia Orientalis* 17–19 (Paris, 1923–25). On the genre of these works, see Susan Ashbrook Harvey, *Asceticism and Society in Crisis: John of Ephesus and the* Lives of the Eastern Saints (Berkeley: University of California Press, 1990), esp. 34–37. Bernard Flusin suggests that Cyril of Scythopolis (ca. 525–558) conceived of his seven *vitae* of Palestinian monks as forming part of an anthology (*Miracle et histoire dans l'œuvre de Cyrille de Scythopolis* [Paris: Études Augustiniennes, 1983], 34–35, 70).

tions of short biographies of saints, or, *synaxaria*, complete the hagiographic trajectory of the *historia*.[22] Thus what began as a hybrid genre combining travel writing and hagiography eventually became a hagiographic genre with secondary travel motifs.

Given this shift toward biography in later monastic collections, it is all the more important to recognize the earlier *historiai* as personal narratives about travel. Their personal nature is reflected in the way each author organized material, choosing to gather anecdotes according to the places where they were received.[23] Occasionally the author turns to literary sources to expand his description of a particular place.[24] Indeed, this borrowing sometimes disrupts the itinerary, leading some to cast doubts on the historicity of the account.[25] But even when specific details of the itinerary have been called into question, few scholars today would argue that the *Lausiac History* or the *History of the Monks* are pure fabrications.

22. "Synaxarion," in *Oxford Dictionary of Byzantium*, ed. Alexander P. Kazhdan et al. (3 vols.; New York: Oxford University Press, 1991), 3:1991.

23. See, for example, D. F. Buck, "The Structure of the *Lausiac History*" *Byzantion* 46 (1976): 292–307.

24. Eva Schulz-Flügel, "The Function of the *Apophthegmata* in *Vitae* and *Itineraria*," *SP* 18 (1989): 281–91, esp. 284. The fact of literary borrowing, however, would not have prevented ancient audiences from recognizing the *historia* as an *itinerarium*. Gabriel Bunge detects traces of a travel memoir Palladius penned several years prior to composing the *Lausiac History* ("Palladiana I: Introduction aux fragments coptes de *L'histoire lausiaque*," *Studia Monastica* 32 [1990]: 79–129, esp. 119–224).

25. For example, P. Peeters, "Une vie copte de S. Jean de Lycopolis," *Analecta Bollandiana* 54 (1936): 359–83. On the larger debate, see Young, *From Nicaea to Chalcedon*, 40–41. Recognizing the use of literary sources in Palladius's travelogue, E. D. Hunt offers this helpful perspective: "The essential facts of his own experience were enriched with tales form the popular tradition to produce a work at once edifying and authentic" ("Palladius of Helenopolis: A Party and Its Supporters in the Church of the Late Fourth Century," *JTS* n.s. 24 [1973]: 456–80, esp. 458–60).

Leaving aside the difficult distinction between fact and fiction,[26] a more meaningful question is whether the early *historiai* were likely to be read as travel guides or travel accounts. Ancient Christians, like readers today, understood the difference between a guide *to* a journey and a narrative *about* a journey.[27] Jerome implied this distinction when he warned his readers that his description of Paula's travels was not to be taken as a travel guide *(odoeporicon)*.[28] He promised no practical travel advice, guiding the reader less toward the actual places and more toward Paula's experiences once there. Jerome's invitation to imagine the journey was hardly novel to ancient audiences, who frequently read about journeys without any intention of ever undertaking the travel themselves.[29] So it was for Palladius, whose aim was to edify his patron, Lausus, rather than offer a map for a physical journey.

Other factors, too, prevent modern readers from understanding the *historiai* as travel books. At first blush, the abundance of miracles in the *historiai* seems alien to any form of travel writing. It makes historians shudder: Derwas Chitty cautions readers of the *History of the Monks*, "The work is full of wonders, and the writer was extremely gullible."[30] Even among generous interpreters, who appeal to the historical or cul-

---

26. See now Claudia Rapp, "Storytelling as Spiritual Communication in Early Greek Hagiography: The Use of *Diegesis*," *JECS* 6 (1998): 431–48, esp. 443–44. Cf. Campbell, *Witness*, 2, 4.

27. As one modern travel editor explains the distinction, "Travel books, unlike guidebooks, contain little useful information. They are meant to be read, not pillaged for practical tips. Some of the best ones describe trips that few readers will ever take." Gary Fisketjon, quoted in Miller, "Literature's New Nomads," 50.

28. Jerome, *Ep.* 108.8.1.

29. A classic example of the fabricated journey from a later period is Mandeville's *Travels;* on Mandeville's use of literary sources, see Iain Macleod Higgins, *Writing East: The "Travels" of Sir John Mandeville* (Philadelphia: University of Pennsylvania Press, 1997).

30. Derwas Chitty, *The Desert a City* (Crestwood, N.Y.: Saint Vladimir's Seminary Press, 1966), 51.

tural context of the work, the scholarly embarrassment over the prominence of miracles is apparent.[31] Benedicta Ward moved this debate over miracles in an important direction when she explored the theological significance of marvels as a form of biblical typology.[32] As Ward reminds modern historians, miracles had a symbolic function in the *History of the Monks*. A miracle, particularly one reminiscent of Jesus, served as a potent device for authenticating the sanctity of the protagonist.

What Ward's analysis does not entertain, however, is the profusion of miracles and marvels in ancient travel writing. Ever since Odysseus landed on the island of the Phaiacians, storytellers have delighted armchair travelers with tales of distant places and mysterious events. In the fifth century B.C.E. writers such as Herodotus and a court physician named Ctesias of Cnidos pushed the boundaries of the geographical imagination with their accounts of exotic peoples, strange beasts, and the marvels of India.[33] This fascination with the foreign and fantastic resurged in Hellenistic times with the appearance of paradoxographies, catalogues of bizarre phenomena verging on the miraculous.[34]

Imaginary journeys also associated distant places with marvels. The title of Antonius Diogenes's fantastic journey, *The Wonders beyond*

31. See, for example, Young, who calls on modern readers to make "some allowance for a tendency to exaggeration and idealization" in reading *historiai* (*From Nicaea to Chalcedon*, 41).

32. Benedicta Ward, "Introduction," in *The Lives of the Desert Fathers: The Historia Monachorum in Aegypto*, trans. Norman Russell (Kalamazoo: Cistercian, 1980), 39–46, expanded in Benedicta Ward, "Signs and Wonders: Miracles in the Desert Tradition," *SP* 18 (1982): 539–42; repr. in id., *Signs and Wonders: Saints, Miracles and Prayers from the Fourth Century to the Fourteenth* (Hampshire: Variorum, 1992).

33. James S. Romm, *The Edges of the Earth in Ancient Thought: Geography, Exploration, and Fiction* (Princeton: Princeton University Press, 1992), 82–120.

34. Texts available in A. Giannini, *Paradoxographorum Graecorum Reliquiae* (Milan: Istituto Editoriale Italiano, 1965). For a recent bibliography on paradoxography, see William Hansen, trans., *Phlegon of Tralles' Book of Marvels* (Exeter: University of Exeter Press, 1996), 2–12. See also Alessandro Giannini,

Thule, says it all: ἄπιστα, or "unbelievable things" take place beyond the edges of existence.[35] Even if, as Strabo remarked, "the distant is difficult to disprove,"[36] the description of marvels required little justification. In a parody of the genre, *A True Story (Verae Historiae)*, Lucian linked marvels with remote places when he promised to "tell all kinds of lies in a plausible and specious way," as generations of travel writers had done before him.[37] Despite his irony, he is pointing to a commonplace of travel writing: a distant place without marvels is not so distant after all.[38]

Some distant lands gained a special reputation for miracles. Egypt, in particular, was famed for its prodigies.[39] In the fifth century B.C.E.

"Studi sulla paradossografia greca," *Rendiconti Istituto Lombardo Accademia di Scienze e Lettere* 97 (1963): 247–66; Roger French, *Ancient Natural History: Histories of Nature* (New York: Routledge, 1994), 299–303. For an anti-paradoxographical writer, see the fourth-century B.C.E. refutations of mythological marvels in Palaephatus's περὶ ἀπίστων (1902 Teubner text, repr. with trans. by Jacob Stern; Wauconda, Ill.: Bolchazy-Carducci, 1996). Within paradoxography, there were first-person accounts about traveling to a distant land in search of saving wisdom, an even closer parallel to the Christian travelogues; see John J. Winkler, *Auctor & Actor: A Narratological Reading of Apuleius's* Golden Ass (Berkeley: University of California Press, 1985), 257–73.

35. *The Wonders beyond Thule* (Sandy, 779). See also James S. Romm, "Novels beyond Thule: Antonius Diogenes, Rabelais, Cervantes," in *The Search for the Ancient Novel*, ed. James Tatum (Baltimore: Johns Hopkins University Press, 1994), 101–16, esp. 103. Cf. Romm, *Edges of the Earth*, 202–14.

36. Strabo, *Geog.* 11.6.4, cited in Romm, *Edges of the Earth*, 98 and n. 37.

37. Lucian, *Ver. Hist.* 1.2–3 (LCL 1:249); among his forebears, he mentions Ctesias, Iambulus, and Homer. On this topos, see Emilio Gabba, "True History and False History in Classical Antiquity," *JRS* 71 (1981): 50–62, esp. 53.

38. François Hartog, *The Mirror of Herodotus: The Representation of the Other in the Writing of History*, trans. Janet Lloyd (Berkeley: University of California Press, 1988), 231–32.

39. See, for example, the mid-fourth-century C.E. geography *Expositio totius mundi et gentium*, 34 (ed. J. Rougé, SC 124 [1966]). For a valuable discussion of Greco-Roman "Egyptomania," see David Frankfurter, *Religion in Roman Egypt:*

Herodotus devoted an entire book of the *Histories* to Egypt for the sole reason that "nowhere are there so many marvellous things (θωμάσια)."[40] Egypt's reputation for exotica and healings endured throughout the imperial period, as young intellectuals from all over the empire set out in pursuit of secret knowledge. Plutarch describes Cleombrotus of Sparta, who "made many excursions in Egypt" and was "a man fond of seeing things and acquiring knowledge."[41] And Greek novelists such as Achilles Tatius set some of their most fantastic adventures in Egypt.[42]

Even to Christians who restricted themselves to Christian texts, the connection between distance and miracle was familiar by the fourth century.[43] Legends of the apostles edified and entertained ancient audiences with marvels about distant places. Audiences followed the travels of the wonder-working apostles Thomas, Philip, and Peter to India, Parthia, and Rome, respectively. More exotic were the exploits of Andrew, who rescued Matthias from the eye-gouging, cannibalistic Myrmidonians, or Philip, who saved his companions from the bloodthirsty Ophians.[44]

Assimilation and Resistance (Princeton: Princeton University Press, 1998), 217–21. Lucien Regnault points to the fascination with Egypt shaping the literary developments in the apothegmatic tradition ("Les apophtegmes des pères en Palestine aux Ve et VIe siècles," *Irénikon* 54 [1981]: 320–30, esp. 328–29).

40. Herodotus, *Hist.* 2.35 (LCL 1:315).

41. Plutarch, *De defectu oraculorum*, 410 a–b: ἀνὴρ φιλοθεάμων ὤν καὶ φιλο-μαθὴς (LCL 5:353). For a historical perspective on this type of inquisitive travel, see E. D. Hunt, "Travel, Tourism, and Piety in the Roman Empire: A Context for the Beginnings of Christian Pilgrimage," *Échos du monde classique* 28 (1984): 391–417, esp. 403–8.

42. Achilles Tatius, 3.18–19. Only in Egypt do Clitophon's eyes "meet [their] match," (5.1), so amazing are the sights.

43. For instance, Macrina (Gregory of Nyssa, *V. Macrinae*, 3); Melania (*V. Mel.* 23).

44. *Acts of Peter* (Vercelli) 4–6; *Acts of Philip*, 3; Richard A. Lipsius and Maximillian Bonnet, eds., *Acta apostolorum apocrypha* (1891–1903, repr. Hildesheim: Georg Olms, 1959), 1:78–103 (Peter); 2.2:1–98 (Philip); 2.2:99–291

Christian storytellers could also draw more subtle connections between miracle and distance. In the *Acts of Thomas*, the apostle's first miracle describes how he underwent a stupefying and sudden change in appearance at a wedding feast: in describing the guests' confusion, the narrator includes several reminders that Thomas is a foreigner, speaking in a foreign tongue.[45] Thus miracles were the stuff not only of an amazing life, but also the stuff of foreign visitors and exotic places.

Even if miracles remain an unlikely feature of travel writing to modern readers, who regard the genre as somehow closer to "fact," they were not so for the ancients. More than mere embellishment, marvels enhanced the sense of distance inscribed in travelers' tales. As François Hartog points out, without miracles Herodotus's construction of Egypt would have failed. Marvels convinced readers to believe in the "otherness" of a place called Egypt. Thus Herodotus relied on marvels to maintain the spatial as well as cultural remoteness of Egypt. As Hartog explains the literary effect of marvels, *"Thoma* translates the difference between there and here and, as such, . . . produces an impression of reality. It declares: I am the reality of otherness."[46] Hartog is making an important point here: however fantastic they might be, accounts of miracles heighten and solidify the writer's claims that a wholly other people

---

(Thomas). *Acts of Andrew and the Acts of Andrew and Matthias in the City of the Cannibals,* ed. and trans. Dennis Ronald MacDonald (Atlanta: Scholars, 1990). Here I follow the translations provided in James K. Elliott, *The Apocryphal New Testament* (Oxford: Clarendon, 1993). On the affinities between travel tales and Christian apocrypha, see Dennis Ronald MacDonald, *Christianizing Homer: The Odyssey, Plato, and* The Acts of Andrew (New York: Oxford University Press, 1994), 77–84.

45. *Acta Thom.* 4, 8: "And they all looked at him, as at a stranger and one come from a foreign land." The staring continued until Thomas's appearance changed, "but they did not understand what he said, since he was Hebrew and what he said was spoken in the Hebrew tongue."

46. Hartog, *Mirror of Herodotus,* 237.

lives in a truly distant land. By this logic, miracles are best understood as tools for constructing reality and not necessarily chinks in truth's armor.

Given the pervasiveness of marvel writing in historical, geographical, and novelistic works,[47] Christian audiences would find it natural to encounter miracles (and many of them) in a travel account.[48] Thus, the *historiai* and travel writing were related precisely because of miracles, not despite them. Within this hybrid genre, miracles provided commentary on both places and persons. As hagiography within travel writing, the *historia*, as a genre, played a key role in shaping the pilgrims' image of desert asceticism. For if hagiography allows the reader to imagine an individual holy life, travel writing has the added effect of connecting that holy existence to a place. In expanding a travel narrative with biographical digressions (and not the other way around), the *historia* allowed ancient audiences to imagine individual ascetics within a separate world. When the evocation of another world—and not just its individual inhabitants—captures the reader's imagination, we are dealing with travel writing. To appreciate the role of travel writing in shaping the Christian religious imagination, I turn to a closer examination of the pilgrim's voice, allusions to distances, travel impressions, and destinations first as they are presented in the *History of the Monks* and then in the *Lausiac History*.

DISPLACEMENT IN THE *HISTORIA MONACHORUM*

The challenge for any travel writer is to draw the reader into another, unfamiliar world, one that is distant and self-contained. To convince the

47. See, for example, Jacques LeGoff, "The Medieval West and the Indian Ocean: An Oneiric Horizon," in *Time, Work, and Culture in the Middle Ages*, trans. Arthur Goldhammer (Chicago: University of Chicago Press, 1980), 189–200, esp. 193; Romm, *Edges of the Earth*, 82–120.

48. Even the title "historia" alerts the reader to a travel genre. In addition to signifying "investigation," the term could also mean "visits" in fourth-century

reader of that separation, the writer uses various techniques to differentiate between the reader's world and the world described in the text.[49]
As a way to preserve a "clear cultural distance,"[50] utopian and exotic
writers invoke boundaries and distances to establish the reader's status
as stranger to the world in the text. Even if the author draws the readers
closer to the world described in the text, they are never assimilated into
it. Every "there" implies a "here"; every "them" suggests an "us."[51] This
displacement is essential if the writer is to succeed at rendering an exotic
world sufficiently familiar to be understood but without undermining
its "otherness."

Late antique Christians were reminded of the distance between
themselves and the Egyptian monks whenever the author of the *History
of the Monks* alluded to his identity as an outsider writing for other outsiders. Sometimes those cues are subtle, as in this description of John of
Lycopolis's miracles: "These are the wonders which [John] performed
before strangers who came to see him (τοὺς ἔξωθεν ἐρχομένους). As
regards his own fellow-citizens (πολίταις συνεχῶς), who frequently came
to him for their needs, he foreknew and revealed things hidden in the
future."[52] Even though both groups benefit from the holy man's powers,
the distinction between outsiders (ἔξωθεν) and those nearby (συνεχῶς)
remains firm and keeps the reader at a remove from the pilgrim's destination, the holy man.

What buttresses that distinction is the continuous rhetorical presence of the first-person traveler-narrator. Whereas use of the third per-

---

writings. See Lampe, *PGL*, *678b*, s.v. "ἱστορία." Eusebius also uses ἱστορία in the
context of (pilgrim) travel, *Hist. eccl.* 6.11.1 (ed. E. Schwartz, 540.27); I thank
E. Mühlenberg for this reference.

49. Hartog, *Mirror of Herodotus*, 212–59.

50. François Hartog, *Mémoire d'Ulysse: Récits sur la frontière en Grèce ancienne*
(Paris: Gallimard, 1996), 60.

51. Cf. Hartog, *Mirror of Herodotus*, 249.

52. *HM* 1.11 (Russell, 53).

son might efface the pilgrim, the *History of the Monks* relies on that authorial presence, particularly in the opening words of many notices. One chapter opens, "We also saw another father in the desert not far from the city, called Theon, a holy man who had lived as an anchorite in a small cell and had practised silence for thirty years . . . One could see him with the face of an angel giving joy to his visitors by his gaze and abounding with much grace."[53] The traveler's direct, visual experience of the holy man—his physical appearance, some loose geographical coordinates, and Theon's hospitality—anchors the pilgrim's presence at the outset of the notice. Such reminders appear throughout the description. The author not only sees for the audience but even controls what is seen. As he says elsewhere, "But what need is there to speak of any of the works of this saint other than those which we perceived with our own eyes?"[54] Wedged between the monks and the implied reader, the traveler's rhetorical presence holds firm the distance between the reader's world and the exotic world that is visited. In this rhetoric of distancing, the eyewitness lays claim not just to veracity but also to distance.[55] It is not surprising that the author of the *History of the Monks* casts himself as an eyewitness, so as to occupy that precarious middle ground between the world of the monks and the reader's world.

53. *HM* 6.1 (Russell, 69).

54. *HM* 1.13 (Russell, 53); cf. 12.12 and 10.1, in reference to Copres, who performed some miracles "before our very eyes." On the significance of eyewitness accounts in the *historiai*, see Rapp, "Storytelling," 431–48, esp. 441; on this topos in pagan historiography, see John Marincola, *Authority and Tradition in Ancient Historiography* (Cambridge: Cambridge University Press, 1997), 63–86.

55. The importance of being an eyewitness—or having consulted with eyewitnesses—figures into many prologues and resurfaces in subsequent notices, as in Palladius, *HL* prol. 2, cf. 35.3; Theodoret, *HR* prol. 11 (Price, 9), cf. *HM* prol. 3, cf. 1.19; 8.50. On the significance of this topos for perceptions of the hagiographer, see Derek Krueger, "Typological Figuration in Theodoret of Cyrrhus's *Religious History* and the Art of Postbiblical Narrative," *JECS* 5 (1997): 393–419, esp. 415–16.

The eyewitness perspective alone, however, cannot sustain this distance. Geographical details, such as place-names, distances, and boundaries, also enhance the "otherness" of Egyptian monasticism. Such markers are part of a larger strategy to define the remoteness of the "other," implying that what cannot be completely understood can at least be measured.[56] Travel writers often marked the limits of human civilization in order to investigate those who dwelt beyond them.[57] Pliny located strange races at the edge of the known world or, as he called it, "the Earth's Door Bolt."[58] One function of these markers was to allow the author to insert a comfortable distance between the audience and the world described in the text.

Distances serve a similar purpose in the *History of the Monks*. In several notices the author emphasizes the distances and difficulties involved in reaching holy people, as if to heighten the hardships and rewards that await the reader. At first, the author hesitates to describe the desert of Antinoë where Abba Elias lived, insisting that "no description can do justice to that rugged desert in the mountain." Despite this compunction, the author proceeds to describe the arduous path one must follow to reach that perfect monk.[59] Even more perilous is the approach to Scetis: "This place is a waste land lying at a distance of a day's and a night's journey from Nitria through the desert. It is a very perilous journey for travelers. For if one makes even a small error, one can get lost in the desert and find one's life in danger."[60]

---

56. Cf. Hartog, who refers to these techniques as "operators of intelligibility" (*Mirror of Herodotus*, 234–35).

57. Lucian, *Ver. Hist.* 5 (Reardon, 622).

58. Pliny, *Nat. Hist.* 7.10 (home to the one-eyed Arimaspi); cf. other exotic peoples who crowd the edge of Pliny's map, as in Lixos (5.1.3) and those beyond Africa (5.8.45–46). On ethnography and the *eschatai*, see Romm, *Edges of the Earth*, 39.

59. *HM* 7.2 (Russell, 69).

60. *HM* 23.1 (Russell, 113).

The epilogue is devoted to enumerating the "great dangers"—starvation, swamps, floods, attacks by humans and beasts, drowning—from which the travelers were delivered. The author introduces that catalogue of torments thus: "In fact, it was not without danger or hardship that we visited those fathers whom we have mentioned. Nor was it without considerable effort that we saw what is reported in this work. On the contrary, we suffered much on our journey and came very near to losing our lives before we were counted worthy to see these things."[61] The catalogue of calamities is explicitly patterned on Job's seven trials, but it also brings to mind the shipwrecks, monsters, desert islands, and other perils found in ancient marvel writing. While these hardships may appear a sobering antidote to the marvels described in previous pages, the dangers of Scetis and of the epilogue in effect heighten the marvelous nature of the destinations. Such dangers are the necessary conditions for being "counted worthy to see these things," a reward that is promised in the chapter on Scetis: "All the monks [in Scetis] have attained perfection."[62]

This litany of hardships and great distances has a larger purpose: to prepare the reader for the marvels interlaced throughout the *History of the Monks*. Displacement and miracles are bound even in the opening lines of the prologue: "For [God] brought us to Egypt and showed us great and wonderful things (μεγάλα καὶ θαυμαστά)."[63] In this introduction one hears the opening words of Herodotus, who introduces the subject of his *Histories* as μεγάλα τε καὶ θαυμαστά.[64] This cue also evokes

---

61. *HM* epil. 3 (Russell, 118).

62. *HM* 23.1 (Russell, 113). A more graphic connection between remoteness and greatness appears in Philostratus's *V. Apoll.* (2.4), which notes that the inhabitants become taller as one approaches India: thus, whereas at the Caucasus Mountain dwellers are said to be eight feet tall, he reports that at the Indus, the men were two feet taller.

63. *HM* prol. 1 (Russell, 49).

64. Herodotus, *Hist.* 1.1 (LCL 1:2).

Egypt's longstanding reputation as a distant land of abundant natural beauty, fertility, strange fauna, antiquity, and wisdom.[65] The *History of the Monks* casts the monks in that exotic glow: "They do not busy themselves with any earthly matter or take account of anything that belongs to this transient world. But while dwelling on earth in this manner, they live as true citizens of heaven. Some of them do not even know that another world exists on earth."[66] Here we find a people oblivious to the audience's world. The language of two worlds erects a one-way glass that permits the reader to observe the monks while the monks remain unaware of the reader's existence. That separation is critical to the work's ability to construct the "otherness" of desert asceticism. Together geographical distance and inviolable containment anticipate further displacement in the body of the travelogue.

Displacement also has a temporal dimension.[67] In the tradition of ancient utopian writing, the author of the *History of the Monks* depicts the desert as a place where the distant past—in this case, the biblical past—is restored among the monks. Several markers denote this temporal divide between reader and monks. In one notice, Apelles tells the story of a monk who is considered to be "a man of another age, who sur-

65. K. A. D. Smelik and E. A. Hemelrijk, " 'Who Knows Not What Monsters Demented Egypt Worships?': Opinions on Egyptian Animal Worship in Antiquity as Part of the Conception of Egypt," in *Aufstieg und Niedergang der römischen Welt*, ed. H. Temporini and W. Haase (Berlin: DeGruyter, 1984), ser. 2, vol. 17, part 4, 1853–2337, esp. 1873–75, 1897, 1938–55; I thank Stephanie West for this reference. For Christian examples, see the *Infancy Gospel of Thomas* in *The Apocryphal New Testament*, 68–83. See also Paul J. Achtemeier, "Jesus and the Disciples as Miracle Workers in the Apocryphal New Testament," in *Aspects of Religious Propaganda in Judaism and Early Christianity*, ed. Elisabeth Schüssler Fiorenza (Notre Dame: University of Notre Dame Press, 1976), 149–86, esp. 155–56.

66. *HM* prol. 5–6 (Russell, 49–50).

67. Elsner detects a similar temporal and mythologizing displacement in Pausanias's description of Greece (*Art and the Roman Viewer*, 140–44).

passes in virtue all the monks of our own time."[68] That sense of "another age" is established early in the prologue, when the author marks the narrative's true beginning with "the coming of our Saviour Jesus Christ."[69] By turning back the clock in this way, the author can easily elide the Egyptian ascetics with Christ and the apostles: "They have performed cures, miracles and acts of power like those which the holy prophets and apostles worked. The Saviour performs miracles through them in the same way."[70] The epilogue observes: "To this day, [the monks] raise the dead and walk on water just like Peter."[71] Both temporal references bracket the entire narrative within biblical time.

Not just in their deeds but also in their physical appearance, the holy men are described as resembling biblical figures. Although I develop the sensory implications of this resemblance in chapter 5, their function as a travel-writing trope is worth mentioning here. Abba Or, we are told, "looked just like an angel. He was about ninety years old and had a brilliant white beard down to his chest. And his face was so radiant that the sight of him alone filled one with awe."[72] Another desert father, Theon, had "the face of an angel giving joy to his visitors by his gaze and abounding with much grace."[73] As any attentive reader of saints' lives might note, moral and even biographical resemblances to specific biblical figures were a common technique for authenticating the holy person's sanctity.[74] By invoking physical resemblances, these travel writers

68. *HM* 13.3 (Russell, 93).

69. *HM* prol. 4 (Russell, 49).

70. *HM* prol. 9 (Russell, 50).

71. *HM* epil. 2 (Russell, 118).

72. *HM* 2.1 (Russell, 63, modified).

73. *HM* 6.2 (Russell, 68);. cf. *HM* 26; 7.1 (Russell, 69): "even the sight of [Elias] was very impressive." Although the connection to Elijah is explicit, no physical description is included.

74. A point underscored by Flusin, *Miracle et histoire*, 85; cf. *HL* 12.1–2; *HR* 6.5; 22.3; Cyril of Scythopolis, *V. Cyriac.* 2; *V. Euthy.* 1, 5, 8; Athanasius, *V. Ant.* 7;

reduce the complexity of a human life to a moment of biblical perception. When cast in biblical language, these portraits arrest the convulsions of ascetic life into a crisp, clear, biblical event. As Mary Campbell once described this double function of biblical language in pilgrims' narratives, it "domesticates the places thus 'described' *and* provides the thrill of strangeness."[75] In the *History of the Monks*, however, it is persons, not places, that are domesticated and exoticized through a biblical idiom.

Separated from the rest of human society both temporally and spatially, the distant peoples enjoy a privileged relation to nature. Utopian descriptions of distant lands often remark on the longevity of the inhabitants, as in Pliny's description of the Hyperboreans, "who live to extreme old age and are famous for legendary marvels. Here are believed to be the hinges on which the firmament turns."[76] In this brief description, Pliny links old age, marvels, and the edges of existence. The *History of the Monks* drew similar inferences about distance and longevity. Apollo was at least eighty years old; both Abba Or and John of Lycopolis were ninety; Elias was expected to be one hundred.[77] Their advanced ages pale in comparison to the biblical patriarchs who lived over nine hundred years (cf. Gen 5:3–32); yet such longevity would surely have earned them a place in the record books of antiquity, such as Phlegon of Tralles's *Long-Lived Persons*, an anecdotal list of people whose sole claim to fame was their advanced age.[78] Although the *History of the Monks* bears no direct resemblance to formal treatises on longevity, the topic constitutes yet another affinity between the Chris-

---

V. Charitonis 8, 24, 43. On the significance of this compositional mimesis, see Krueger, "Typological Figuration," esp. 403–5.

75. Campbell, "The Object of One's Gaze," 6 (Campbell's emphasis).

76. Pliny, *Nat. Hist.* 4.87; cf. 7.28, 153–55; *Expositio totius mundi et gentium*, 7.

77. *HM* 2.1; 1.17; 7.1.

78. Hansen, *Phlegon*, 50–57; on the background of this genre, see ibid., 17–20.

tian travelogue and pagan works dealing with utopias and geographical wonders, including paradoxographies.[79]

The utopian qualities of the *History of the Monks* are hard to miss. On the Island of the Sun, as Iambulus describes it, inhabitants live to the age of 150 years, when they voluntarily remove themselves from society.[80] Likewise, within Isidore's monastery, the monks lived a self-sufficient existence. "Within the walls," as the pilgrims learned from the lone guest master, "were such saints that all could work miracles and none of them ever fell ill before he died."[81] That the monastery was enclosed and "fortified with a high brick wall" is a detail that both isolates and insulates these monks from the life-threatening forces of the desert,[82] as well as from the mortality-ridden world of the reader.

Both walls and the desert demarcate a space where a charmed existence and a new relation to nature can unfold. Wild animals are no menace to these wonder-working monks (although they pose a threat to travelers, as the epilogue reminds us).[83] A new relation to nature is introduced in the prologue, which states that with the monks, "There is ... no anxiety for food and clothing."[84] Several stories echo that reassurance. When stranded in the desert without food or water, Abba

---

79. Indeed, later manuscripts often combined *Long-Lived Persons* with the *Book of Marvels* (Hansen, *Phlegon*, 17; cf. 19).

80. Diodorus Siculus, 2.57 (LCL 2:72); cf. Pliny's description of the Hyperboreans (*Nat. Hist.* 4.87). For a useful analysis of utopian writings, see David Winston, "Iambulus' *Islands of the Sun* and Hellenistic Literary Utopias," *Science Fiction Studies* 3 (1976): 219–27, esp. 221–23.

81. *HM* 17. 1–3 (Russell, 101).

82. Antoine Guillaumont, "La conception du désert chez les moines d'Egypte," *Revue de l'histoire des religions* 188 (1975): 3–21; repr. in id., *Aux origines du monachisme chrétien* (Spiritualité Orientale, 30; Bégrolles-en-Mauges: Abbaye de Bellefontaine, 1979), 69–87, esp. 77–78.

83. See *HM* 4.3; 9.9; cf. epil., 11–13. On this topos see Ward, "Introduction," in Russell, *Lives of the Desert Fathers*, 43.

84. *HM* prol. 7 (Russell, 50).

Apollo and his disciples were visited by a "number of men . . . complete strangers to them, who said that they had traveled a long distance." The strangers brought enough food to last for months, including "things that do not grow in Egypt": exotic fruit, fresh milk, even bread that was still hot from the oven—an oven in a distant land![85] In this brief tale, where a stranger (the author) tells a story about strangers (Apollo and the monks) who encounter strangers (the gift-bearers), distance and miracle go hand in hand.

With supplies of food assured, a moderate diet becomes a privilege conferred by abundance rather than a necessity. Iambulus's islanders, for instance, follow a prescribed diet.[86] And the Camarines, according to the fourth-century C.E. *Expositio totius mundi et gentium*, live off wild honey and pepper drinks.[87] Likewise, the monks practice remarkable moderation. More than half of a brief notice on Ammon (3.1–2) details, with ethnographic precision, the spectacle of mealtime at a Pachomian monastery. The visitor scrutinizes every move: the three spoonfuls of soup that satisfy one monk; the singular gesture of raising food to mouth (one or two such moves make up the entire meal), or the monk who slowly chews on the same piece of bread, for he will eat nothing else that day.[88] Although this restraint may seem less sensational than angels who deliver hot bread,[89] the writer is nevertheless astonished by it: "I marvelled at these things, as was fitting."[90]

Often, however, the excess of marvel was too much to bear, or describe. Perhaps the most striking resemblance between the *History of*

---

85. *HM* 8.40 (Russell, 76); cf. *HM* 12.15 and Ps 78.19.

86. Diodorus Siculus 2.57.4; 2.59.1–5. Cf. Pliny's description of the Astomi (*Nat. Hist.* 7.25), who, as their name suggests, have no mouths and must live on odors alone.

87. *Expositio totius mundi et gentium*, 4 (SC 124).

88. *HM* 3.1–2 (Russell, 65).

89. *HM* 8.40.

90. *HM* 3.2 (Russell, 65). Several notices (usually brief ones) close with details about dietary habits, such as 6.4; 7.3; 15.4; 20.

the Monks and exotic travel writing is the way in which the author confronts the inexplicable. Often paradoxographers as well as geographers resorted to rapid-fire lists whenever distant wonders defied explanation.[91] The *History of the Monks* also relies on lists. Each notice presents a collage of personal traits and concrete details about the individual ascetic or community. Typically the following details find their way into even the briefest notice: the ascetic's name, some information about his followers, characteristic physical features (*eikonismos*), noteworthy ascetic practices, and special supernatural powers.[92] Even the longer chapters appear as a list of separate anecdotes and sayings.[93]

The meaning of these lists depends on the literary context. As Patricia Cox Miller suggests, the repetitive language of ascetic discourse mimics the repeated movements and utterances typical of monastic practice.[94] In travel discourse, however, lists are part of a larger strategy to exoticize the other rather than to imitate it. The final notice, which appears as a straightforward list, can illustrate the difference: "We also visited another John in Diolcos, who was the father of hermitages. He too was endowed with much grace. He looked like Abraham and had a beard like Aaron's. He had performed many miracles and cures, and was especially successful at healing people afflicted with paralysis and gout."[95] The biblical content of these characterizations is far less exotic than Herodotean descriptions of "dogheaded men and

---

91. Romm, *Edges of the Earth*, 102–6. Cf. Michael Roberts's observation that detailed lists had the effect of "creat[ing] the impression of exhaustivity" (*The Jeweled Style: Poetry and Poetics in Late Antiquity* [Ithaca: Cornell University Press, 1989], 41).

92. For example, *HM* 2.1; 6.1; 26. See Eva Schulz-Flügel, ed., *Tyrannius Rufinus, Historia monachorum sive De Vita Sanctorum Patrum* (PTS 34; Berlin: DeGruyter, 1990), 8.

93. For example, *HM* 12 (Helle).

94. Patricia Cox Miller, "Desert Asceticism and the 'Body from Nowhere,'" *JECS* 2 (1994): 137–54, esp. 144.

95. *HM* 26 (Russell, 117).

headless that have their eyes in their breasts."[96] The effect on the reader, however, is the same: lists consolidate disparate facts, leaving no room for explanation or connection. As James Romm observes in his survey of ancient geographical writing, "Lists present the wonders of the East as an aggregation of facts; they demand that the multiplicity of eastern nature be accepted on its own terms."[97] Likewise, the author of the *History of the Monks* used list-making to fragment the wonders of desert asceticism and then rearrange the pieces into an intelligible picture for the reader.

The short notices that comprise the *History of the Monks* also serve to fragment the author's picture of desert asceticism. The brevity of the notice allows the travel writer to control what the reader "sees" and knows. In as little as two or three sentences this author puts the stilted and stunted notice to effective use as a focusing device. As soon as readers peer over high walls, through small openings, or across expansive deserts to catch a glimpse of Egyptian asceticism, the author cuts the gaze short to preserve that distance and fascination between the audience and those living saints.

Often, however, the author himself senses when those controlling techniques buckle and collapse. One hears the breathless exhaustion in remarks that admit to the inadequacy of language: "They saw and heard a host of other wonders, such as the tongue does not dare to utter or the ears to hear." Or, as he says of Abba Apollo's signs and wonders, "They defy description." Hyperbole also breeds silence, as when the narrator warns, "If anyone should wish to see . . . all [the fathers], the whole of his life would not be long enough to make a complete tour."[98] Such remarks are frail placeholders for the complex experience of encountering a living saint. In his efforts to show the excessiveness of monastic

---

96. *Hist.* 4.191 (LCL 2:395), cited in Romm, *Edges of the Earth*, 91.
97. Romm, *Edges of the Earth*, 91.
98. *HM* 8.7, 34, 62 (Russell, 71, 75, 79).

marvels, this author at times can only stumble into silence, less out of a sense of taboo or secrecy[99] than out of amazement.

Distance, nature, miracle, and sacred time, then, are integral to the construction of the world portrayed in the *History of the Monks*. With them, the writer strings together moments of biblical perception. These moments, viewed as a whole, say more about the region than about any single inhabitant. By demarcating the desert through distances and walled structures, then populating it with so many patriarchs, prophets, and angels, the author of the *History of the Monks* wraps Egyptian monastic culture in a biblical haze. Anything and anyone resonate with biblical significance. Seeking biblical reminders in every rock, tree, and plain was a common pursuit among Holy Land pilgrims, who relied on monks to help them identify those resonances.[100] What the *History of the Monks* achieved—in a way that pilgrims' writings did not—was to cast every monastic as a biblical figure in that *tableau vivant*. By examining this work through the lens of travel writing, one can appreciate the collective effect of these tropes.

DISPLACEMENT IN THE *LAUSIAC HISTORY*

In the *Lausiac History*, the trio of miracle, distance, and Bible are put to a different use. Like the author of the *History of the Monks*, Palladius writes from an outsider's perspective, using the itinerary as a framework for brief hagiographic notices, all contained between a prologue and epilogue.[101] And yet Palladius's collection of travel memories has a dif-

99. Cf. Pausanias, *Description of Greece*, 1.38.7; cf. Elsner, *Art and the Roman Viewer,* 145–49.

100. Leyerle, "Landscape as Cartography," 126–32; see also Campbell, *Witness,* 17–20.

101. The similar organization and subject matter facilitated the later conflation of these two works. For a concise overview of the textual history, see Young, *From Nicaea to Chalcedon,* 38–39. One important difference is the fact that Pal-

ferent tone. Recounting fewer miracles, this work provides some of the most poignant portraits found in monastic literature. In his efforts to present the varieties of monasticism, Palladius also shows the human price for such pursuits. His condemnation of ascetic zeal reveals psychological wounds, fallen heroes, and a simple recognition that the demands of an elusive perfection can be too much to bear for a fragile and brittle ascetic will.[102]

Leaving others to judge the veracity of Palladius's travelogue,[103] I instead consider its function. Palladius was faced with the problem of how to recount his voyage to an audience primarily concerned with advancing their own spiritual progress. He solved it by appealing to one biblical exemplar in particular: the Apostle Paul. In the prologue the reader learns that Palladius travels and writes for the same reasons Paul did. Just as Paul "was not satisfied merely to hear of Peter's virtue, but he longed for a meeting with him,"[104] so does Palladius accept "the hardship of travel gladly in order to meet a man full of the love of God."[105] And just as Paul felt compelled to record (or "boast") of his experiences "as an incentive to those who lived in self-satisfaction and idleness,"[106] so does Palladius determine the need to write down his

---

ladius devotes several notices to female ascetics and benefactors (*HL* 5, 6, 28, 33, 34, 37, 41, 46, 54–57, 59–61, 63, 64, 67, 69)—a high percentage compared to other anthologies (cf. Elizabeth A. Clark, "Holy Women, Holy Words: Early Christian Women, Social History, and the 'Linguistic Turn,'" *JECS* 6 (1998): 413–30, esp. 414 nn. 3–6).

102. For example, *HL* 2.1 (the ailing Palladius abandons a life he finds "squalid and harsh"); 12.3 (on the importance of mentioning sickness of "just men"); and 25–28 (tales about proud hermits), the list being echoed and expanded in 47 (Paphnutius and Chronius on the moral failings of monks).

103. Rousseau (*Ascetics*, 17) deems the *Lausiac History* to be "more balanced and more credible than the *Historia Monachorum*," qualifying Chitty (*Desert a City*, 52).

104. *HL* prol. 6 (Meyer, 25).

105. *HL* prol. 5 (Meyer, 24–25).

106. *HL* prol. 5 (Meyer, 24–25).

memories, even twenty years after the fact. Moreover, Palladius points out, Paul himself was following the example of other pilgrims turned writers. Palladius remarks, "For even those who wrote down the lives of the Fathers, Abraham, . . . Moses, Elias, and John, wrote not to glorify them, but to help their readers."[107] Thus Palladius bathes his travelogue in the glow of a grander biblical lineage. Whereas the *History of the Monks* biblicized the desert, Palladius biblicizes himself as a new Paul, who narrates his physical travels to promote spiritual progress.[108]

As an imitator of Paul, Palladius devotes considerable attention in the prologue to his own "trials" and perseverance: "I would make a journey of thirty days, or twice that, and covered on foot, God help me, the whole land of the Romans."[109] In specifying the extent of his travel in both time and space, as well as the fact that he covered those distances on foot, Palladius lends spiritual significance to his physical experience. His willingness to accept hardship permits Palladius to identify with the physical austerities of his subjects: an *askesis* of travel qualifies him to explore the *askesis* of the desert.

Given that Palladius's audience is unlikely to repeat the journey, it is ironic that he alludes often to the physicality of his own travels.[110] Palladius later includes many details of the physical journeys that brought him to these remote places. To reach Mount Nitria, Palladius tells his readers, one must spend a day and a half crossing the seventy-mile span of Lake Marea.[111] Geographical coordinates also appear: "Beyond the mountain (of Nitria) stretches the Great Desert reaching as far as Ethiopia, Mazi-

---

107. *HL* prol. 7 (Meyer, 25).

108. It is fitting that Palladius returns to *imitatio Pauli* in the epilogue (*HL* 71.1–2). Here, however, the allusion is to Paul's mystical ascent (2 Cor 12), signaled by the reference to a nameless "brother who has been with me from youth until this very day." The oblique third person was also used by Paul to refer to his strange but wonderful journey to the third heaven (2 Cor 12:2–5).

109. *HL* prol. 5 (Meyer, 24–25).

110. *HL* prol. 15–16 (Meyer, 28–29).

111. *HL* 7.1 (Meyer, 40).

cae, and Mauretania."[112] He maps out much of his physical experience, noting the arrangement of monastic complexes,[113] the accommodations, and detailed descriptions of ascetics' physical appearance.[114] Macarius, he tells us, "was slight and without a beard, having hair only about the lips and at the end of the chin, for the asceticism he practiced did not allow hair to sprout on him."[115] And Chronius "measured 15,000 steps from his village" before choosing his desert settlement.[116] Whether these details are accurate is beside the point. Their collective effect is what matters: to convey the palpable sense of bodies in a landscape. Like the exotic travel writers of his day, Palladius invokes the experience of physical space, from the ascetic body to the desert vistas, as a way to draw his readers to a place much closer to the edges of the world.[117]

Toward the middle of the collection, the emphasis on Palladius's own physical experiences becomes even more pronounced. He remarks that he had had the option to remain home and hear stories about John of Lycopolis. His venerable teacher, Evagrius, chose that course when he resigned himself with these words: "Gladly would I learn what kind of man he is from the testimony of one who knows how to interpret mind and speech. Since I myself cannot see him, I could hear exactly from another man of his way of life, but I shall not go so far as the mountain."[118] Evagrius's remark launches Palladius on yet another journey through the Thebaid to act as Evagrius's eyes and ears. The contrast

112. *HL* 7.2 (Meyer, 40).

113. *HL* 4.

114. See the descriptions of Palladius's extended stay in the Kellia with Macarius of Alexandria (*HL* 18.22, 26)

115. *HL* 18.29 (Meyer, 67).

116. *HL* 47.1 (Meyer, 125).

117. On this topos see Romm, *Edges of the Earth*, 11–20. On the role of the desert in the ascetic construction of space, see James Goehring, "The Encroaching Desert: Literary Production and Ascetic Space in Christian Egypt," *JECS* 1 (1993): 281–96.

118. *HL* 35.3 (Meyer, 99). The remark foreshadows Palladius's own actions: as the notice draws to a close, Palladius mentions the report he delivered "to the

between the sedentary teacher and his galloping disciple is even more pronounced in Palladius's subsequent description of hardships he endured. Much of the journey is depicted as an endurance test: it took "eighteen days, partly on foot, partly by sailing along the river."[119] He also mentions that he was slowed by disease.[120] All this detail allows the reader to empathize with Palladius's physical exhaustion and disappointment on discovering John's cell locked and having to wait several days for an audience with him.

The physical act of travel, along with its the rewards and hardships, is also described in other chapters. The previous chapter (34), about a nun who appeared insane, tells how a traveler named Piteroum set out to find a holy woman more pious than himself at Tabbenisi. There he discovered this hidden saint and shamed the sisters who abused her. Most striking in this tale is the way the two central characters, Piteroum and the holy nun, struggle between stability and movement. An angel instructs Piteroum, a monk who "had never gone away [from] the monastery," to abandon his solitude and "cease wander[ing] about cities in your mind."[121] As the story draws to a close, both characters are on the road: Piteroum has left the convent, and the holy nun takes flight, unable to bear the sisters' remorse. Fittingly, Palladius keeps silent about their ultimate destinations. By pairing these two wandering monks, Palladius valorizes physical travel over the sedentary life.

---

blessed fathers." The fact that he appends further discussion of his own physical ailments (*HL* 35.11–13) draws attention to the messenger's weary body. No doubt this rhetorical move establishes Palladius's reliability as a desert reporter not just to the fathers in Egypt but also, by extension, to his readers in Constantinople. As Claudia Rapp remarks ("Storytelling," 440), this story establishes "an intrinsic connection between hearing a *diegesis*, seeing a holy person, and actively sharing his life."

119. *HL* 35.4 (Meyer, 99).
120. *HL* 35.4; cf. 35.12.
121. *HL* 34.3 (Meyer, 97).

The importance of displacement also appears in Posidonius's tale (36), which immediately follows the John of Lycopolis notice. Like Piteroum, Posidonius led a solitary existence until he found himself on the point of starvation, with no choice but to return to "civilization." Weak from hunger, he managed to crawl only two miles the first day, when he had a vision. He immediately returned to his cave and discovered there abundant supplies of food. Beyond the allusions to manna in the wilderness, the story also contains a comment on travel. The fact that Palladius specifies the exact, if meager, distance Posidonius traveled allows us to ponder the spiritual rewards of travel.[122] When read together, the stories about Piteroum, the nun who feigned madness, John of Lycopolis, and Posidonius highlight the spiritual progress that comes from physical movement.

These rewards are most pronounced, however, in the tale of an Egyptian named Sarapion (*HL* 37), a traveler par excellence. Palladius describes this monk's adventures in Greece and aboard a ship bound for Rome. In Rome he went in search of the great ascetics, including a famous holy woman. Mirroring Palladius in his excruciating wait for an audience with John of Lycopolis, Sarapion also endures several delays. When Sarapion finally meets the holy woman, the question of who is the true traveler comes to the fore:

HE MET HER AND ASKED HER:	"Why do you keep sitting?"
SHE SAID:	"I do not sit, but I travel."
HE SAID:	"Where do you travel?"
AND SHE:	"To God."
HE ASKED HER:	"Are you living or dead?"
SHE ANSWERED:	"I believe in God that I am dead, for no one in the flesh makes that journey."[123]

---

122. *HL* 36.3 (Meyer, 104).
123. *HL* 37.13.

Significant here is the fact that Palladius never mocks Sarapion's intensely physical journey. Rather than add Sarapion to his catalogue of fallen heroes,[124] Palladius leaves ambiguous the question of who is the true pilgrim.

By bringing together an ascetic who has endured an intense physical journey with one who is engaged on a spiritual journey, Palladius signals the crucial intersection of physical and spiritual displacement that he anticipates in the prologue. In the remainder of the story, Sarapion challenges the woman to prove that she is dead to the world: she must undress and parade nude in the middle of Rome. He is prepared to do the same. She balks at the prospect, proving to Sarapion (and the reader) that no one is entirely dead to the world. And, as Palladius draws the story to a close, the woman is left "humbled," her pride "shattered."[125] Sarapion's dare makes clear to the reader that the woman, if she has truly reached her goal, must undergo one more physical journey: into the heart of the city. The interdependence of both types of travel is noteworthy.

This complex tale about wandering, desired centers, and elusive goals marks a new direction in Palladius's larger narrative, which progresses from physical journeys (described through chapter 37) to spiritual journeys. The effects of this transition, which takes place in Sarapion's simple conversation about travel to God, are found in subsequent notices. Ephraem of Edessa, we are told, "had accomplished the journey of the spirit in a right and worthy manner, never deviating from the straight path."[126] Whereas in earlier notices spiritual and literary journeys compete, by the time of the Philoromus story they converge. In this tale, Palladius describes how Philoromus wandered on foot to Rome, then to Alexandria to pray at Saint Mark's shrine, and finally to

124. For example, *HL* 25–27, 47.
125. *HL* 37.16 (Meyer, 110).
126. *HL* 40.1 (Meyer, 116).

Jerusalem. For one who logged so many miles, his final remark, "Never do I remember being absent from God in thought,"[127] highlights the complex interaction of distance, movement, and spirituality. All these encounters between physical and spiritual travelers set the stage for the brief story of a virgin who leaves her cell only after sixty years of seclusion in order to "make the journey to the Master and see all the saints."[128] The reader follows her to her mother's home and to a church as she makes preparations for her own death. Among its other messages, the tale reminds us that even on the cusp of death, physical movement and spiritual progress are intertwined.

For Palladius, the journey remains an enduring metaphor for the spiritual life.[129] Yet, unlike critics of pilgrimage who advocated interiorizing all journeys,[130] Palladius viewed the physical journey positively. These episodes attest that any spiritual advancement must stem from the physical journey. Physical distance and movement are indispensable to the efforts to gauge one's distance from and movement toward God. At the center of his collection, he included a cluster of notices (34–37) that accentuated physical journeys, including his own, as a way to bring the reader gradually to deeper reflection on spiritual journeys. By this arrangement, the physical journey may invite allegory, but it never dissolves in it. Even when physical and spiritual journeys appear at odds, any attempts to separate the two prove disastrous for protagonists. That message is borne out by the overall structure of the work.

In the *Lausiac History*, displacement creates the effect of a real journey so as to provide a template for the reader's own spiritual displacement. To measure one's journey toward a holy man or woman provides

127. *HL* 45.4 (Meyer, 123).

128. *HL* 60.1 (Meyer, 141).

129. On this metaphor, see Margaret Miles, *Practicing Christianity: Critical Perspectives for an Embodied Spirituality* (New York: Crossroad, 1988), 43–62.

130. For instance, Gregory of Nyssa, *Ep.* 2.16 (SC 363:120).

a scale for measuring one's journey toward God. Already in the prologue, Palladius sets his audience in motion: "Go to a clear window and seek for meetings with holy men and women so that you may see clearly your own heart as in the case with a book of small writing."[131] Not only does the metaphor elide a better reading of the written page with a closer reading of the heart, but it also makes all benefits at the "window" involve some physical displacement. On this spiritual journey, even armchair travelers have their marching orders. Palladius also offers himself as a model for how a physical journey gradually leads to a spiritual journey. Displacement also has an additional function in this work. By including so many travelers' tales, the travelogue recreates the effect of moving and pausing to look, and it thereby casts the reader as a passerby who stops long enough to gaze on the monastic but never fully enters the monastic space. Through this literary effect of moving and watching, the *historiai* had a profound influence on the image of the monastic, the object of the pilgrim's gaze, ultimately endowing him with the qualities of a monument.

THE MONASTIC AS MONUMENT

Narrowly defined, the word *monumentum* stood for anything "written or produced for the sake of memory."[132] To Romans any tangible reminders like a tomb inscription, statue, building, or temple could be regarded as a *monumentum*. Yet, poets, orators, and historians also applied the term to their works. Livy, for example, referred to his history of Rome as an *inlustris monumentum*, on which the reader "beholds

131. *HL* prol. 15–16 (Meyer, 28–29).
132. Varro, *De lingua latina* 6.49 (Spengel and Spengel [1885; repr. 1979]), quoted and translated in Mary Jaeger, *Livy's Written Rome* (Ann Arbor: University of Michigan Press, 1997), 15–26, esp. 15–16; cf. Andrew Feldherr, *Spectacle and Society in Livy's* History (Berkeley: University of California Press, 1998), 1–7.

the lessons of every kind of experience."[133] Underlying this broad use of the term was the assumption that *monumenta* were visible remnants from the past.[134]

The metaphor is particularly fitting for pilgrims' depictions of Christian monastics. As Livy's comments suggest, the monument required the sustained gaze of an audience. Or, as with the epitaphs that lined the road, the passerby was expected to pause, reflect, and enter another time while remaining in the same place. Some Roman epitaphs "addressed" the passerby directly, assuming the voice of a speaker from the grave that invited the reader to gaze. "Stop for a little, stranger," one epitaph begged, "and then go on your way; do not leave the stele at once, but first see what it says."[135] The still monument was rife with contradictions, a voice from the past beckoning to those in the present, detaining passersby long enough to make them beholders, and demanding that a fleeting glance turn into a stationary gaze. Such were the connotations of these "hybrid places," to borrow Mary Jaeger's words.[136]

---

133. Livy, *Ab urbe condita*, praef. 10 (trans. B. O. Foster; LCL 1:7). Cf. Livy, *Ab urbe condita*, praef. 6; Cicero, *De off.* 3.4.3; Cat. 95; Horace, *Carm.* 3.30.1 (cited along with other examples in Jaeger, *Livy's Written Rome*, 17 n. 9); cf. Cicero, *II Verr.* 4.69. It is worth wondering if the inclusion of speech acts as *monumenta* was facilitated by the emphasis on *enargeia* in historical writing (e.g., Plutarch, *De glor. Ath.* 347a). On Livy's contribution to the notion that the historian renders the past visible, see Feldherr, *Spectacle and Society*, 32; cf. Miles (*Livy*, 10) for the etymological gloss on *historia* as derived from the Indo-European root **weid*, "to see."

134. As Gary Miles (*Livy*, 17) defines the term, *monumenta* "represent an unbroken link with the past, a part of the past still available for direct personal inspection."

135. *EG* 388, 1–2 (Apamea) quoted by Richmond Lattimore, *Themes in Greek and Latin Epitaphs* (Urbana: University of Illinois Press, 1962), 230–37, esp. 232.

136. Jaeger, *Livy's Written Rome*, 17. On the political function of monuments, see Feldherr, *Spectacle and Society*, 12–37. On *ergon* in Greek historiography, see Henry R. Immerwahr, "*Ergon*: History as a Monument in Herodotus and Thucydides," *American Journal of Philology* 81 (1960): 261–90.

Christians were also attracted to the visualizing and nostalgic possibilities of monuments.[137] Theodoret of Cyrrhus, like many other hagiographers, described the saint's life as an "aid to memory," a verbal equivalent of the types of pagan memorials erected for athletes so as to "extend their memory as long as possible."[138] More explicit in its use of the metaphor is an anonymous work from the fifth or sixth century, the *Poem on the Passion of the Lord*.[139] This work assumes the voice of a monument to Christ: "Whoever you are who approach . . . stop a little and look upon me, who, though innocent, suffered for your crime."[140] Like a monument, the poem draws the reader into the past. In just over twenty verses of this eighty-line poem, a condensed gospel told in the first person, Christ recounts his birth, ministry, and trial. Only at the point of recalling the trial is the reader-viewer invited at last to enter the drama. The tense switches from the past to the present: "Fasten in your mind *(fige animo)*" the witnesses, Pilate, "and the immense cross pressing on my shoulders and wearied back."[141] With increasing physicality, the poem moves from past to present, from remembrance to visualization: "Now survey me from head to foot. . . . Behold and see my locks clotted with blood, and my blood-stained neck under my very hair . . . survey my compressed and sightless eyes . . . see the blood streaming from [my wound], and my perforated feet, and blood-stained limbs."[142]

---

137. Cf. *HM* 8.8 (*ergon* used for exemplary deeds); closer to our more architectural monuments are the pyramids, or, "Joseph's granaries," as they are called (*HM* 18.3; Russell, 102); cf. the Piacenza pilgrim (ca. 570), who also refers to the "twelve granaries of Joseph," noting their miraculous replenishment ("and they are still full"), *Pseudo-Antonini placentini itinerarium*, 43 (Wilkinson, 88).

138. *HR* prol. 3 (Price, 4). Cf. Athanasius, *V. Ant.* prol.; Cyril of Scythopolis, *V. Euthy.*, 1.

139. Pseudo-Lactantius, *De passione Domini* (ed. Samuel Brandt, CSEL 27, 148–51; trans. ANF 7:327–28). On this text, see Angelo Roncoroni, "Sul De passione Domini Pseudolattanziano," *VC* 29 (1975): 208–21.

140. *De passione Domini*, 1–3.

141. *De passione Domini*, 37.

142. *De passione Domini*, 38–45.

The audience is bidden to inspect every inch of the dying body. As the voice explains, "These *monumenta*, if at any time you find pleasure in thinking over them . . . will be incitement to virtue."[143] In this poem about a talking monument, Christ extends a personal invitation to the audience to enter his story and relive it.

Like the poem, pilgrims' narratives generated the circumstances for perceiving the living saint as a monument. The first-person voice, however, is that of the passerby and not the monument. By adopting various travel-writing tropes such as measurements, topographical details, and boundaries, the authors of the *historiai* distanced readers from their own world and the world visited in order to control the diversity of Egyptian asceticism.[144]

To a great extent, that control was achieved through tropes that both domesticated and exoticized the desert. Thus, Palladius's portraits of vulnerable ascetics make them painfully familiar to the audience, whereas the *History of the Monks* delights in making monks strangers to the audience. Like an impression on putty stretched and pinched, the image of desert asceticism shifts before the audience, which learns to recognize how the same image can contain both the alien and the familiar. The shape of the narrative also sustains that paradox.

Instrumental to this shift in perception is the narrator's ability to reposition the reader within the world of the text. Readers are first directed to positions that allow them to view the ascetics from afar, then immediately brought up close for a face-to-face encounter. In the *History of the Monks* this kind of sweep is best captured in the transition from the Oxyrhynchus chapter to the notice on Abba Theon (5–6). At

---

143. *De passione Domini*, 58, a term also used at 64: "If these *monumenta* shall turn away your senses, which are devoted to a perishable world . . ."

144. Campbell (*Witness*, 3) understands this predicament: "The traveler in foreign parts is faced with a world for which his language is not prepared: no matter how naïve the writer's understanding of language, the option of simple transparence, of verbal equivalences, is not open."

Oxyrhynchus, a city recalled for the "marvels we saw there," the narrator mentions "temples and capitols of the city." But their identity as *monumenta* is constituted strictly by the fact that they were "bursting with monks."[145] Moreover, the reader remains positioned outside the town's walls, reported to contain five thousand Christians, in company with the "watchmen posted at the gates and entrances" to care for the needs of "strangers." From outside the walls, the reader can observe those within, but the vantage point is panoramic, as the rather round numbers suggest: churches come in tidy packages of a dozen, and monks and nuns are bundled by the tens of thousands.[146] That emphasis on exteriority is especially noticeable once the reader is brought into the city. At this point, the notice rushes to an ending, with a perfunctory description of profligate hospitality and of the "many great fathers who possessed various charisms."[147] The shift from big picture to minute observation does not take place until the following notice, which describes how Theon had the "face of an angel," read "Greek, Latin, and Coptic," and preferred raw vegetables.[148] The closeup is complete when the notice specifies the animals whose tracks are discerned outside the hermitage: "antelope and wild asses and gazelle."[149] Thus, in the course of two brief notices, totaling just over sixty lines in the critical edition, the narrator has moved the reader from a distant view to a close inspection.

This repositioning and movement through space shapes the meaning of the *monumentum*, which, as Mary Jaeger observes, is "determined jointly by the reminder, its physical context, and the circumstances of

145. *HM* 5.2 (Russell, 67).
146. *HM* 5.5–6 (Russell, 67): In response to his question, "How can one convey an adequate idea of the throngs of monks and nuns past counting?" the narrator ventures a guess of "ten thousand monks and twenty thousand nuns."
147. *HM* 5.6–7 (Russell, 67).
148. *HM* 6.2–4 (Russell, 68).
149. *HM* 6.4 (Russell, 68).

each viewer."[150] No single position can prove satisfactory; the reader is brought nearer and farther but never stands still. As Jaeger explains this continuous repositioning, "The closer one is to the *monumentum*, the clearer one sees it. However, the viewer who stands too close cannot take in the *monumentum* in its entirety."[151] Although Jaeger is commenting on Livy, her words could just as well apply to the Christian travelogues, which also prevent the reader from taking the desert "in its entirety." The oscillation between distance and proximity assures that the reader will never have to contend with all the complexities of Egyptian monasticism. There is sufficient distance to allow readers to recognize the familiar world of the biblical past, but there is only enough proximity to remind them of the strangeness of desert existence. Against such a panoramic literary landscape, the holy person was rendered a monument, a visible proof. From the reader's various positions the monks appear as visible traces of past greatness, individual entities that can be displayed and examined apart from their historical, religious, or cultural contexts.[152]

The appeal of the monument for travelers and their audiences is not hard to understand. For those who "love France but hate the French," as the old joke goes, a postcard, painting, or château provides a device with which to encounter (or, as the case may be, avoid) the otherness of French culture. Likewise, the literary image of monks provided a device by which to avoid the complexities of desert existence yet enter the biblical past.

150. Jaeger, *Livy's Written Rome*, 18. For an insightful discussion of how viewers interact with public monuments, see Mary Carruthers, *The Craft of Thought: Meditation, Rhetoric, and the Making of Images, 400–1200* (Cambridge: Cambridge University Press, 1998), 35–44.

151. Jaeger, *Livy's Written Rome*, 24; cf. Livy, *Ab urbe condita* 6.1.2, on history as long-distance vision.

152. Immerwahr, *"Ergon,"* 271; John Elsner, "From the Pyramids to Pausanias and Piglet: Monuments, Travel, and Writing," in *Art and Text in Ancient*

The monument's paradoxical status as an object that simultaneously belongs to the present and the past affords rich insights into pilgrims' perceptions of monks. Like monuments, these ascetics bear the legacy of the biblical past while living in the present. What bridges past and present in the *historiai* is the Bible itself. Together, distance and marvel move the readers to the edges of existence and to a biblical time, permitting them to imagine a place where figures from the sacred past spring to life against a tidy desert backdrop. The brief, formulaic notices also play a decisive role in reducing the complexity of ascetic culture to a "convenient and accessible miniature," as John Elsner describes the perceptual shrinkage that monuments invite.[153] Every ascetic life was reduced through the fragmentation and recombination of details. The brief notice "froze," as it were, these living artifacts of a distant culture. Marvels further crystallized the ascetics' identity as biblical monuments by merging the wonders of distant places with the miracles of a biblical past.

The stilted style of pilgrims' reports, then, served a significant purpose: it acted to stabilize and consolidate the sheer variety of monasticism in Egypt at the end of the fourth century.[154] As James Goehring and others have noticed, the *History of the Monks* skewed its picture of monasticism toward male ascetics, and particularly those in the desert.[155] Whatever the motives behind such choices, it is clear that these pilgrim-authors needed a way to control, manage, and even reduce the diversity of the pilgrim's destinations. Using the form of the brief notice and var-

Greek Culture, ed. Simon Goldhill and Robin Osborne (Cambridge: Cambridge University Press, 1994), 224–54, esp. 224, 228–29.

153. Elsner, "From the Pyramids,", 228.

154. *HM* prol. 10; 1.32, 45, 46.

155. Cf. Goehring, "Encroaching Desert," 288–96, esp. 288 and n. 28. On women in Egyptian monasticism, see Susanna Elm, *"Virgins of God": The Making of Asceticism in Late Antiquity* (Oxford: Clarendon, 1994), 227–372, esp. 311–30.

ious techniques of displacement, these travel writers demarcated and recast the desert as a biblical land where Paradise was restored and gospel miracles could find their full realization. And, judging by the popularity of pilgrimage to living ascetics at this time, the strategy worked.

If travel writing was the solution, what was the problem? Clearly, the need for an "accurate" account of monasticism was not foremost in these writers' minds. The challenge was that of the audience. John Chrysostom's homilies to the newly baptized offer a rich insight into the audience for the *historiai*. While still in Antioch, Chrysostom welcomed a group of monks who had come from the countryside to join the catechumens. In John's greetings one detects how unsettling the visitors' presence would have appeared to the new converts: "Let us learn . . . that [the monks] prove in deeds the things we, in our love of true doctrine strive to teach by words. . . . Let us not look simply at their appearance and the language they speak, while we overlook the virtue of their lives. Let us observe carefully the angelic life they lead."[156] Apparently the new converts were having a difficult time reconciling the scriptures with the appearance of the monks before them. "Are such men the fullest expression of these scriptures' ideals?" they must have asked. Ever the pastor, Chrysostom hastened to concede that the monks' appearance might indeed appear at odds with the converts' biblical ideals and to find ways to reconcile the disparity. Dealing with "cognitive dissonance," as theorists of conversion remind us, is no light matter. Chrysostom insisted that the problem was not the monks' appearance but rather the converts' misperception. Only proper perception would allow the true believer to see how the monks embodied the highest truths of scripture. By acknowledging the initial contradiction, he could help these new Christians see how vision, rightly used, would achieve the necessary synthesis.

Central to this rhetoric of reconciliation was the careful control of the converts' gaze. Chrysostom provided detailed instructions about what to notice and what to overlook. As the monks stood before these

---

156. *Catech.* 8.4 (Harkins, 120).

gawking converts, he carefully directed their gaze: the congregants were instructed to overlook any rusticity of dress or speech and instead to gaze intently at the virtue of the monks' deeds. Only then, he promised his flock, would the "true doctrine" be made visible.

The preacher's reasons for reshaping the converts' perceptions are difficult to understand at first. With his insistence that things are not as they seem, he may appear a mere spin doctor. By that interpretation, however, we risk misreading Chrysostom, who implored his audience to recognize how the world of the Bible and the world of monks are one and the same. To elide those two worlds, he assumed a two-pronged approach: he pointed out how the monks embody the Bible and simultaneously erased any perceptions that could undermine this biblical image. Thus he demanded that details of appearance, speech, and physical context be ignored to allow what is "angelic" to shine through. By this strategy of directing and erasing, John was in effect fragmenting his audiences' perceptions, then reassembling only those parts that would constitute his desired biblical image.

This baptismal homily offers an inverted image of the challenges faced by travel writers such as Palladius and the author of the *History of the Monks*. Like Chrysostom, these pilgrim-authors strove to show how the world of the monks and the world of the Bible were one and the same. And they had to help their audience to experience the Bible where they did not expect to find it.

Whereas John Chrysostom had to deal with the fallout from a collision between expectation and reality, the authors of the *historiai* dealt only with their own experiences and the audience's expectations. They could omit and supply details as they saw fit, an option Chrysostom clearly did not have with the "rustic" monks standing in plain view of his audience. Circumstances notwithstanding, it is tempting to ask if the authors of the travelogues were in some indirect way responsible for Chrysostom's predicament. Might travelers like Palladius or the author of the *History of the Monks* have given rise to the inflated expectations and idealizations that Chrysostom addressed? Whether or not there exists a historical connection between those who generated idealized images of monasticism and those who dealt with the consequences of that image, one thing is clear: the power of travel writing is more complex than many are willing to admit. By definition, travel writing is a retrospective genre, one that reports on past experiences. Yet it could also shape how pilgrims might construct and anticipate their own experiences. To ancient audiences, at least, the excitement of what was possible on pilgrimage was more captivating than the assurance of what actually happened. Chrysostom's converts would not have had to be familiar with pilgrims' reports to acquire such an idealized image of monasticism. As the next chapter demonstrates, other types of Christian journey literature could also sow the seeds for a fascination with the desert.

THREE

Imagined Journeys
Literary Paradigms for Pilgrimage to Holy People

For this is the journey which leads to God.

Apocalypse of Paul, 19

If it is possible for the desert to have "urban legends," the *Life of Onnophrius* offers one of the best candidates. It opens with an eerie description of pilgrimage to holy people.[1] After several days' journey without food or water, a monk named Paphnutius discovered an anchorite's cave in the "farthest reaches of the desert." After a hesitant knock met no reply, Paphnutius leaned into the cool darkness of the cave. As his vision adjusted to the shadows, he slowly discerned a seated figure. Paphnutius was a patient man, but this silence was too much to bear. He thrust his hand into the darkness to shake the hermit from his contemplation. No sooner had he tugged on the hermit's arm, Paphnutius recalls, than it "came off in my hands and disintegrated into dust. I felt his body all over and found that he was clearly dead and had been

---

1. Paphnutius, *V. Onnophr.*, 2 (Vivian, 145–46). I follow Vivian's translation as well as his paragraph divisions.

dead a long time." The same happened when he groped for the dead man's tunic hanging on the wall. Everything disintegrated beneath his touch, leaving this pilgrim with the palpable realization that instead of beholding ascetic splendor, he breathed its dust.

Although Paphnutius's story is not repeated in any travelogue, it offers rich insights into the expectations, emotions, and even the horrors that pilgrimage to holy people engendered. In the previous chapter, I focused on how pilgrims' own writings communicate expectations. Paphnutius's tale reminds us that pilgrims' ideals, hopes, and fears were formed in and by other types of literature as well. Literary depictions of pilgrimage merit consideration precisely because they fostered interest in desert asceticism and helped to shape perceptions of that culture.

For late antique Christians the mutual influence between literature and pilgrimage is well known.[2] Before she set sail for Egypt, Melania the Younger read saints' lives "as if she were eating dessert,"[3] as her biographer put it. And Jerome was familiar with (and even composed) lives of desert saints long before he joined Paula on pilgrimage.[4] It is hardly surprising that accounts of holy people inspired readers to travel to them, even after the saints were dead. Such reading by pilgrims in preparation for their journeys causes us to rethink how we might reconstruct their experiences. Should our investigation be limited to pilgrims' testimonies, or might there be other types of evidence that might illumine for us pilgrims' fears, hopes, and expectations?

This chapter expands the discussion of pilgrims' writings to consider how texts that enticed pilgrims to visit the desert also shaped their perceptions of their journey and destinations. One is tempted to begin with the diaries of pilgrims who visited the Holy Land, but I prefer to leave

---

2. See Philip Rousseau, *Ascetics, Authority, and the Church in the Age of Jerome and Cassian* (Oxford: Oxford University Press, 1978), 93–95.

3. *V. Mel.* 23 (Clark, 45).

4. J. N. D. Kelly, *Jerome: His Life, Writings, and Controversies* (New York: Harper and Row, 1975), 61.

the discussion of holy places until the next chapter. This chapter focuses instead on fourth- and fifth-century texts about pilgrimage to *people*, or, more precisely, to destinations conceived as people. This criterion admits a broader range of works, including imaginary journeys to biblical heroes in heaven and paradise.

The journey to a person was a familiar motif in spiritual works that described journeying to God. The anthropomorphic language that often appears in such works—as in references to God's "back" or "face"—was often accompanied by allusions to the traveler approaching that presence. Gregory of Nyssa's description of the soul's ascent to God in the *Life of Moses* illustrates this type of journey well. Hagiographic episodes of holy people seeking holy people, such as Paphnutius's encounter, offer special insights into the idealized pilgrim. A particularly good illustration of this ideal appears in Jerome's *Life of Paul the First Hermit*, in which Anthony the Great is cast in the role of a pilgrim and thus models the desires and rewards of pilgrimage.

All these imagined journeys provided paradigms for pilgrimage to holy people. Literary journeys illumine what pilgrims expected and how those expectations affected their interior experiences. Moreover, as literary models, these journeys reveal habits of speech that shaped how pilgrims later expressed their memories. If pilgrimage can be defined as "journeying to an ideal,"[5] it is important to ask what ideal of journeying is operative.

RELIGIOUS EXPERIENCE
AND THE STUDY OF PILGRIMAGE

How can we know what pilgrims—and especially pilgrims from the past—once felt, anticipated, or perceived? Social scientists have paid little attention to this question, since their investigations tend to focus on

5. Alan Morinis, "Introduction," in *Sacred Journeys: The Anthropology of Pilgrimage*, ed. Alan Morinis (Westport, Conn.: Greenwood, 1992), 1–28, esp. 4.

external and collective behaviors rather than on inner states.[6] Yet the pilgrim's experience is never completely beyond our reach. As Barbara Nimri Aziz points out, we can have access to what she calls "the personal dimensions" of the sacred journey through the myths, songs, and poetry shared by pilgrims. "Pilgrimage," she says, "remains strongly anchored in our mythologies."[7] Those mythic journeys and spiritual quests are expressions of, as well as models for, earthly pilgrimage. As Aziz explains, "Expressing the ideals of inner experience in pilgrimage, these literary sources create a template for actual pilgrims to follow."[8]

Although Aziz's comments pertain to her interviews with South Asian pilgrims, she is making a larger point about the role of literary sources in the study of pilgrimage. Myths, legends, and stories about real and imagined journeys influence the shape and language of pilgrims' testimonies.[9] Moreover, they "are likely to be the only means available to know about pilgrims' experience in the past."[10] Yet it does

6. See, for example, *Contesting the Sacred: The Anthropology of Christian Pilgrimage*, ed. John Eade and Michael J. Sallnow (New York: Routledge, 1991). An interesting exception is E. Valentine Daniel, *Fluid Signs: Being a Person the Tamil Way* (Berkeley: University of California Press, 1984), 245–87.

7. Barbara Nimri Aziz, "Personal Dimensions of the Sacred Journey: What Pilgrims Say," *Religious Studies* 23 (1987): 247–61, esp. 247. Cf. Victor Turner and Edith Turner, *Image and Pilgrimage in Christian Culture* (New York: Columbia University Press, 1978) esp. 23–25. For a fruitful integration of poetic literature in the study of Hindu pilgrimage, see David Haberman, *Journey through the Twelve Forests* (New York: Oxford, 1994), xiii, 50–55, 120–21.

8. Aziz, "Personal Dimensions," 251.

9. Donald R. Howard, *Writers and Pilgrims: Medieval Pilgrimage Narratives and Their Posterity* (Berkeley: University of California Press, 1980), 10. Cf. Barbara Metcalf, "The Pilgrimage Remembered: South Asian Accounts of the Hajj," in *Muslim Travelers: Pilgrimage, Migration, and the Religious Imagination*, ed. Dale F. Eickelman and James Piscatori (Berkeley: University of California Press, 1990), 85–107, esp. 87–89.

10. Aziz, "Personal Dimensions," 252.

not seem necessary to take such a concessive stance. As Margaret Miles has argued, imaginary journeys can deepen our understanding of real ones.[11] The question of how ideals and practices interact remains underexplored in the study of pilgrimage.[12] Important, too, in any study of early Christian pilgrimage is a consideration of how texts generated and mediated that convergence of ideal and practice.

Late antique Christians were particularly attentive to the dynamic interaction between spiritual ideals and practices. Recent scholarship on asceticism has extended this approach in useful directions, identifying bodily practices that grew out of spiritual concepts in late antiquity. James Goehring, for instance, has examined how the monastic literature in Egypt translated the ideal of separation from the world, or *anachorēsis*, into a lived reality.[13] According to some ascetic biographers, for the heroes of the desert the resurrection body was no longer a biblical hope but now a visible reality.[14] And, as Susan Ashbrook Harvey has observed of early Syrian Christianity, there was a tendency to evoke

11. Margaret R. Miles, *Practicing Christianity: Critical Perspectives for an Embodied Spirituality* (New York: Crossroad, 1988), 43–85.

12. Anthropologists Victor Turner and Edith Turner raise interesting possibilities when they link pilgrimage and mysticism: pilgrimage is "an extroverted mysticism, just as mysticism is introverted pilgrimage" (*Image and Pilgrimage*, 33).

13. James E. Goehring, "The Encroaching Desert: Literary Production and Ascetic Space in Christian Egypt," *JECS* 1 (1993): 281–96, esp. 282. See also Antoine Guillaumont, "La conception du désert chez les moines d'Egypte,"and "Le dépaysement comme forme d'ascèse dans le monachisme ancien," both in Antoine Guillaumont, *Aux origines du monachisme chrétien: Pour une phénoménologie du monachisme* (Spiritualité orientale, 30; Bégrolles-en-Mauges: Abbaye de Bellefontaine, 1979), 67–88, 89–116, respectively.

14. Anthony, *Ep.* 1.4.25–28 (*Saint Antoine: Lettres*, trans. André Louf et al. [Spiritualité orientale, 19; Maine & Loire: Abbaye de Bellefontaine, 1976], 48); cf. Pseudo-Macarius, *Hom.* 5.9 (Maloney, 73). See Patricia Cox Miller, "Desert Asceticism and 'The Body from Nowhere,' " *JECS* 2 (1994): 137–54; and David Brakke, *Athanasius and the Politics of Asceticism* (Oxford: Clarendon, 1995), 242–44.

"extreme action through a spirituality that called for lived symbols."[15] She points to the pillar saint Symeon the Elder, who stood with arms extended in continuous prayer, a "lived symbol" of the psalmist's image of incense rising up to God.[16] These are but a few examples of the ways Christians integrated spiritual ideals and physical realities.

Amid this climate of literalizing, embodying, and enacting spiritual ideals, it is natural to ask what spiritual ideals informed pilgrimages to holy people. Yet the idea of manifesting spiritual ideals through physical pilgrimage was a troublesome one for some Christians. Gregory of Nyssa, for instance, cautioned that pilgrims run the risk of over-literalizing the ideal of seeing God. "A change of place," he warned, "does not amount to approaching God, rather, wherever you are, God will come to you."[17] I elaborate on this complex statement in the next section. For now, it bears reminding that the ever-thinning line between spiritual ideal and spectacle alarmed some Christian leaders. Pilgrims to holy people, however, showed no misgivings over whether physical pilgrimage could disrupt one's interior journey toward God. (One need only recall Sarapion's confident challenge to the contemplative nun in chapter 37 of the *Lausiac History.)* Nor was travel among the excessive austerities that worried Palladius.[18] To him, pilgrimage was a practice that mirrored

15. Susan Ashbrook Harvey, *Asceticism and Society in Crisis: John of Ephesus and the* Lives of the Eastern Saints (Berkeley: University of California Press, 1990), 7.

16. Susan Ashbrook Harvey, "The Sense of a Stylite: Perspectives on Simeon the Elder," *VC* 42 (1988): 376–94, esp. 382–86. The liturgical dimensions of these symbols are further developed in id., "The Stylite's Liturgy: Ritual and Religious Identity in Late Antiquity," *JECS* 6 (1998): 523–39. Cf. Miller, "Desert Asceticism," 145–47.

17. Gregory of Nyssa, *Ep.* 2.16 (SC 363:120). Cf. *HR* 6.8; 9.2

18. For example, *HL* 25–27. On Palladius's use of scripture to justify certain ascetic practices, see Elizabeth Ann Schechter, "Domesticating the Desert: The Literary Function of Scripture Citations in the *Historia Lausiaca,* " unpublished paper, summarized in *AAR/SBL Abstracts 1995* (Atlanta: American Academy of Religion, Society of Biblical Literature, 1995), 14.

spiritual goals, so long as it did not ape them or, worse yet, detract from these ideals.

In this context, the question of whether pilgrimage undermines spiritual goals is a misplaced one. More helpful is the simpler question, "Where did ancient Christians learn to imagine pilgrimage to the living?" In the previous chapter, I considered the influence of the Bible in shaping the imagination of pilgrims. This chapter continues this line of inquiry by asking how travels in visionary, apocalyptic, and fictionalized hagiographies also shaped pilgrims' goals and expectations. I focus on three themes that are common in literary depictions of journeys to persons: the desire for a face-to-face meeting with the divine; paradisiac descriptions of the desert; and holy persons' journeys to even holier persons.

THE JOURNEY TOWARD GOD

"When you see a man who is pure and humble," Pachomius is reported to have said, "that is a vision great enough. For what is greater than such a vision, to see the invisible God in a visible man, his temple?"[19] Pachomius's comment could just as well have appeared in either the *History of the Monks* or the *Lausiac History*. It echoes the notion that holy people offer an intimation of divine presence.[20] Often in these works, the descriptions of luminous, fiery, or even withered faces suggest that the pilgrim's desire is fulfilled in a face-to-face meeting.[21] The notion that the face is the locus of the holy takes on a special force in stories about the lengths to which pilgrims went in order to see a holy person.

19. *(First Greek) Life of Pachomius*, 48, in *Pachomian Koinonia*, trans. Armand Veilleux (3 vols.; Kalamazoo: Cistercian, 1980), 1:330.

20. Peter Brown, "The Saint as Exemplar in Late Antiquity," in *Saints and Virtues*, ed. John Stratton Hawley (Berkeley: University of California Press, 1987), 3–14.

21. The descriptions are the subject of chapter 5 (below). See also Miller, "Desert Asceticism," 141.

In these episodes, beholding the holy person's face is a privilege reserved for a few. Melania the Elder admitted to Palladius that she never beheld the immured Alexandra "face to face."[22] Other pilgrims were devastated when denied even a glimpse of the ascetic's face.

Many pilgrims settled for the solace of proximity and remained outside the cell,[23] but some refused to take no for an answer. Both the author of the *History of the Monks* and Theodoret tell stories of nameless noblewomen who persisted (and schemed) until they saw the ascetic's face.[24] The elusiveness of the ascetic face is even more dramatic in the story of Cyrus, a monk who lived in Egypt during the fifth century. His biographer, Pambo, makes much of the fact that he alone was permitted to see Cyrus's face,[25] no doubt a privilege that enhanced Pambo's authority among his audience. And Pambo recounts even greater privileges: in a vision, Pambo watched Christ himself enter the cell and kiss Cyrus on the lips.[26] The fact that Pambo failed to recognize Christ, taking him for a monk, is significant insofar as it makes perfectly understandable to the reader why Pambo did not receive a kiss. The reader can recognize a clear order of spiritual authority: Christ comes face to face with Cyrus, who in turn comes face to face with Pambo. This lineage of encounters with the divine ultimately might benefit the pilgrim who gazes into a monk's face.

The ambiguous status of the holy face as an object beheld or withheld is also found patristic discussions of Moses' ascent to God (Exodus 33).

---

22. *HL* 5.2 (Meyer, 36).

23. For example, *V. Ant.* 48; cf. 62, 88.

24. *HM* 1.6; cf. *HR* 3.22.

25. "Truly, no human shall see my face except Abba Pambo" (Vivian, 33). Pambo's experiences are described in "The Life of Apa Cyrus" (Vivian, *Journeying to God*, 25–36). Internal evidence suggests a terminus post quem of 474; see ibid., 25 n. 2. Theodoret claimed a similar privilege for himself with regard to James of Cyrrhestica (*HR* 22.3).

26. "Life of Apa Cyrus" (Vivian, *Journeying to God*, 34).

Gregory of Nyssa's *Life of Moses* exposes the problems of withholding the divine face. The work is divided into two parts: first, a *historia* (here meaning a narrative) about the exploits of Moses described in Exodus and Numbers, followed by the spiritual interpretation of the narrative, or *theoria*. In the *theoria* Gregory explores the implications of Moses' ascent up Mount Sinai and his efforts to meet God face to face.

In Gregory's reading, Moses represents the soul's approach toward God, a quest that is endless but never futile.[27] Gregory underscores the point: Moses neither "stopped in his ascent, nor did he set a limit for himself in his upward course . . . because he always found a step higher than the one he attained."[28] This continuous ascent did not bring him to the face of God; instead, he perpetually contemplated God's backside. Gregory describes the spiritual paradox: "And the bold request which goes up the mountains of desire asks this: to enjoy the Beauty not in mirrors and reflections, but face to face. The divine voice granted what was requested in what was denied. . . . The munificence of God assented to the fulfillment of his desire, but did not promise any cessation or satiety of the desire."[29] In identifying an insatiable longing to see God, Gregory offers a rationale for pilgrims to the living: the prospect of gazing at a face that is partially or even completely hidden is not to be feared. Such occlusion, ironically, induces deeper and more intense modes of seeing. As Gregory explains, "One must always, by looking at what he can see, rekindle his desire to see more."[30]

No amount of desire, however, could overcome the fundamental paradox of God's corporeality. Even as Gregory insists that God is by

---

27. For a clear introduction to the concept of "eternal progress," see *Gregory of Nyssa: The Life of Moses*, trans. Everett Ferguson and Abraham Malherbe (CWS; New York: Paulist, 1978), 12–13.

28. Gregory of Nyssa, *V. Moysis*, 227 (Ferguson/Malherbe, 113–14).

29. Gregory of Nyssa, *V. Moysis*, 232 (Ferguson/Malherbe, 114–15).

30. Gregory of Nyssa, *V. Moysis*, 239 (Ferguson/Malherbe, 116).

nature incorporeal and invisible, he retains the language of the back and the face.[31] In his *Commentary on the Song of Songs*, Gregory revisits that paradox, again through the Moses story:

> Moses still had an insatiable desire for more. He implored God to see him face to face, despite the fact the scripture already says that he had been allowed to speak with God face to face. . . . "If I have found favor before you, show me your face clearly." . . . God passed Moses by at the divine place in the rock shadowed over by his hand. Moses could hardly see God's back even after he had passed by. I believe we are taught that the person desiring to see God can behold the desired One by always following him. The contemplation of God's face is a never-ending journey toward him accomplished by following right behind the Word.[32]

This passage is stuffed with God's body parts—face, hand, back—with the face as the object of Moses' desire and destination.

If we recall that Gregory himself was once a pilgrim, the overlap between his notion of progress and his views of actual pilgrimage seems even greater. In a letter on Jerusalem pilgrimage, he offered several arguments against the practice: some practical, some scriptural, and some theological. His final argument, interestingly enough, is spatial: "A change of place does not amount to approaching God," but "God will come to you, if he finds the inn (καταγώγιον) of your soul such that the Lord can inhabit (ἐνοικέω) and walk about (ἐμπεριπατέω) in you."[33] Drawing on pilgrimage vocabulary, Gregory describes the soul as a setting for pilgrimage, where God becomes the pilgrim, walking, peram-

---

31. See Everett Ferguson, "God's Infinity and Man's Mutability: Perpetual Progress according to Gregory of Nyssa," *Greek Orthodox Theological Review* 19 (1973): 59–78, esp. 63–64.

32. Gregory of Nyssa, *In Cant.* 12 (McCambley, 219).

33. Gregory of Nyssa, *Ep.* 2.16 (SC 363:120).

bulating, and occupying the guesthouse or inn (καταγώγιον).[34] Clearly, Gregory's aim is to substitute a spatial movement toward God with a nonspatial movement of God toward the soul. But this metaphoric reversal works only if God is conceived as a pilgrim, embodied and occupying spaces. Thus, even for Gregory of Nyssa, who resisted any notion of a visible or embodied God,[35] the embodied language of pilgrimage was irresistible.

Gregory of Nazianzus, a close friend of Gregory of Nyssa, also found in Moses' ascent a personal metaphor for the pursuit of God. In his second *Theological Oration*, Gregory announced to his Constantinopolitan audience in 380, "I eagerly ascend the mount."[36] His efforts to understand God are presented as a journey to a person: "I was running with a mind to see God and so it was that I ascended the mount. . . . But when I directed my gaze I scarcely saw the averted figure of God."[37] Although he insists that "to know God is hard, to describe him impossible,"[38] and that "God is not a body," he can also speak of seeking God's face.[39] Despite language that strikes us as frankly corporeal, the Cappadocian theologians were not timid about using terms connoting parts of God's body. They would probably have been surprised by how rapidly such embodied language was dropped from later interpretations of Moses' ascent. In the sixth-century *Mystical Theology*, Pseudo-Dionysius avoids

---

34. Lampe, *PGL*, 706b, s.v. "καταγώγιον."

35. See Robert S. Brightman, "Apophatic Theology and Divine Infinity in St. Gregory of Nyssa," *Greek Orthodox Theological Review* 18 (1973): 97–114.

36. Gregory of Nazianzus, *Orat.* 28.2 (Norris, 224). On the metaphor of ascent in Christian spirituality, see Miles, *Practicing Christianity*, 63–86.

37. Gregory of Nazianzus, *Orat.* 28.3 (Norris, 225–26). Cf. Exodus 33:22–23.

38. Gregory of Nazianzus, *Orat.* 28.5 (Norris, 226).

39. Gregory of Nazianzus, *Orat.* 28, 4–5; on the connection to *Life of Moses*, see Paul Gallay, *Grégoire de Nazianze, Discours 27–31 (Discours théologiques)* (SC 250:106–7 n. 2).

God's body altogether, explaining that Moses "does not meet God himself, but contemplates not him who is invisible, but rather where he dwells."[40] What Pseudo-Dionysius leaves us with, after removing all references to hands, face, or back, is a divine body missing in action. Moses, like Paphnutius in the cave, finds himself alone contemplating an empty space.

Pseudo-Dionysius's modifications notwithstanding, the ideal of journeying toward a divine human body was a powerful one in the fourth and fifth centuries. Christian liturgists also seized on this motif. Catechumens in Theodore of Mopsuestia's church at Antioch were invited to understand the Eucharist as a visualization of future salvation: "We wait here in faith until we ascend into heaven and set out on our journey to our Lord, where we shall not see through a glass and in a riddle but shall look face to face."[41] Salvation is achieved by a journey that culminates with the vision of God's face. The central mystery of Christian faith, the Eucharist, anticipates that journey.

In the Christian imagination of the fourth century, the concept of the journey to God implied a desire to see God face to face. The sentiment

40. *Mystical Theology* 3 = 1000D (Luibheid, 137): Cf. the discussion of biblical corporeal language in relation to God, id., *Divine Names* 8.597B (Luibheid, 57). For background on Pseudo-Dionysius's anagogical theology, see Paul Rorem, "The Uplifting Spirituality of Pseudo-Dionysius," in *Christian Spirituality*, vol. 1: *Origins to the Twelfth Century*, ed. Bernard McGinn and John Meyendorff (New York: Crossroad, 1989), 132–51, esp. 143–44. See also Paul Rorem, *Pseudo-Dionysius: A Commentary on the Texts and an Introduction to Their Influence* (New York: Oxford University Press, 1993), 189–92. On Pseudo-Dionysius and the larger problem of representing God in linguistic terms, see Averil Cameron, "The Language of Images: The Rise of Icons and Christian Representation," in *The Church and the Arts*, ed. Diana Wood (Studies in Church History; Oxford: Blackwell, 1992), 1–42, esp. 24–29. On various interpretations of Moses' ascent, see Jean Daniélou, *From Shadows to Reality: Studies in the Biblical Typology of the Fathers* (Westminster, Md.: Newman, 1960), 215.

41. Theodore of Mopsuestia, *Hom.* 5, in *Woodbrooke Studies* 6, ed. A. Mingana (Cambridge: Heffer & Sons, 1933), 82.

was so powerful that it resisted any theological reservations about corporeal language for God. Stories about journeying toward a person (or toward God) spoke both to beginners in the faith, such as the catechumens in Theodore of Mopsuestia's congregation, and monastics, such as those addressed in the *Life of Moses*. It should come as little surprise, therefore, to find a similar desire for a face-to-face encounter with holy men in the writings of pilgrims, who, like Moses, were equally energized and frustrated by the desire to behold the divine.

In these echoes of Moses' ascent, pilgrims to the living would discover how elusive but glorious the divine face could be. As much as pilgrims identified with Moses, however, they nevertheless sought to behold many faces. This desire was patterned less on Moses' ascent than on other types of tales.

THE JOURNEY TO PARADISE

Tours of Paradise figure prominently in pilgrims' writings, since the desert was often thought to be closer to Paradise.[42] The *History of the Monks* describes a journey the desert father Patermuthius experienced: he had been "transported physically to paradise . . . and had seen a vast company of saints."[43] As proof of this embodied experience, he returned with a "large, choice fig" from Paradise, a fruit with which he healed both the sick and the skeptical.[44] Patermuthius's journey echoes almost

42. On this theme, see Jean Daniélou, "Terre et Paradis chez les pères de l'Eglise," *Eranos Jahrbuch* 22 (1953): 433–72.

43. *HM* 10.21 (Russell, 85). On ascent and return journeys, see Jacqueline Amat, *Songes et visions: L'au-delà dans la littérature latine tardive* (Paris: Études Augustiniennes, 1985), 363–66; Claude Carrozi, *Le voyage de l'âme dans l'au-delà dans la littérature latine, Ve–XIIIe siècles* (Paris: Boccard, 1994).

44. *HM* 10.21–22. This fruit is even more significant precisely because it imitates fourth-century pilgrim practices. Bringing home a fruit from the sacred destination was a practice that went back to the earliest days of holy land pilgrimage. These souvenirs, or, "blessings," *(eulogiae)*, as they were called, not only were regarded as a gesture of monastic hospitality but also, as many pil-

verbatim the prologue of the *History of the Monks*. In both instances, the author describes "seeing" a "great number" of holy figures, combining variant forms of ὁράω with πλῆθος.[45]

As the language crosses over from desert to Heaven and back, so too monastic identities shift. In the *Life of Onnophrius* the desert is so near the heavens that the distinction is easily forgotten. As Onnophrius says to the pilgrim Paphnutius: "If desert anchorites desire to see anyone, they are taken up into the heavenly places where they see all the saints and greet them. . . . Afterwards, they return to their bodies and they continue to feel comforted for a long time. If they travel to another world (αἰών) through the joy which they have seen, they do not even remember that this world (κόσμος) exists."[46] In this desert there is no solitude, because heavenly companions are readily available. And such crossings are so common that monastics can enter the "heavenly places" when they please. Closer to homecoming weekend than the apostle Paul's bewildered memories of the "third heaven," Onnophrius's Paradise represents a closing of the gap between heaven and earth.

Also unlike the "third heaven" where Paul heard the mysteries, the "heavenly places" here are visually alluring, offering perceptions so intense that all memories of this world are erased. The emphasis on visuality in Paradise is underscored in Paphnutius's response to this speech: "Blessed am I that I have been worthy to see your holy face and hear your

---

grims later claimed, were believed to hold magical powers even away from the holy places. See, for example, *It. Eg.* 3.6–7; 11.1; 15.6; 21.3. On the variety of *eulogiae* and their powers, see Cynthia Hahn, "Loca Sancta Souvenirs: Sealing the Pilgrim's Experience," in *The Blessings of Pilgrimage*, ed. Robert Ousterhout (Urbana: University of Illinois Press, 1990), 85–96; and Gary Vikan, "Early Byzantine Pilgrimage *Devotionalia* as Evidence of the Appearance of Pilgrimage Shrines," in *JAC Suppl. 20*, 1:377–88.

45. Cf. *HM* prol. 10: εἶδον . . . πλῆθος ἄπειρον μοναχῶν; 10.21 ἑωρακέναι πλῆθος ἁγίων.

46. Paphnutius, *V. Onnophr.* 17–18 (Vivian, 156–57, modified).

sweet words."[47] By his emphasis on seeing and hearing the holy man, the pilgrim identifies with the monks who see and hear those in the heavenly places. This-worldly and otherworldly journeys intertwine in these accounts; everyone seems to "travel to another world through joy."[48]

In contrast to the apostle Paul, who reports having "heard things that are not to be told" (2 Cor 12:4), it seems odd that Onnophrius chooses to broadcast the visual experiences of his journey. Tours of Paradise were common in the Jewish and Christian literature of antiquity.[49] The *Apocalypse of Paul*, or the *Visio Pauli*, a late-fourth-century work deriving from Egypt, became widely known not only in Greek but also in Latin, Coptic, and Syrian translations.[50] This popular work, composed within a decade or so of the *historiai*, offers another literary model of physical journeys to holy people.[51]

47. Ibid., 18, a sentiment echoed by the apostle Paul in *Visio Pauli* 22.5 (in Claude Carozzi, *Eschatologie et au-delà: Recherches sur L'apocalypse de Paul* [Aix-en-Provence: Publications de l'Université de Provence, 1994]): "Ego autem admiratus sum, et benedixi dominum Deum in omnibus quae uidi."

48. Paphnutius, *V. Onnophr.* 17 (Vivian, 156).

49. See Martha Himmelfarb, *Ascent to Heaven in Jewish and Christian Apocalypses* (New York: Oxford University Press, 1993); and *Death, Ecstasy, and Other Worldly Journeys*, ed. John J. Collins and Michael Fishbane (Albany: State University of New York Press, 1995), esp. Alan F. Segal, "Paul and the Beginning of Jewish Mysticism," 93–120.

50. Text in Carozzi, *Eschatologie et au-delà*, 186–263. James K. Elliott's English translation, which is based on older editions, is available in *The Apocryphal New Testament* (Oxford: Clarendon, 1993), 620–44. The consulships mentioned in the introduction point to a terminus post quem of 388 (*Visio Pauli*, 1; Elliott, 617, 620). Those who cast doubts on R. Casey's argument for an early-third-century origin ("The Apocalypse of Paul," *JTS* 34 [1933]: 28, 31) include Martha Himmelfarb (*Tours of Hell: An Apocalyptic Form in Jewish and Christian Literature* [Philadelphia: University of Pennsylvania Press, 1983], 18–19) and Pierluigi Piovanelli ("Les origines de *l'Apocalypse de Paul* reconsidérées," *Apocrypha* 4 [1993]: 25–64, esp. 55–57).

51. Piovanelli dates the work to 395–416, a span that would coincide with

The *Apocalypse of* Paul takes the reader on a magnificent tour of Paradise, to see its flora and fauna and to hear the sun, moon, stars, and sea speak to the Lord.[52] Prominent on this tour are monks as well as biblical prophets and patriarchs.[53] Thus Paul meets Elijah, Isaiah, Jeremiah, Ezekiel and Amos.[54] As he moves to higher realms, he meets those who "have given hospitality to strangers," specifically the patriarchs Abraham, Isaac, Lot, and Job, "and other saints," who praise Paul for having "observed humanity and helped pilgrims."[55] Monks cohabit easily with biblical heroes, and, conversely, biblical heroes behave as monks, visiting each other and extending hospitality.[56]

Another striking parallel with the *History of the Monks* lies in the many references to the facial or bodily appearance of those in heaven. Paul witnesses several grotesque faces, including "angels without mercy" with buckteeth and eyes that "shone like the morning star . . . and from the hairs of their head or from their mouth sparks of fire went out."[57] More common are the luminous faces of the righteous. Thus Enoch's countenance, like David's, "shone as the sun."[58] And the Coptic version specifies that prophets' faces "shone like the sun, [only] seven times [brighter]."[59] Later in the journey, Paul sees "three men coming . . . very beautiful in the likeness of Christ, and their forms were shin-

---

the composition of the *History of the Monks* (395–400) and anticipate the *Lausiac History* (ca. 420–21) by as little as five years ("Les origines," 55).

52. *Visio Pauli* 22–23; 4–6.

53. Monastics appear both in Heaven and Hell; see, for example, *Visio Pauli* 9, 24, 26, 29, 39, and 40.

54. *Visio Pauli*, 25.

55. *Visio Pauli* 27 (Elliott, 631).

56. For example, *HM* 1.13, 62; 5.5; 8.55; 14.13. On monastic visiting and hospitality, see Graham Gould, *The Desert Fathers on Monastic Community* (Oxford: Clarendon, 1993), esp. 147–50.

57. *Visio Pauli* 11.3 (Elliott, 623); cf. "very black faces" of adulterers and fornicators (38).

58. Enoch: *Visio Pauli* 20 (Elliott, 628); David: *Visio Pauli* 29.

59. *Visio Pauli* (Coptic) in E. A. Wallis Budge, *Miscellaneous Coptic Texts in the*

ing." Even when Paul requires the assistance of his guide to identify holy people in the distance, as with these three men, who turn out to be Abraham, Isaac and Jacob,[60] the text makes frequent reference to the fact that this is an embodied journey.[61]

The holy people Paul meets appear to be engaged in no activity except to approach Paul, greet him, and be seen. Any further movement, it seems, might interrupt the larger purpose of Paul's journey: to gaze on figures from the sacred past. What exactly he is gazing at is also difficult to determine. Instead of furnishing details about the dress, hair, eyes, and other features of the patriarchs and prophets,[62] this author is more likely to differentiate degrees of beauty or brilliance. Thus, Moses and Lot are described as "beautiful of countenance," while Job is "*very* beautiful of countenance"; a Coptic version takes it one step further, mentioning Adam, "taller than them all and very beautiful."[63] While I reserve a fuller discussion of these descriptions for chapter 5, these examples already indicate an intense interest in reporting on the visual experience of bodies.[64]

Dialect of Upper Egypt (London: British Museum, 1915; repr. 1977) fol. 33b (trans. p. 1078).

60. *Visio Pauli* 47 (Elliott, 640). Cf. 29 (on eventually recognizing David).

61. Whereas the *Visio Pauli* opens in doubt as to whether Paul experienced his tour of Heaven "in the body or out of the body" (prol. quoting 2 Cor 12:2), the work concludes on the side of embodiment: the Virgin Mary refers to the saints who "pray that [Paul] might come here in the body that they might see [him] . . . in the flesh" (*Visio Pauli* 46; Elliott, 640). Cf. the Syriac description of Abel (J. Perkins, trans. in *Journal of the American Oriental Society* 8 [1864]: 183–212, excerpts appended to Elliott's translation). Here Abel rushes to see the Apostle, since "there will be deliverance for us if we see him while he is still in the body" (Elliott, 644).

62. As in the self-description provided by Noah "in the time of the flood": "In those one hundred years not a hair of my head grew in length, nor did my garments become soiled" (*Visio Pauli* 50; Elliott, 643).

63. *Visio Pauli* 47–49 (Elliott, 640–42; emphasis mine). Coptic: Elliott, 644.

64. As in the vision of Christ (44), when the tormented cry out in unison, "For since we have seen you we have refreshment"; cf. the references to per-

All these descriptions of otherworldly journeys, whether in the body or out of the body, point to the common desire to see a holy person in the flesh. The narrator underscores this desire not just by presenting luminous bodies of the heavenly dwellers but also by reversing roles so as to make these figures pilgrims to Paul. Thus an exuberant Noah makes pilgrimage "saying, 'Blessed are you, Paul, and blessed am I because I saw you.' " The Virgin Mary announces to Paul that she stands ahead of "all the righteous men" who are "coming to meet [Paul]," because they "desire to see him in the flesh."[65] At first Paul is baffled by these supplicants and turns to his angel to ask, "Sir, who is this?" Yet this role reversal does not change the fact that pilgrimage here is to an embodied destination, as the copious details regarding dress, hair, and faces demonstrate.[66] This emphasis on visual perception of bodily sanctity is not limited to otherworldly journeys, as a consideration of saints' lives will demonstrate.

THE JOURNEY TO THE SAINT

So far, my discussion has focused on otherworldly encounters with embodied sanctity. In this final section, I turn to this-worldly encounters between pilgrims and holy people, as described in popular saints' lives. During the fourth and fifth centuries, anyone familiar with Athanasius's *Life of Anthony* would have known of the practice of visiting holy people.[67] In an effort to rival Athanasius's hero, Jerome composed the *Life of Paul the First Hermit*. Writing some twenty years after the *Life of Anthony* first appeared, Jerome acknowledged the growing popularity of the Greek and Latin versions of Athanasius's work and borrowed sub-

---

ceiving those "coming from afar" or perceived from afar: e.g., 29 (David), 47 (Abraham, Isaac, and Jacob), 48 (Moses), 49 (Lot and Job), 50 (Noah).

65. *Visio Pauli* 50 (Elliott, 642); 46 (Elliott, 640).

66. *Visio Pauli* 50 (Elliott, 643); cf. Coptic ending, Elliott, 644.

67. A fuller discussion appears in chapter 5 (below).

stantially from it.[68] Yet whereas Athanasius's interest remained focused on the holy man and his battles—with wild animals, demons, and heretics—Jerome swiftly reversed the lens to direct the reader's attention to the pilgrim, Anthony himself. As Jerome remarks, Anthony may have "stirred others to emulation" through ascetic withdrawal, but he ought best be remembered as a pilgrim in search of "another and better monk."[69] Jerome insists that a less famous monk named Paul of Thebes was the "first monk to dwell in the desert."[70] Whether Paul of Thebes was real mattered little to Jerome.[71] Nor did the question prevent the *Life of Paul* from gaining a large audience, which grew with each new translation.[72] Between the *Life of Anthony* and the *Life of Paul*, then, Anthony undergoes two significant transformations: from exemplar of desert ascetics to an imitator of them, and, more important, from pilgrims' goal to pilgrim proper.

Lest we concern ourselves too much with Anthony's demotion,[73] we should consider what the work says about pilgrimage. Pilgrimage shapes

68. Jerome, *V. Pauli* 1, following Harvey's paragraph divisions. On the *Life of Anthony's* widespread influence, see, for example, Jerome, *Ep.* 127.5; G. J. M. Bartelink, *Athanase d'Alexandrie, Vie d'Antoine* (SC 400; Paris: Cerf, 1994) 68–70; Quasten, 3:40; Frances M. Young, *From Nicaea to Chalcedon: A Guide to the Literature and Its Background* (Philadelphia: Fortress, 1983), 81, 302 n. 81; Rousseau, *Ascetics*, 3; and Bernard Flusin, *Miracle et histoire dans l'œuvre de Cyrille de Scythopolis* (Paris: Études Augustiniennes, 1983), 44–45.

69. Jerome, *V. Pauli* 7 (Harvey, 363).

70. Jerome, *V. Pauli* 1 (Harvey, 359).

71. The extent to which the narrative and even its subject, Paul of Thebes, are fictional is debated. See Rousseau, *Ascetics*, 133; Quasten, 4:237 (for Chalchis); Kelly, *Jerome*, 60–61 (for Antioch); Samuel Rubenson, *The Letters of St. Antony: Origenist Theology, Monastic Tradition and the Making of a Saint* (Lund: Lund University Press, 1990), 172, 175.

72. *PL* 23.17–28. Kelly (*Jerome*, 60) mentions six Greek translations, one Coptic, one Syriac, and one Ethiopic translation.

73. E. Coleiro, "St. Jerome's Lives of the Hermits," *VC* 11 (1957): 161–78, esp. 168–70.

the characters and structure of the *Life of Paul*. After a relatively short description of the sixteen-year-old Paul's decision to settle in the uninhabited desert, Jerome abruptly moves to the holy man's 113th year. By this time, Anthony too is quite elderly, but when a dream instructs him to seek out "another and better monk," he immediately sets out on the journey.[74] Along the way he encounters strange and fearsome creatures: first a centaur, then a "dwarf, whose nostrils were joined together, with horns growing out of his forehead, and with the legs and feet of a goat."[75] In this new role, Anthony is made to experience the hopes, frustrations, and fears of the very pilgrims he once turned away. Whereas other pilgrims' tales reassure readers with tales about holy men who tame wild animals and rescue travelers from savage beasts,[76] Jerome's offers an entirely different picture. His beasts may at first frighten pilgrims but ultimately become their greatest allies. The centaur offers roadside assistance by pointing Anthony in the right direction, and the dwarf supplies him with dates "as pledges of peace."[77] In this Oz-like, pilgrim-friendly desert, the traveler, as well as the monks, enjoys a paradisiac existence.

More so than the journey, the destination highlights how frightening desert pilgrimage can be. When Anthony finally reaches the cave (having been led there by a thirsty she-wolf), he hesitates before entering. Although Jerome sets up the reader for a horrifying discovery like that of Paphnutius, he takes the story in a different direction. As Anthony follows the trail of a sound and then a dim, distant light, he accidentally knocks against a stone and startles Paul, who immediately slams his cell door shut. More persistent than the pilgrims described by Athanasius, Jerome's Anthony now must see at all costs.[78] Shut out from Paul's cell,

---

74. Jerome, *V. Pauli* 7 (Harvey, 363).
75. Jerome, *V. Pauli* 8 (Harvey, 363).
76. For example, *HM* 4.3; 9.6–10; 12.5–9; 20.12.
77. Jerome, *V. Pauli* 7–8 (Harvey, 363); cf. 10.
78. That desire to see Paul contrasts with the privileged role of hearing in Athanasius's *Life of Anthony*. Apart from the theophanic episode (*V. Ant.* 14),

Anthony begs, "I realize that I am not worthy of your glance. Nonetheless, I shall not go away until I have seen you."[79] Although Paul has not yet revealed himself to his visitor, he provides a detailed verbal self-portrait: "Look at the unkempt hair covering a body decayed with age. This is the man whom you have sought with such hard work. You see before you a man soon to become dust."[80] All the visual cues in this passage signal the beginning of the visit.

Even deeper visual experiences mark the farewell episodes. As part of his preparation for death, Paul instructs Anthony to bury him in a cloak Anthony had received from Athanasius. Jerome did not need to explain to his audience how potent this garment was as a symbol of spiritual authority; that much was already apparent in Athanasius's *Life of Anthony*.[81] More miraculous are Paul's clairvoyance and prophetic powers, which trigger a visionary experience for Anthony: "Anthony was dumbfounded at hearing that Paul knew of Athanasius and his cloak. He saw, it seemed, Christ himself in Paul. Worshipping God dwelling within Paul, Anthony dared not reply."[82] The recognition scene, extended by visual exchanges, underscores the importance of seeing holy faces as a means to seeing Christ himself. Missing here is a verbal response to that vision.

Anthony finds words to describe what he has seen only after he has left Paul. After much pleading from his disciples, Anthony finally divulges the experience in three simple phrases: "I have seen Elijah, I have seen John in the desert, and truly have I seen Paul in paradise."[83]

Athanasius stresses the auditory dimensions of Anthony's sanctity, both in the divine voices he hears (e.g., *V. Ant.* 10, 49, 60, 80) and in the extensive discourses.

79. Jerome, *V. Pauli* 9 (Harvey, 365).

80. Jerome, *V. Pauli* 10 (Harvey, 365).

81. *V. Ant.* 91.

82. Jerome, *V. Pauli* 12 (Harvey, 366–67). On seeing Christ in the person of a monk, cf. Jerome, *Ep.* 108.14 (NPNF 1.6.202).

83. Jerome, *V. Pauli* 13 (Harvey, 367).

Then he gathers the cloak and returns to the desert. As Jerome describes Anthony's hasty return, "he thirsted for him, he longed to see *(videre desiderans)* him, he embraced him with his eyes and mind *(oculis ac mente complectens)*."[84] Such decidedly visual language crystallizes the pilgrim's purpose: to see the holy.

As all these visual desires and visionary experiences attest, the *Life of Paul* defines pilgrimage to people as a visual practice. For Jerome, at least, pilgrimage to holy people synthesizes the ideals of spiritual pilgrimage (seeing God face to face), the paradisiac tour (seeing biblical figures), and physical pilgrimage (seeing the desert ascetic). Anthony's remark about seeing Elijah, "John in the desert," and "Paul in paradise," itself unites these face-to-face encounters in a setting where the desert and Paradise elide. The fullest meaning of this remark becomes clear only when it is read against the background of allegorical journeys and apocalyptic voyages, where devotions are determined by the process and effects of vision.

Just as Palladius artfully integrated spiritual and physical journeys in his travelogue, so other texts achieve a synthesis between this-worldly and otherworldly journeys to holy people. To some extent, the imaginary journeys discussed here echo details from actual pilgrims' practice. But it is equally clear how much pilgrims borrowed from these invented journeys. The *History of the Monks*, with tours of Paradise and gleaming faces of biblical prophets, shows how deeply pilgrims integrated their own practices with the spiritual quest. Action and ideal, perception and desire all merge in the travelogues, so that physical journey and spiritual progress are indistinguishable. From a pilgrim's perspective, is there any meaningful difference between the biblical figures who behave as monks in the *Apocalypse of Paul* and a monk who behaves as a biblical figure in the *Life of Paul?* Here is religious imagination that draws no firm distinction between holy men such as Paul, who lives "a heavenly life on earth," and those who live an earthly life

84. Jerome, *V. Pauli* 14 (Harvey, 367).

in Heaven, as the *Apocalypse of Paul* would have us see the patriarchs, angels, and prophets.[85]

It becomes easier to understand from these otherworldly journeys and fictionalized pilgrimages how actual pilgrims could draw from these stories the metaphors and expectations by which to represent their own journeys. When Anthony uttered his three phrases about Elijah, John, and Paul, he signaled to his disciples (and to Jerome's audience) that pilgrimage to people is about movement across both space and time. One seeks out holy people to encounter faces from a biblical time, to look the past in the eye. The apostle Paul's tour of Paradise offers a similar reminder: to be prepared for special moments of recognition, when unfamiliar silhouettes in the distance become the distinctive faces of Elijah or Abraham. And that moment, as we have seen in these ancient travelogues and imaginary journeys, tends to be not only visual but also biblical. The places may change from mountain to desert to heavens, but the sensory dimensions of the experience are constant: vision defines the moment of recognition, whereby the gaze is returned in a face-to-face encounter with a figure from the biblical past. Why vision, in particular, was invested with the power to perceive and penetrate the past is the subject of the next chapter.

85. Jerome, *V. Pauli* 7 (Harvey, 363).

FOUR

Pilgrims and the Eye of Faith

All travel writing is a form of seeing for the reader, who must rely on the eyes of another. Some travelers draw attention to that responsibility, as Egeria did. In her diary, the fourth-century pilgrim promised her readers that if she described the holy places in sufficient detail, her audience might "see more completely *(pervidere)* what happened in these places" when they read the Bible.[1] She knew that travel writing both represents what has been seen and creates what can be seen.[2]

Travel writers' claims to re-present sensory perceptions provide a useful point of entry into pilgrims' religious experiences. Pilgrims to the Holy Land record physical details about what they saw, such as how shrines and markers were decorated and designed.[3] More interesting for our purposes are the subtle messages these reminiscences carry

1. *It. Eg.* 5.8 (Wilkinson, 97–98, modified). Cf. 7.1; 12.3.
2. As François Hartog explains, "To describe is to see and make seen. It is to say what you have seen. . . . But if you can only say what what you have seen, you can only see what can be said" (*The Mirror of Herodotus: The Representation of the Other in the Writing of History*, trans. Janet Lloyd [Berkeley: University of California Press, 1988], 248).
3. For example, on the value of Egeria's testimony for reconstructing the appearance of the Holy Sepulchre, see Cynthia Hahn, "Seeing and Believing:

about the value placed on visual experiences. The intensity of those experiences suggests to modern interpreters that pilgrims did not necessarily see the way *we* see. As cultural anthropologists and art historians point out, certain features of sensory perception are universal, including the physiological structure of the eye. Yet the quality of perceptions can differ according to the complex attitudes and beliefs assigned to sensory impressions. Thus it is helpful to distinguish between "vision"—the physiological and neurological processes involved in the act of seeing—and "visuality"—the meanings, properties, or values that a given culture assigns to sight.[4] "Vision" is explored through the study of optics, ophthalmology, neurology, and other disciplines concerned with the mechanics of sight. Understanding "visuality," however, is largely a reconstructive process, one that considers how language, symbols, myths, and values become attached to the act of seeing. Exploring visuality in a particular cultural context requires careful attention to the poetics and organization of visual experiences.

This chapter explores the visuality inherent in the recorded memories of pilgrims to the Holy Land, many of whom testify that their most transformative experiences were linked to the act of seeing. Pilgrims to the holy places have left us with more testimonies to their visual experiences, spanning two centuries of reports, than those who traveled in

The Construction of Sanctity in Early-Medieval Saints' Shrines," *Speculum* 72 (1997): 1079–1106, esp. 1084–86; and for liturgical practices, see John F. Baldovin, *The Urban Character of Christian Worship: The Origins, Development, and Meaning of the Stational Liturgy* (Rome: Pontificale Institutum Studiorum Orientalium, 1987), 55–64.

4. I have been influenced by Michael Baxandall, *Painting and Experience in Fifteenth-Century Italy* (Oxford: Oxford University Press, 1972), 29–40; Martin Jay, "Vision in Context: Reflections and Refractions," in *Vision in Context: Historical and Contemporary Perspectives on Sight*, ed. Teresa Brennan and Martin Jay (New York : Routledge, 1996), 1–12; *The Varieties of Sensory Experience: A Sourcebook in the Anthropology of the Senses*, ed. David Howes (Toronto: University of Toronto Press, 1991); James Elkins, *The Object Stares Back: On the Nature*

search of living saints. With a better understanding of how and why pilgrims to the holy places valued visual experience, one can eventually arrive at a deeper appreciation for the visual experiences of pilgrims to the living.

My investigation focuses less on how the holy places appeared than on what it meant for pilgrims to *behold* these places. Two main questions emerge: How did pilgrims use their senses, and what qualities of vision were inherent in those perceptions? The first question relates to the importance of visual perceptions. Pilgrims to holy places valued the sense of sight as a primary mode for religious understanding, even when their devotions at the holy places became increasingly tactile. Although a tactile visuality might appear a contradiction in terms, it was not so for the ancients, as essayists, philosophers, novelists, and poets of the day articulated the powers of visual perception.

VISION AT THE HOLY PLACES

"The man who has seen Judaea with his own eyes ... will gaze more clearly upon Holy Scripture."[5] This comment by Jerome alerts us to an important feature of pilgrimage in the late fourth century. Although pilgrimage engages every physical sense, late antique Christian pilgrims believed that seeing offered special benefits. In diaries and letters they claimed a more genuine understanding of scripture precisely because the sense of sight allowed them to internalize and embody that knowledge. The vocabulary of pilgrimage was primarily visual. Writers described pilgrimage as "seeing with the senses (αἰσθητῶς) the holy places" and

---

of Seeing (New York: Simon & Schuster, 1996). For antiquity, see David Chidester, *Word and Light: Seeing, Hearing, and Religious Discourse* (Urbana: University of Illinois Press, 1992), esp. 1–24.

5. Jerome, *Praef. in Lib. Paralip.* (PL 29.401; quoted in E. D. Hunt, *Holy Land Pilgrimage in the Later Roman Empire (A.D. 312–460)* ([Oxford: Clarendon, 1982], 94).

"seeing the signs of Christ's sojourn."[6] According to the Syr
Theodoret of Cyrrhus, the purpose of pilgrimage was to "fea
eyes" on the holy places.[7] One prominent feature of Egeria's La\ ...₃ ner
frequent use of verbs for seeing used in the sense of "visiting."[8]

Habits of expression can reflect habits of viewing. In letters home, pilgrims described both visual and visionary experiences. One privilege Christian pilgrims claimed was to "see" what others had only heard. Jerome put it this way: "I entered Jerusalem, I saw a host of marvels, and with the judgment of my eyes I verified things of which I had previously learned by report."[9] When the Empress Helena entered Jerusalem, as Paulinus, bishop of Nola, describes her experiences, she "avidly visited all the places . . . which bore the marks of God's presence. She was eager to absorb through her eyes the faith which she had gained by devoted listening and reading."[10] Whether to verify information, as Jerome did, or to "absorb" it, as Helena did, both pilgrims deepened their knowledge of the scriptures through the faculty of sight.

With such an emphasis on seeing, it is puzzling that these pilgrims tell us little about what they actually saw. The site of Jesus' crucifixion, for example, appears strikingly empty in Jerome's description of Paula's

6. A distinction made by Gregory of Nyssa, *Ep.* 3.3 (SC 363:126–127). On the frequent use of the verbs *see* and *was shown* in pilgrims' writings, see Robert Wilken, *The Land Called Holy: Palestine in Christian History and Thought* (New Haven: Yale University Press, 1992), 300 n. 46; Pierre Maraval, *Lieux saints et pèlerinages d'Orient: Histoire et géographie des origines à la conquête arabe* (Paris: Cerf, 1985), 137–38.

7. *HR* 9.2 (Price, 82).

8. G. F. M. Vermeer, *Observations sur le vocabulaire du pèlerinage chez Égérie et chez Antonin de Plaisance* (Latinitas Christianorum Primaeva 19; Utrecht: Dekker & Van de Vegt, 1965), 42, citing *It. Eg.* 19.4 as an example: "Ac sic ergo vidi in eadem civitate martyria plurima nec non et sanctos monachos."

9. Jerome, *Apol.* 3.22, translated in J. N. D. Kelly, *Jerome: His Life, Writings, and Controversies* (San Francisco: Harper & Row, 1975), 124.

10. Paulinus of Nola, *Ep.* 31.5 (Walsh, 2:130).

veneration: she "fell down and worshipped before the Cross as if she could see the Lord hanging on it."[11] Paula's viewing assumes greater importance than the physical artifacts others might see at the same place. A similar visionary experience occurred at Bethlehem: "With the eye of faith, she saw a child wrapped in swaddling clothes, weeping in the Lord's manger," along with the Magi, Mary, Joseph, and the shepherds.[12] Were images of Christ's birth displayed at the cave of the Nativity? On this matter, both Jerome and the archaeological and literary records are silent.[13] Jerome shows no interest in satisfying our curiosity about what the eyes of the body saw. He directs the reader's attention instead to the "eye of faith" and its power to conjure and display a biblical event.

In these accounts, the "eye of faith" signals a vivid perception of a past biblical event that is triggered by seeing the physical holy place. One might refer to these visualizing moments as "biblical realism," by which I mean instances when the viewer claims to become an eyewitness to a biblical event. Paula's experience of the Nativity resembles a type of consciousness that Ewert Cousins, a historian of spirituality, has called "mysticism of the historical event," by which "one recalls a significant

11. Jerome, *Ep.* 108.9.2. See John Wilkinson, *Jerusalem Pilgrims before the Crusades* (Warminster: Aris & Phillips, 1977), 49 n. 29. Although Paula's expression is more than visual (kissing the stone, licking the spot where the Lord's body had lain), vision triggers this multisensory reponse.

12. Jerome, *Ep.* 108.10 (Fremantle, 199).

13. As Hunt (*Holy Land Pilgrimage*, 104) comments: "It has to be admitted that, if pilgrims at the holy places really had remarked what covered the interior walls of the churches in which they worshipped, we should have expected them to have provided more detail in their descriptions." Lately, art historians have called into question the existence of *loca sancta* art at this relatively early period. See, for example, Robert John Grigg, "Images on the Palestinian Flasks as Possible Evidence of the Monumental Decoration of Palestinian Martyria" (Ph.D. diss., University of Minnesota, 1974), 117–23; and Gary Vikan, "Early Byzantine Pilgrimage *Devotionalia* as Evidence of the Appearance of Pilgrimage Shrines," *JAC Suppl.* 20, 1:377–88.

event in the past, [and] enters into its drama."[14] Like the pilgrims who are depicted standing beside the Magi on decorated flasks from the Holy Land, Paula inserts herself among the eyewitnesses to the birth of Christ. As Gary Vikan has shown for these sixth-century flasks, pilgrims entered into the world of the Magi through the imitative gestures built into the Jerusalem Liturgy.[15] In Paula's case, over a century earlier, the eye of faith gives her access to this scene, closing any perceived gap between the present and the past.

The type of realism Paula experienced begins to appear only in late-fourth-century accounts. One narrative by an anonymous pilgrim from Bordeaux, who journeyed to the Holy Land during the 330s, is steeped in the past tense, indicating a detachment from biblical events.[16] He recalls Golgotha as the place "where the Lord was crucified"[17] but gives no indication of any personal experience of that event. Paula, visiting the same place almost a half-century later, claimed actually to see Christ crucified. A letter attributed to Paula, inviting the Roman aristocrat Marcella to the Holy Land, achieves a similar vividness: "As often as we enter [the Lord's sepulchre] we see the Saviour in His grave clothes, and if we linger we see again the angel sitting at His feet, and the napkin folded at His head."[18] In closing the invitation, the writer anticipates the sensory wonders of Marcella's pilgrimage:

14. Ewert Cousins, "Francis of Assisi: Christian Mysticism at the Crossroads," in *Mysticism and Religious Traditions*, ed. Steven T. Katz (Oxford: Oxford University Press, 1983), 163–90, esp. 166–67.

15. Gary Vikan, "Pilgrims in Magi's Clothing: The Impact of Mimesis on Early Byzantine Pilgrimage Art," in *The Blessings of Pilgrimage*, ed. Robert Ousterhout (Urbana & Chicago: University of Illinois Press, 1990), 97–107.

16. See the interesting work of Laurie Douglass, "A New Look at the *Itinerarium Burdigalense*," *JECS* 4 (1996): 313–34.

17. *It. Burg.* 593 (Wilkinson, 158).

18. Jerome, *Ep.* 46.5. (ed. Labourt 2:105; Fremantle, 62): "quod quotienscumque ingredimur, totiens iacere in sindone cernimus Saluatorem, et paululum ibidem commorantes rursum uidemus angelum sedere ad pedes eius, et ad caput sudarium conuolutum." On Jerome's pilgrimages, see Pierre Maraval,

> Then shall we touch with our lips the wood of the true cross. . . . We
> shall see *(videre)* Lazarus come forth bound with grave clothes. . . .
> We shall see *(conspicere)* the prophet Amos. . . . We shall see *(videre)*
> the fountain in which the eunuch was immersed by Philip. . . . If
> only you will come, we shall go to see *(videbimus)* Nazareth. . . . Not
> far off Cana will be visible *(cernetur)* . . . we shall see *(videbimus)* the
> spots where the five thousand were filled with five loaves. Our eyes
> will look on Capernaum, the scene of so many of our Lord's signs.[19]

Apart from mentioning the standard practice of kissing the wood of the
Cross, the journey is arranged as a series of visual events. One is
tempted to liken this verbal itinerary to a glossy brochure, but there is a
key difference: whereas tourists see the markers of the biblical events,
pilgrims "linger" to see the event itself.[20]

The power of that lingering vision to connect the viewer to biblical
events is prominent in another set of reminiscences of a Jerusalem pilgrimage undertaken in the fourth century. This account, however, is
written by a non-pilgrim, Athanasius, who welcomes home a group of
female ascetics returning from their journey to the Holy Land. Known
today as the "Letter to Virgins Who Went and Prayed in Jerusalem and
Returned,"[21] and joined to a treatise on virginity, the letter reimagines
the women's pilgrimage to the Holy Land through a series of vignettes.

"Saint Jérôme et le pèlerinage aux lieux saints de Palestine," in *Jérôme entre
l'Occident et l'Orient (Actes du Colloque de Chantilly, 1986)*, ed. Yves-Marie Duval
(Paris: Études Augustiniennes, 1988), 345–53.

19. Jerome, *Ep.* 46.13 (Labourt, 2:113–115; Fremantle, 65, slightly modified).

20. Jonathan Culler, *Framing the Sign: Criticism and Its Institutions* (Norman:
University of Oklahoma Press, 1988), 153–67, esp. 159–60.

21. Hereafter cited as *LVJer.* The text survives only in a Syriac translation
from the sixth or seventh century, edited by J. Lebon, "Athanasiana Syriaca II,"
Le Muséon 41 (1928): 169–216. Eng. trans.: David Brakke, Appendix B, "Second
Letter to Virgins" in id., *Athanasius and the Politics of Asceticism* (Oxford: Clarendon, 1995), 292–302. References are to Brakke's paragraph divisions. On the

Part reminiscence, part consolation, Athanasius's letter extends a sympathetic welcome home to the virgins. Athanasius remarks on their sense of loss after leaving Bethlehem, Golgotha, and the "holy mountain," probably the Mount of Olives.[22] The place-names alone reveal little about the experience of being a pilgrim. When he comes to Bethlehem, however, Athanasius provides more details: "You saw the cave of the Lord, which is the image of Paradise."[23] "You have not journeyed far from the holy places," he consoles them, "for where Christ dwells, there is holiness. And where Christ's presence is, there too is an abundance of the joys of holiness."[24] The virgins' nostalgia, as Athanasius constructs it, is not just for the places but also for the divine presence they perceived there.[25]

More perplexing is the way Athanasius uses biblical allusions to fill out these reminiscences: "Peter saw our Lord Jesus, abandoned his net, and followed him. Zacchaeus the tax-collector saw him, rejected fraudulent profits, and accepted the Savior. That evil-doing woman saw him and wiped his feet with her tears and hair. Mary [the sister of Martha] saw him and did not depart from before his feet."[26] There is nothing odd in invoking biblical stories when discussing the land of the Bible. What is strange about this passage is that Peter, Zacchaeus, and Mary have no connection to the sites on the virgins' itinerary. Normally, pilgrims preferred to recall biblical stories that were read at the holy

---

debated authorship of this letter, see J. Roldanus, *Le Christ et l'homme dans la théologie d'Athanase* (Leiden: Brill, 1968), 400–401; Brakke, *Athanasius*, 36–41; and Susanna Elm, "Perceptions of Jerusalem Pilgrimage as Reflected in Two Early Sources on Female Pilgrimage (Third and Fourth Centuries, A.D.)," *SP* 20 (1987): 219–23.

22. *LVJer* 1 (Brakke, 292).

23. *LVJer* 1 (Brakke, 292).

24. *LVJer* 3 (Brakke, 293).

25. An assumption that was often criticized; see Gregory of Nyssa, *Ep.* 2.10. On critics of pilgrimage, see Maraval, *Lieux saints,* 153–55.

26. *LVJer* 5 (Brakke, 294).

places.[27] Egeria, for example, noted the excitement she felt when she listened to the story of Israel's wanderings as she stood in the Sinai desert.[28] Athanasius's inclusions, however, suggest a new emphasis: the pilgrims are reminded not that they *stood* where Mary, Peter, and Zacchaeus once stood, but that they *saw* what Jesus' contemporaries saw. As Athanasius puts it, "In the life-giving places you saw, so to speak, Christ walking."[29] The immediacy of Christ's presence is perceived by the faculty of sight. For Athanasius, at least, "being there" is less important than "seeing there."

Athanasius's curious choice of exemplars has a subtle but forceful effect on the reminiscences. By separating biblical places from the stories that are traditionally associated with them, he subtly shifts attention away from sacred topography to visual piety. This move leaves him free to invoke other biblical paradigms. When he recalls Bethlehem, he makes no mention of the Magi, the archetypal pilgrims.[30] Instead, the virgins are to identify with Mary, the sister of Martha and model disciple, who sat at Jesus' feet (Luke 10:38–42); likewise, the virgins listened obediently to the "exhortations" of the "holy ones" there.[31] Whereas Paula predictably encountered the Virgin Mary at Bethlehem, Athanasius puts there an entirely different Mary, not the mother of God but an attentive disciple.

Although Athanasius does not evoke visionary experiences or a biblical realism comparable to Paula's eye of faith, he nevertheless places great emphasis on seeing: "You have seen the place of the Nativity: he

27. For an insightful discussion of this practice, see Jonathan Z. Smith, *To Take Place: Toward Theory in Ritual* (Chicago: University of Chicago Press, 1987), 89–90; and Mary Carruthers, *The Craft of Thought: Meditation, Rhetoric, and the Making of Images, 400–1200* (Cambridge: Cambridge University Press, 1998), 44–46.

28. *It. Eg.* 3.6; cf. 4.3, 5.

29. *LVJer* 5 (Brakke, 294).

30. Vikan, "Pilgrims in Magi's Clothing," 103.

31. *LVJer* 1 (Brakke, 292).

has given birth to your souls anew. You have seen the place of the crucifixion: let the world be crucified to you and you to the world. You have seen the place of the ascension: your minds are raised up."[32] Seeing engenders change in the viewer. The repeated "you have seen" links each act of seeing with a transformation. Modeled on Jesus' companions, the virgins have changed as a result of seeing Christ. As Athanasius constructs these correspondences, time cannot separate the pilgrims from those who knew the "historical" Jesus precisely because the act of seeing is what unites them. Although Athanasius does not suggest that the virgins were participants or eyewitnesses to the actual events, theirs is a visual piety unfettered by temporal distance. Whether one is speaking of Zacchaeus or of the fourth-century virgins, visual perception triggers an immediate bond with divine presence, a bond that is edifying and permanently transforming.[33]

Although Athanasius's consolation offers an alternative to holy places, his message is not far removed from the sermons delivered in Jerusalem. When preaching to Jerusalemites and pilgrims, Bishop Cyril reminded them that they alone had the privilege of seeing Jesus.[34] As Cyril explained, the chance to see a holy place could affirm sacred mysteries more effectively than hearing, since "we know that sight is more trustworthy than hearing."[35] When he introduced a group of newly

32. *LVJer* 6 (Brakke, 294). Everett Ferguson detects a similar seeing-conversion pattern in Gregory of Nyssa's *Life of Moses:* "Each of the experiences of Moses in 'seeing' the divine is followed by an act of service" ("Progress in Perfection: Gregory of Nyssa's *Vita Moysis*, " *SP* 14 [1976]: 307–14, esp. 312).

33. Given that the consolation is juxtaposed with a treatise praising female virginity, the section on pilgrimage can be read as a polemic against physical pilgrimage. The author attempts to show how the sense of divine presence can be perpetuated away from holy places by means of the ascetic life. (Cf. Elm, "Perceptions," 220–21, 223).

34. On how this letter relates to fourth-century *loca sancta* debates, see Georgia Frank, "Pilgrims' Experience and Theological Challenge: Two Patristic Views," *JAC Suppl.* 20 2:787–91.

35. Cyril of Jerusalem, *Cat. Myst.* 1.1 σαφῶς ἠπιστάμην ὄψιν ἀκουῆς πολλῷ

baptized Christians to the sacraments, he demonstrated the importance of sight by directing his audience to gaze on the holy places, since the proof of his words was before their eyes.[36] The resurrection is not an illusion, Cyril insisted, for the simple reason that "the place itself, [is] still visible," as well as the church that adorns it.[37] He affirmed the truth and immediacy of the biblical past by calling on his audience to see for themselves. As these fourth-century texts reveal, vision was capable of conjuring, constituting, and responding to the presence of the divine.

Why did these bishops so readily single out vision as a bridge between the pilgrim's present and the sacred past? Changes in the political and religious environment offer some explanations. As historians of Christianity have pointed out, the legalization of Christianity fostered among Christians a more positive valuation of the material world.[38] In this climate, the developing doctrine of the Incarnation took on a new significance. According to several fourth-century theologians, the sanctifying effect of God's incarnation extended to the physical, material world. Even Evagrius of Pontus, a proponent of imageless prayer, felt that a full understanding of the "sensible and corporeal creation" was indispensable to any contemplation of invisible realities; for, whoever has "probed the visible creation in diligence and purity, knows what it tells about the invisible creation."[39] In this broader understanding of the

---

πιστοτέραν εἶναι (FC 64:153). Cf. *Cat.* 13.22 and *Cat. Myst.* 5.21–22 (FC 64:203), which couple seeing with touch.

36. Cyril of Jerusalem, *Cat.* 10.19, 13.4; *Cat. Myst.* 2.4 (FC 61:207–9; 64:6, 164).

37. ὁ τόπος αὐτὸς ἔτι φαινόμενος. *Cat.* 4.10 (FC 1:124).

38. See for example, Wilken, *The Land Called Holy*, 90–91.

39. Evagrius of Pontus, *Ep. ad Melaniam* 3 (*CPG* 2438; trans. M. Parmentier, "Evagrius of Pontus' 'Letter to Melania' I," *Bijdragen, tijdschrift voor filosofie en theologie* 46 [1985]: 2–38, esp. 9–10, cf. 22). On Cyril of Jerusalem regarding the Incarnation, see P. W. L. Walker, *Holy City, Holy Places? Christian Attitudes to Jerusalem and the Holy Land in the Fourth Century* (Oxford: Clarendon, 1990), 37–38, 81–83.

Incarnation, God was revealed not only in Jesus and humanity but also throughout creation. The words of the eighth-century theologian John of Damascus (d. ca. 749) defending icons could well have been spoken in the fourth century: "I boldly draw an image of the invisible God, not as invisible, but as having become visible for our sakes by partaking of flesh and blood."[40] What had once been inaudible would now be heard; what had once been invisible could now be seen.

The Incarnation endows all sensory experience with a theological significance, including pilgrims' delight in remembering their experiences at the holy places. God could be experienced in the sweeping arc of burning incense or in the rich melody of a hymn.[41] Even mystical theologians such as Gregory of Nyssa or Augustine, whose distrust of the physical senses led them to propose an alternative and higher order of spiritual senses, still used sensory language to structure the language of spiritual experience.[42] But if the Incarnation, in theory, legitimated all forms of sense perception as a means of knowing God, why did pilgrims, in practice, favor vision over the other senses? What prompted pilgrims to disparage the sense of hearing, as in the pilgrim who reminded on holy man that "the ears are naturally (πέφυκεν) less reliable

---

40. *Contra imaginum calumniatores orationes tres* 1.4 (Anderson, 16).

41. Susan Ashbrook Harvey, "St. Ephrem on the Scent of Salvation," *JTS* n.s. 49 (1998): 109–28.

42. See Aimé Solignac, "Oculus," *DS* 11:591–601, esp. 593–96; Mariette Canévet, "Sens spirituel," *DS* 14:598–617; Robert J. Hauck, "'They Saw What They Said They Saw': Sense Knowledge in Early Christian Perspective," *HTR* 81 (1988): 239–49; Margaret R. Miles, "Vision: The Eye of the Body and the Eye of the Mind in Saint Augustine's *De Trinitate* and *Confessions*," *Journal of Religion* 63 (1983): 125–42; Jean Daniélou, *Platonisme et théologie mystique: Essai sur la doctrine spirituelle de Saint Grégoire de Nysse* (Paris: Aubier, 1944), 222–52. On the background and legacy of this idea, see K. Rahner, "Le début d'une doctrine des cinq sens spirituels chez Origène," *Revue d'ascétique et de mystique* 13 (1932): 113–45. B. Fraigneau-Julien, *Les sens spirituels et la vision de Dieu selon Syméon le Nouveau Théologien* (Paris: Beauchesne, 1985).

than the eyes"?[43] The cultural assumptions behind this preference for vision and distrust of hearing are worth investigating.

VISION IN LATE ANTIQUE THEOLOGY

The cultural privileging of vision ran deeper than any incarnational theology that valorized all the senses. Ironically, the problem of blindness allows us to understand why pilgrims cherished visual experience. Of all the healing miracles reported in the gospels, the story of the man born blind (John 9:1–41) was particularly perplexing to preachers. Jesus heals the blind man, who goes on to expose the arrogance and ignorance of the Pharisees. In many respects, this story follows the symbolic inversions of light and dark, seeing and blindness, that are so prominent in Johannine literature.[44] The irony of the situation was unmistakable. As John Chrysostom summed it up: "A blind man was teaching those with sight how to see,"[45] a reversal that lent itself well to condemnations of spiritual blindness in all its forms.[46]

More disturbing was the fact of real blindness. Perhaps it was part of the human condition to *become* blind, but the idea that God would cre-

---

43. *HM* 1.19 (Russell, 54–55).

44. Esp. Jn 1:5; 9:1–41; 12:40; 1 Jn 2:11. See Judith M. Lieu, "Blindness in the Johannine Tradition," *New Testament Studies* 34 (1988): 83–95.

45. John Chrysostom, *De incomprehensibili* 10.34 (FC 72:257).

46. Unbelief: Jn 9:39–41; Mt 15:14; cf. Isa 6:9–10, quoted in Mt 13:10–15; Mk 4:12; Lk 8:10; Jn 12:39–41; Acts 9:1–19a (cf. Ephrem's commentary on Saul's "infamous mark of blindness," *Sermo de Domino nostro* 30.4 [FC 91:308–9]); Acts 28:26–27. Heresy: John Chrysostom, *De incomprehensibili* 2.54 (FC 72:93); Augustine, *Ep.* 185.22; cf. blinding diseases as a metaphor for unbelief in Augustine, Sermon Mayence 61/Dolbeau 25.14 (ed. F. Dolbeau, *Vingt-six sermons au peuple d'Afrique* [Paris: Études Augustiniennes, 1996]: 257), I thank Michael Gaddis and Peter Brown, respectively, for these two references. Immorality: John Chrysostom, *In Ioh. hom.* 22; 57.3; Gregory of Nyssa, *De virginitate* 10–11. See also Jean Daniélou, *L'être et le temps chez Grégoire de Nysse* (Leiden: Brill, 1970), 133–53 (chapter 7, "Aveuglement"), esp. 151.

ate a blind person was particularly distressing to Christian preachers. To the fourth-century bishop Asterius of Amasea, such neglect on the part of the Creator was almost inconceivable: "Among the created things . . . the eye is worthy of wonder. For when perceiving the entire creation accurately, and from this activity perceiving the crafter, it explains even God to me. Thus from visible things it explains the invisible things to the soul. . . . For if the eye did not exist, the creation would grow old unwitnessed (ἀμάρτυρος), since no one would observe (καθορῶντος) the wisdom and power of God."[47] Underlying this praise of the eye is a painful question: if the healthy eye is both teacher to the soul and link to the Creator, why would God deprive his creatures of the very instrument by which he can be known? Isn't God forgetting himself by forgetting the eye? To Asterius, blindness posed not just an aesthetic or practical problem but also a theological one with grave implications both for the Creator and the creature.

Asterius's vocabulary for blindness is taken from theologians' praise of the healthy eye. He echoes the author of the *De structura hominis* (a work falsely attributed to Basil of Caesarea), whose entire understanding of sight and blindness rested on the conviction that all humans "were born to see God."[48] Thus, God equipped us with *two* eyes, not only to sharpen perception but also to ensure uninterrupted vision of God should one eye become damaged. No doubt this author was aware that many body parts come in pairs; but only the eyes were regarded as having a backup system in place. Several writers, including Gregory of Nyssa, called attention to the position of the eyes: the fact that they are situated higher than any other sense organ is ample proof that they are closest to God.[49] Thus, by divinizing the eye, Asterius managed to diminish the horror of blindness.

47. Asterius of Amasea, *Hom.* 7.5.
48. Pseudo-Basil, *De structura hominis* 2.15.
49. Gregory of Nyssa, *De opificio hominis* 8.1. Cf. John Chrysostom, *In Ioh. hom.* 56 (FC 41:91); Augustine, *De Trinitate* 11.1.1. See also Canévet, "Oculus," *DS* 11:593.

John Chrysostom also devoted considerable attention to the man born blind. In both the *Homilies on John* and *On the Incomprehensibility of God* he praised the eye: it was, as he put it, "a small organ in size, but . . . more important than all the rest of the body."[50] According to John, its importance rested on the fact that it is "the light not merely of the body, but also of the soul more than of the body."[51] Chrysostom follows Asterius when he points out that the eye is essential to all life: "If you should extinguish the sun, you would destroy everything and create chaos; if you should extinguish the light of the eyes, the feet would also be useless, and the hands and even life."[52] Thus Chrysostom too concludes that only by the eyes does the creature know God. "If the eyes have been disabled," Chrysostom claims, "wisdom also departs, because by them we know God."[53] Neither writer could have entertained the notion of a "blind seer"; wisdom and vision were too closely tied.

For all his praise of the eye and sight, Chrysostom stands out for his efforts to fit blindness into the divine plan. To him the eye was as revelatory as it was capable of perceiving revelation: "The heavens may be silent, but the sight of them emits a voice, that is louder than a trumpet's sound; instructing us not by the ear, but through the medium of the eyes; for the latter is a sense which is more sure and more distinct than the former."[54] Not only are the eyes most receptive to this revelation, but the revelation itself chooses the visual medium precisely for its universality. As the preacher goes on to explain, "Of the things that are

50. John Chrysostom, *In Ioh. hom.* 56 (FC 41:90).

51. John Chrysostom, *In Ioh. hom.* 56 (FC 41:90); cf. *Mir. Thec.* 24.10–19. Tales such as these prompt the editor, Gilbert Dagron, to dub the *Miracles of Saint Thecla* "une littérature des yeux grands ouverts" (SH 62:138).

52. John Chrysostom, *In Ioh. hom.* 56 (FC 41:90); cf. Plato, *Republic* 508b.

53. John Chrysostom, *In Ioh. hom.* 56 (FC 41:90).

54. John Chrysostom, *De stat.* 9.4 (NPNF 1.9.401); cf. *De stat.* 11.6 (NPNF 1.9.415).

seen, there is one uniform perception; and there is no difference, as is the case with respect to languages."[55] As Chrysostom understands vision, it is not only preferred but essential to any knowledge of God.

To give this priority to vision renders the problem of blindness even more distressing, prompting Chrysostom to insist that God has no intention of blinding sighted people.[56] To reconcile these conflicting claims about God, Chrysostom reminds his audience that the man born blind suffers only a temporary affliction. By this reasoning, God is to be understood as a "first-class sculptor" who "leaves out a part [of a statue] so that, by the omission, he may prove his skill and ability to make the statue whole."[57] This is not the first time Chrysostom has invoked an argument for a deliberate manufacturing defect. In a sermon on the Gospel story of Jesus healing the man born blind, he likens God to an architect who, as he puts it, "may complete part of the house and leave a part unfinished, so as to prove to the skeptical that the whole building is his work, when he supplies what is has been left incomplete."[58] By this reasoning, blindness—and not the eye—has become the proof of divine craftsmanship. All claims to the divine origins of the eye become undermined by the notion of temporary blindness. Thus, Chrysostom exclaims, "O blessed blindness!" so long as it is strictly temporary.[59] Unable to fathom long-term blindness, Chrysostom avoids any embarrassment to God. Blindness is transformed into a matter of unfinished business; the restoration of vision is God's way of signing off on a job well done, nothing less than a coda to creation. Troubled by a God who would inflict blindness, John Chrysostom and Asterius each found a different way to ascribe divine purpose to it. Asterius drew from the lan-

55. John Chrysostom, *De stat.* 9.5 (NPNF 1.9.401–2).
56. John Chrysostom, *In Ioh. hom.* 56 (FC 41:89).
57. John Chrysostom, *De incomprehensibili* 10.32 (FC 72:256)
58. John Chrysostom, *In Ioh. hom.* 56 (FC 41:89); cf. Jn 9:1–41.
59. John Chrysostom, *De incomprehensibili* 10.35 (FC 72:257).

guage of the healthy eye, and Chrysostom turned the affliction into a temporary ailment.

SEEING AND TOUCHING THE HOLY PLACES

In a theological environment that privileged sight, pilgrims discovered the further powers of vision at holy places. Seeing the holy places threw open the weighted curtains of the sacred past and so of the scriptures. More difficult to understand in this theological context is why pilgrims also desired to link themselves to holy places by touch. How does one reconcile John Chrysostom's notion of God's exclusively visible revelation with pilgrims' tendency to touch holy places?

The desire to touch the holy manifests itself wherever pilgrims gather dirt, rub statues, or run their fingers along the words of an inscription.[60] In the fourth century Cyril of Jerusalem boasted to catechumens that "others merely hear, but we see and touch."[61] From as far away as Italy, Paulinus, bishop of Nola, echoed this sentiment: "No other sentiment draws men to Jerusalem but the desire to see and touch the places where Christ was physically present. . . . So if the desire is a truly religious one to see the places in which Christ walked, suffered, rose again, and ascended into heaven . . . there is a blessing in taking and keeping a pinch of dust from these places or a mere mote from the wood of the cross."[62] For Paulinus, at least, the fulfillment of that "desire . . . to see" comes only in the act of touching. The conjunction of sight and touch is even more puzzling when one recalls all the pilgrims who noted memorable experiences of seeing and hearing biblical stories at the holy places[63] yet never cited hearing as a privilege of pilgrimage. To understand why pilgrims began giving special attention to what they touched,

60. Wilken, *Land Called Holy*, 114.
61. Cyril of Jerusalem, *Cat.* 13.22 (FC 64:19).
62. *Ep.* 49.14 (Walsh, 2:273).
63. For example, *It. Eg.* 3.6; cf. 4.3, 5.

it is worth recalling how much the pilgrimage sites changed over the course of the century that followed Constantine and Helena's promotion of the Holy Land.

The rapid increase in the display and transfer of relics was one factor that contributed to pilgrims' desire to touch the holy. In a letter that accompanied the transfer of a relic of the Cross, Paulinus of Nola described the sand surrounding the place of Jesus' ascension: not only is it "visible," he said, but it is also "accessible to worshippers," a qualification not found in earlier pilgrim reports.[64] The Holy Land, as it were, was up for grabs. And grab the pilgrims did. When they processed before the True Cross, as Egeria describes the scene, they first touched the relic with their foreheads and eyes, then kissed it.[65]

By the sixth century, the architectural, monastic, and liturgical settings for pilgrims had changed considerably. One gets a sense of those changes from the crudely executed images on souvenirs pilgrims brought home as well as from the Jerusalem skyline depicted on the apse mosaic at Santa Pudenziana in Rome.[66] Even where artifacts from that time are missing, the anonymous diary of a pilgrim from Piacenza in Italy reminds us of how cluttered the holy places had become by the mid-sixth century. This pilgrim describes handling the flagon and the bread basket that were with Mary at the Annunciation, the book and bench that Christ used in his synagogue at Nazareth, the bucket "from which the Lord drank" at the well of the Samaritan woman, and the

---

64. Paulinus of Nola, *Ep.* 31.4 (Walsh, 2:129–30). This description of Helena's building activities also indicates the presence of sacred substances associated with holy places. On the accessibility of sacred substances, see Hunt, *Holy Land Pilgrimage*, 128–54.

65. *It. Eg.* 37.3. After one pilgrim bit off a piece of the True Cross, kissing continued, but under the close supervision of church personnel. On the pattern of forehead, eyes, and mouth, cf. Cyril of Jerusalem, *Cat. Myst.* 5.21. On the kiss compared to other tactile gestures, see Pierre Adnès, "Toucher, Touches," *DS* 15:1075.

66. Wilken, *Land Called Holy*, 177.

sponge and reed from the Crucifixion.[67] All these items—and more—were within his reach. He describes how he touched, carried, and reclined on various relics, displaying a hands-on piety unmatched by earlier pilgrims' reports.

These "vessels of divine power,"[68] as John of Damascus would later refer to relics, proliferated at a rate that alarmed some bishops in other lands but delighted pilgrims.[69] Indeed, the Piacenza pilgrim could be considered a poster child for what some historians herald as a "new tactile piety."[70] On rare occasions the Piacenza pilgrim managed to resist the impulse to touch; for instance, he and other pilgrims "venerated" the head of John the Baptist by simply looking at it "with our own eyes."[71] Since the head is kept "in a glass vase" (*in doleo vitreo*), one begins to suspect that without that physical barrier, he would also have touched the head. In contrast to Paula's reliance on visualization, more senses came into play as pilgrims responded to the new abundance of relics. With the Piacenza pilgrim's fingerprints all over the Holy Land, one is tempted to doubt that vision could ever again have the effect it had during the fourth century. In this context, a new tactile piety offered the devotee genuine and immediate access to these concrete manifestations of sanctity.

67. *Ps.-Antonini Placentini Itinerarium*, 22 (Wilkinson, 83–84).

68. *C. imag.* 3.34 (Anderson, 85–86).

69. R. A. Markus, "How on Earth Could Places Become Holy? Origins of the Christian Idea of Holy Places," *JECS* 2 (1994): 257–71. On efforts to control pilgrims' sensory access to the holy places and the emotional effects of those changes, see Hahn, "Seeing and Believing," 1086–92, 1100–1.

70. See, for example, Maraval, *Lieux saints*, 144–45 and id., "Égérie et Grégoire de Nysse, pèlerins aux lieux saints de Palestine," in *Atti del convegno internazionale sulla* Peregrinatio Egeriae (Arezzo: Accademia Petrarca di lettere arti e scienze, 1987), 315–31, esp. 330–31. Wilken's discussion of the "new tactile piety" appears in *Land Called Holy*, 115.

71. *Ps.-Antonini Placentini Itinerarium*, 46 (Wilkinson, 89); cf. 44 (Wilkinson, 88).

One is tempted to conclude that touch replaced sight.[72] If there was a shift in sensory priorities, however, it was a relatively rapid one. Not too long before, in Athanasius's *Life of Anthony*, for instance, touch was discredited as the sensory mode used by pagans and demons.[73] More problematic still is the assumption that vision is somehow incompatible with the "localization of the holy," an apt term for, among other things, the increasing materiality inherent in late antique notions of sanctity.[74]

To frame the problem in terms of the replacement of sight or an increasing dissatisfaction with sight leads to greater misunderstandings. These questions are entirely appropriate to our own culture. Inundated as we are by cyberspace, spectator sports, television, and virtual reality, sight can seem impotent compared to touch. The very idea of "hands-on" experience implies that visual experience is somehow less genuine and more passive epistemologically.[75] Such oppositions, however, are not helpful in exploring how ancients understood the relation between sight and touch.

Recent cross-cultural studies of sense experience are helpful. As Constance Classen and David Howes have argued, a culture may ascribe dif-

---

72. For example, Maraval, *Lieux saints*, 144: "Or cette vénération implique un contact physique, où le toucher accompagne le voir et finit par devenir plus important que lui."

73. *V. Ant.* 40; 70 cf. 63.

74. Peter Brown, *The Cult of the Saints* (Chicago: University of Chicago Press, 1981), 86–88.

75. To be sure, the ancients also used tactile metaphors for intellection: see Philostratus, *V. Apoll.* 2.5 (LCL 1:129), an exhortation for the pure soul to see clearly (διοράω), in order to touch (ἅπτω) the virtues and thereby soar to contemplative heights. See also Plotinus, *Enn.* 1.6.4, 6.9.4, 7–8, 11; cf. J. H. Sleeman and Gilbert Pollet, *Lexicon Plotinianum* (Brill: Leiden, 1980), esp. s.v. "ἅπτεσθαι," "ἁφή," "συνάπτειν" (cols. 136, 178, 965–66); cf. Adnès, "Toucher," 1073–98, and David Katz's instructive sampling of tactile expressions for intellection (*The World of Touch*, trans. Lester E. Krueger [Hillsdale, N.J.: Lawrence Erlbaum Associates, 1989], 238–39).

ferent emphases and meanings to individual senses and even privilege the knowledge gained from one particular sense. Some cultures, for instance, may place greater meaning and emphasis on knowledge derived from smell than on sight or hearing. It is up to the cultural interpreter to discern "how the patterning of sense experience varies from one culture to the next"[76] by examining a given culture's myths, rituals, language, and social organization.[77] For late antique pilgrims, then, a survey of the larger culture can yield a better understanding of the relative quality of perceptions afforded by touch and sight.

While the emergence of a new tactile piety is certainly conceivable, it would have been a countercultural piety, one at odds with Greco-Roman and Christian attitudes toward vision, as the ancients understood its anatomical and therefore theological superiority. A Christian valorization of touch is certainly possible, given the example of Jesus, who healed many by touch.[78] Once again, however, it is important to consider what qualities of perception the ancients assigned to touch.

Ancient discussions often ranked the senses from the most sophisticated to the most vulgar. Typically, sight and touch were assigned to opposite ends of the hierarchy.[79] For Aristotle, touch was necessary for survival but hardly a noble sense.[80] A passage from the Hellenistic

76. David Howes, "Introduction: 'To Summon All the Senses,'" in Howes, ed., *Varieties of Sensory Experience*, 3–21, esp. 3. Another useful collection of essays in this field is Constance Classen's *Worlds of Sense: Exploring the Senses in History and across Cultures* (New York: Routledge, 1993); see also Classen, "Sweet Colors, Fragrant Songs: Sensory Models of the Andes and the Amazon," *American Ethnologist* 17 (1990): 722–34, esp. 722.

77. Howes and Classen outline an approach in "Conclusion: Sounding Sensory Profiles," in Howes, ed., *Varieties of Sensory Experience*, 257–88.

78. For example, Mt 8:3; 9:20–22; 14:36; Mk 1:41; 3:10; 5:27–30; 6:56; 7:33; cf. Jn 7:24, 27; 20:17; 1 Jn 1:1.

79. For example, Aristotle, *De anima*, discusses sight (II.7), hearing (II.8), smell (II.9), taste (II.10), and, finally, touch (II.11). This order is also preserved in another work attributed to Aristotle, *Problemata*, 31–35.

80. Despite being the first sense mentioned in Aristotle's *De anima* (II.2 [414a3]; II.3 [415a3–5]), touch still figures last in his systematic discussion of the senses

Jewish philosopher Philo amplifies the polarity between sight and touch:

> Now of the five [senses], the three most animal and servile are taste, smell, and touch. . . . The other two have a link with philosophy and hold the leading place—hearing and sight. But the ears are in a way more sluggish and womanish than the eyes. The eyes have the courage to reach out to the visible objects and do not wait to be acted on by them, but anticipate the meeting, and seek to act upon them instead. . . . [S]pecial precedence must be given to sight, for God made it the queen of the other senses and set it above them all, and . . . has associated it most closely with the soul.[81]

In Philo's understanding of the sensorium, sight is superior to all the other senses, so much so that its nimble acuity can be compared only to hearing. Touch, that "animal and servile" sense, does not even merit comparison. And yet, the fact that Philo ascribes vision's "courage" to its haptic powers, permitting it to "reach out to the visible objects," is a choice of metaphor worth exploring.

Philo's choice is hardly idiosyncratic. Ancient philosophers often described vision as a series of contacts. In the *Timaeus*, Plato explained that in the act of seeing, a fire within the eye flows outward to create a visual ray of such force that it "collides" with its object.[82] One Christian

---

(cf. II.11 [422b17]; III.13 [435a13–14]). See also Cynthia Freeland, "Aristotle on the Sense of Touch," in *Essays on Aristotle's* De Anima, ed. Martha C. Nussbaum and Amélie Oksenberg Rorty (Oxford: Clarendon, 1992), 227–48. Translations are available in *The Complete Works of Aristotle: The Revised Oxford Translation*, ed. Jonathan Barnes, 2 vols. (Princeton: Princeton University Press, 1984).

81. *De Abr.* §§ 149–50 (LCL 6:147–48). See David Chidester's commentary on Philo's treatment of vision in *Word and Light*, 30–43.

82. *Timaeus* 45c (LCL 7:102). Cf. Empedocles, *Fr.* 84 = Aristotle, *De sensu*, 437b23; cf. 438a26f.; Plato, *Tim.* 46b (LCL 7:104), where Plato borrows language associated with the sense of touch (ἐπαφή). For a helpful overview of

summary of this Platonized theory characterized the eyes as having tentacle-like rays, which "lay hold with their ends upon external bodies, as though grasping them with hands."[83] Or, as Gregory of Nyssa adapted the concept of the tactile gaze, "Who can help but love such a [divine] beauty provided that he has an eye capable of reaching out to its loveliness?"[84]

Even philosophers who rejected the notion of a ray flowing from the eye retained the idea of vision occurring through contacts, only in the opposite direction. Aristotle claimed that vision produces a movement in the eye that leaves an impression as if stamped in wax.[85] Zeno the Stoic, in contrast, spoke of stressed air that stretches out from the eye to object of vision "as if by a stick."[86] And the Epicureans, who described vision as images flowing off objects, still spoke of those images striking (ἐμπίπτειν) the eye.[87]

---

ancient optics, see David C. Lindberg, *Theories of Vision from al-Kindi to Kepler* (Chicago: University of Chicago Press, 1976), 1–17; David E. Hahm, "Early Hellenistic Theories of Vision and the Perception of Color," in *Studies in Perception: Interrelations in the History of Philosophy and Science*, ed. Peter K. Machamer and Robert G. Turnbull (Columbus: Ohio State University Press, 1978), 60–95; D. W. Hamlyn, *Sensation and Perception: A History of the Philosophy of Perception* (London: Routledge and Kegan Paul, 1961), esp. 1–42. Still useful is John I. Beare, *Greek Theories of Elementary Cognition: From Alcmaeon to Aristotle* (Oxford: Clarendon, 1906), esp. 86–92.

83. Taken from Hipparchus of Nicaea (fl. 146–126 B.C.E.), *On the Opinions of the Philosophers*, 4.13; quoted in the Christian theologian and doxographer Nemesius (fl. ca. 390), *De nat. hom.* 28 (trans. in *Cyril of Jerusalem and Nemesius of Emesa*, ed. William Telfer [Library of Christian Classics, 4; Philadelphia: Westminster, 1955], 324–25).

84. *In Cant.* 1 (Jaeger, 38; McCambley, 53–54).

85. Aristotle, *De anima* 435a9.

86. As reported in Diogenes Laertius, *De clarorum philosophorum* 7.157 (LCL, 2:261).

87. Alexander of Aphrodisias, *Commentary on Aristotle's De sensu* 438a5ff; text: H. Usener, ed., *Epicurea* (Leipzig: Teubner, 1887) §319; = "Text 98," in

Two observations are in order here: first, all three theories remained current into the late antique period. Aulus Gellius was typical of other intellectuals from the second century when he cursorily summarized several theories, instead of attempting to fully discredit any.[88] Christian summaries of optics likewise implied that several theories were, to varying degrees, viable.[89] This leads to the second observation: that several theories making competing—sometimes conflicting—claims remained plausible over many centuries. It is significant, I think, that the most enduring theories were those that incorporated notions of contact, penetration, and even collision.[90] The idea of continuous contact between the viewer and the object explains a great deal about why vision was considered to ensure unmediated knowledge.

Ancient conceptions of memory most forcefully illustrate this combination of seeing and touching. In a treatise devoted to the nature and function of memory, Aristotle defined a discrete memory as the "imprint" a sense-affection leaves on the soul, "as a seal-ring acts in stamping."[91] Aristotle's conception of memory remains closely tied to the sense of sight. By treating each memory as a "picture" (ζωγράφημα) of the real thing, Aristotle implies that each sensation, on entering the mind, assumes a visual form. So the taste of honey, the smell of incense,

The Epicurus Reader, ed. Brad Inwood and L. P. Gerson (Indianapolis: Hackett, 1994), 94.

88. Aulus Gellius, *Noctes Atticae* 5.16.3 (LCL 1:430–31); Plutarch, *Quaest. conviv.* 1.8.625–26 (LCL 8:82–87).

89. The three theories also appear in Christian doxographies of the fourth century, including Nemesius of Emesa, *De nat. hom.* 7.28 (ed. F. Matthaei, 178.3–182.3; trans. Telfer, 324–26).

90. For example, Lucretius, *De rer. nat.* 4.220–269 (LCL 295–97).

91. καθάπερ οἱ σφραγιζόμενοι τοῖς δακτυλίοις (*De mem.* 450a34; ed. Ross, 104–5). This common haptic metaphor allowed Plato to account for strong and weak memories. Thus in the *Theaetetus* (191c–d), Socrates explains that if the "wax" of one's memory is too soft or too hard, or even too dirty, whatever impressions it captures will be distorted; cf. Aristotle, *De mem.* 450 b (Ross, 105.10–12).

and the melody from a hymn, to take a few examples, would be translated into mental pictures and then stored in the memory.

In later centuries, Cicero and other Romans continued to marvel at the image-making power of memory, a faculty Pliny deemed "the boon most necessary for life."[92] More specifically, it was a sine qua non of oratory, as Cicero explained: "A memory for things is the special property of the orator—this we can imprint on our minds by a skilful arrangement of the several masks (*personis*) that represent them, so that we may grasp ideas by means of images and their order by means of localities."[93] By referring to these mental pictures as "masks," Cicero reinforced the close relation between the tactile process of imprinting and its imagistic result. Recollection is understood as a visual process by which the mind's eye scans and retrieves specific visual images.[94] As with supermarket produce stretch-sealed on styrofoam trays, vision ensured that each memory was neatly processed, packaged, and stored for easier handling.

To some extent the proper placement of memory-images was vital to their successful retrieval; hence the spatial metaphors of writing tablets, treasuries, and palaces.[95] More important than order, however, was the

92. Pliny, *Nat. hist.* 7.24.88 (LCL 2:563): "memoria necessarium maxime vitae bonum." On the arts of memory, see the landmark study by Francis Yates, *The Art of Memory* (London: Routledge & Kegan Paul, 1966), esp. 17–62; and Mary Carruthers, *The Book of Memory: A Study of Memory in Medieval Culture* (Cambridge: Cambridge University Press, 1990), esp. 1–45. A more descriptive survey appears in Janet Coleman, *Ancient and Medieval Memories: Studies in the Reconstruction of the Past* (Cambridge: Cambridge University Press, 1992).

93. Cicero, *De orat.* 2.86.351–2.87.360 (LCL 1:465–73); cf. Quintilian's more detailed description of techniques for cultivating memory, *Inst. orat.* 11.2.1–51, esp. 17–22.

94. Quintilian, *Inst. orat.* 11.2.32.

95. On the importance of an "abode" or locus, see Cicero, *De orat.* 2.87.358; on types of backgrounds, see *Rhet. ad Her.* 3.17.30–3.19.32. More specifically, ancients compared memory to a *tabula:* for example, Cicero, *De part. orat.* 26; *thesaurus:* Quintilian, *Inst. orat.* 11.2.1, 21–22 (LCL 4:213, 223); cf. Augustine,

sense of sight. All storage and organization of memories depended on assumption of a visual form. If properly stored, memory could avoid being "crushed beneath a weight of images," a meltdown of sorts that Cicero refused to contemplate.[96] The most effective "backgrounds," advised the author of the rhetorical treatise *Ad Herennium*, were those that were properly spaced so as to permit accurate inspection.[97] As Cicero explained this priority of vision: "The most complete pictures are formed in our minds of the things that have been conveyed to them and imprinted on them by the senses, but that the keenest of all our senses is the sense of sight, and that consequently perceptions received by the ears . . . can be most easily retained in the mind if they are also conveyed to our minds by the mediation of the eyes."[98] By this scheme, the eyes must intervene for the memory to retain all sense impressions. This was the lesson Cicero drew from the story he relates about the poet Simonides, who had stepped out of a banquet hall just moments before the roof collapsed, killing all the diners. The destruction was so great that friends and family were unable to identify the bodies of the dead. Simonides, however, identified each body by remembering where everyone had been reclining, a feat facilitated by the careful arrangement of visual memories by places.[99] Indeed, the "best aid to clearness of memory consists in orderly arrangement,"[100] but his reconstruction depended primarily on his eye for detail.

Of course the ancients knew that it was possible to remember a song or a smell. Yet even in their imagistic forms, sense impressions derived from smell, taste, touch, or hearing were believed to be more fragile.

Conf. 10.8. Carruthers offers a rich analysis of these locational and architectural metaphors in *Book of Memory*, 16–45, esp. 21–22, and *Craft of Thought*, 7–24.

96. Cicero, *De orat.* 2.88.360 (LCL 1:471).

97. *Rhet. ad Her.* 3.19.32 (LCL [Cicero] 1:213); on the dangers that arise from crowding mental images, see Carruthers, *Craft of Thought*, 82, 99.

98. Cicero, *De orat.* 2.87.357 (LCL 1:469).

99. The story of this father of memory appears in *De orat.* 2.86.352–54.

100. Ibid., 2.86.353 (LCL 1:467).

Even after they assumed a pictorial form, Cicero claimed, they remained *incomplete* images. As he remarked, "Things not seen and not lying in the field of visual discernment are earmarked by a sort of outline and image and shape so that we keep hold of as it were by an act of sight things that we can scarcely embrace by an act of thought."[101] He implies that only the memories of things seen retain their full substance and appearance, whereas memories of things heard, and, by extension, anything smelled, tasted, or touched, are only partially remembered, in a sketchy outline and undifferentiated shape. If memory is the "firm mental grasp of matter and words," as Cicero defined memory elsewhere,[102] the firmest grasp was reserved for things seen.

The orators relied on memory for their livelihood; hence their interest in mnemonic techniques. But biographers of holy men offer deeper insights into the meaning of memory. For instance, Philostratus, in describing Apollonius of Tyana's period of self-imposed silence, remarks on the importance of memory for this period: "[He] kept absolute silence, though his eyes and his mind were taking note of many a thing, and though most things were being stored in his memory."[103] In later years, the hymn he would sing to Memory—sung entirely from memory, Philostratus adds—credited Memory with keeping time itself immortal, even as time erodes and wears away all else.[104] That permanence and divinity of memory says as much about vision, the premier sense that stilled the passage of time.

This preference for visual memory is sustained in Christian pilgrims' writings. In the *History of the Monks*, the narrator recalls justifying his visit to John of Lycopolis: "We have come to you . . . for the good of our souls, so that what we have heard with our ears we might perceive with

101. Ibid., 2.87.357 (LCL 1:468–69).
102. Cicero, *De inv.* 1.7.9 (LCL 2:20–21): "memoria est firma animi rerum ac verborum perceptio."
103. Philostratus, *V. Apoll.* 1.14 (LCL 1:37).
104. Ibid.

our eyes—for the ears are naturally less reliable than the eyes—and because very often forgetfulness follows what we hear, whereas the memory of what we have seen is not easily erased but remains imprinted (ἐντετύπωται) on our minds like a picture (ἱστορία)."[105] The echoes from Cicero are striking here, including the visual framework of memory, connoted by the imagistic ἱστορία, the tenuous nature of aural memory, and the haptic metaphor of imprinted, hence, permanent memory. Although this pilgrim claims no formal mnemonic system or framework, as Quintilian did for orators,[106] he appeals to inherent properties of vision and touch to make his case. With the memory of the eyes nothing is "lost in translation."

One detects an even more concrete persistence of haptic language in discussions of the evil eye.[107] In a dinner discussion about whether and how a glaring eye can injure another person, Plutarch recalls how "everybody [but the host] pronounced the matter completely silly and scoffed at it."[108] But it was a nervous derision that ran throughout the conversation, as several participants offered up tales of the erotic and exotic eye, reporting cases of healing amulets, jaundice cured by looking at the yellow-feathered *charadrios*, and an entire people known for their lethal gaze. Some reported cases of "self-bewitchment," a boomerang affliction brought on when an evil eye catches its own reflection.[109] As

---

105. *HM* 1.19. Cf.: "If we want to convince someone, we say 'I have seen with my own eyes,' not, 'I know by hearsay.' " John Chrysostom, *In Ioh. hom.* 26 (FC 33:257). On this topos in ancient historiography, see John Marincola, *Authority and Tradition in Ancient Historiography* (Cambridge: Cambridge University Press, 1997), 63–69.

106. Quintilian, *Inst. orat.* 11.2.1–51, esp. 11 (*ars memoriae*), 32–34 (on role of the eye in memorization). On the relation between Ciceronian arts of memory and monastic ones, see Carruthers, *Craft of Thought*, 81–82.

107. Plutarch, *Quaest. conviv.* 5.7.680c–683b (LCL 8:417–33).

108. Ibid., 5.7.680c (LCL 8:417).

109. Ibid., 5.7.680e (Thibeans); 681c–d (jaundice); 681f (amulets); 682e (self-bewitchment). To this list one might add Pliny's claim (*Nat. hist.* 7.18) that all women with double pupils have an injurious glance.

one speaker conceded, "it is not paradoxical or incredible" that the glance from the envious is like a "poisoned arrow."[110] Closer to paradoxography than sustained investigation, the conversation closed with a series of explanations invoking authorities such as Hippocrates and the atomist philosopher Democritus. Despite these mental gymnastics, however, no single explanation apparently proved satisfactory. More significant for our purposes, no symposiast managed to "explain away" the evil eye by some appeal to an inherent contradiction between sight, to us an essentially (and not just apparently) immaterial phenomenon, and injury, a material chain of events.[111] Immateriality was simply not an option. Like the thin stream of smoke that rises from an extinguished candle, the materiality of sight curled in the air as the conversation drew to a close. Thus, Plutarch's parting assurances, "Don't think that I want to make your flesh creep and throw you into panic late at night," must have had a hollow ring.[112]

More than any ancient treatise on optics, conversations such as Plutarch's allow us to understand the properties of vision that induced fear, bewilderment, and sometimes even wonder. Even when the phenomenon of the evil eye defied logical explanation, it retained a force in the ancient imagination.[113] It resurfaced in Christian discussions in

110. Plutarch, *Quaest. conviv.* 5.7.681f (LCL 8: 424–27).

111. H. J. Blumenthal makes the interesting point that Aristotle's notion of sense data as *tupoi*, or, impressions, on the soul (citing *De anima* 68,5, 10–11) remained unquestioned by his Hellenistic commentators. In the late antique period, however, Philoponus (ca. 490–ca. 570) and, to a lesser extent, Plotinus before him introduced a markedly antimaterialist reading of the *De anima* (*Aristotle and Neo-Platonism in Late Antiquity: Interpretations of the* De Anima [Ithaca: Cornell University Press, 1996], 123, 134–35). Cf. Aristotle, *De mem.* 450a; Plotinus on the non-haptic nature of vision (4.4.2; 4.5.2, 4).

112. Plutarch, *Quaest. conviv.* 5.7.683a (LCL 8:433).

113. On the persistence of extramissionist notions of vision, see Dale C. Allison, "The Eye is the Lamp of the Body (Matthew 6.22–23=Luke 11.34–36)," *New Testament Studies* 33 (1987): 61–83, esp. 63–65; Hans Dieter Betz, "Matthew vi.22f and Ancient Greek Theories of Vision," in *Text and Inter-*

which the evil eye was believed to cast injurious rays.[114] One commentator was the fourth-century bishop Basil of Caesarea, who discredited many beliefs surrounding the evil eye but still described how the eye can hurl lethal arrows.[115] As these examples suggest, average Christians would not have concerned themselves directly with debates over optical theories, but they readily used haptic metaphors to describe vision. They retained the assumption that seeing involved something reaching out and touching its object.

Perhaps the immediacy and contact associated with seeing can explain why Christians could simultaneously praise and fear the power of the gaze. As the window or mirror of the soul, the eye could lead the soul to God, but it could also swiftly distract it from divine purposes.[116] Some ascetics immured themselves to protect others from the dangerous consequences of the erotic gaze.[117] Most dangerous was vision's power to connect the viewer so intimately to its object that the adhesion could damage the soul beyond repair. As a Coptic preacher warned his flock, "What the eye sees it appropriates."[118]

---

pretation: Studies in the New Testament Presented to Matthew Black, ed. Ernest Best and R. M. Wilson (Cambridge: Cambridge University Press, 1979), 43–56.

114. On the evil eye in the patristic period, see Vasiliki Limberis, "The Eyes Infected by Evil: Basil of Caesarea's Homily, *On Envy*, " *HTR* 84 (1991): 163–84; Matthew Dickie, "The Fathers of the Church and the Evil Eye," in *Byzantine Magic*, ed. Henry Maguire (Cambridge: Harvard University Press, 1995), 9–34; Blake Leyerle, "John Chrysostom on the Gaze," *JECS* 1 (1993): 159–74, esp. 165. For cross-cultural perspectives, see Clarence Maloney, ed., *The Evil Eye* (New York: Columbia University Press, 1976); Alan Dundes, ed., *The Evil Eye: A Casebook* (Madison: University of Wisconsin Press, 1992).

115. See Limberis, "Eyes Infected by Evil," 165.

116. For example, Jerome, *Ep.* 54.3. On the seduction of the eyes, see Theodoret, *De providentia* 9.25, trans. in Thomas Halton, *Theodoret of Cyrus, On Divine Providence* (ACW 49; Mahwah, N.J.: Newman, 1988). See also Leyerle, "John Chrysostom on the Gaze," 165–69.

117. *HL* 5.

118. Pseudo-Shenoute, *On Christian Behaviour* 40.7 (Kuhn, 30:55).

Christians cultivated a religious epistemology that combined the noblest of the senses (sight) with the most animalistic one (touch). That combination was a natural one for Nemesius of Emesa (fl. ca. 390), a bishop who drew from pagan medicine and philosophy for his Christian anthropology, *On the Nature of Man*. As Nemesius ranked the senses, sight came first, followed by touch, and only then taste, hearing, and smell.[119] By drawing sight and touch closer together, Nemesius could entertain a more complementary, even self-correcting, relation between the two: "For one sense shows up the errors of the other."[120] Although touch would never be considered superior to sight, both continued to share the same vital properties: contact, participation, and initiative. These functional affinities between sight and touch invite further reflection on this "new tactile piety" evidenced in pilgrims' devotions at the holy places. When pilgrims reached across the crowded bodies at the holy places to touch a sacred stone, column, or fragment of the True Cross, that gesture did not subvert or even invert the sensorium. Nor did that outstretched hand mime a dissatisfaction with vision's power. Instead, the pilgrims extended a hand that embodied the visual ray of optics. To see and touch, then, were not exclusive activities but rather convergent senses. That sight and touch were so polarized in philosophical and theological hierarchies of the senses did not prevent pilgrims from using both senses in concert at the holy places. Sight was not replaced by touch; it had always been a form of touch.

At the holy places, pilgrims created the conditions for an encounter with the sacred past as a present event. A fourth-century bishop described pilgrims at the Oak of Mamre, a site associated with Moses and the tomb of the patriarchs in Hebron: "With the sight of the holy places, they renew the picture in their thinking, and behold in their minds the faithful patriarch . . . they reflect too on his descendants Isaac and Jacob, and with the recollection of these men they become specta-

119. Nemesius, *De nat. hom.* 7.29 (Matthaei, 182.4–189.2; Telfer, 329).
120. Nemesius, *De nat. hom.* 8.30 (Matthaei, 189.3–195.7; Telfer, 334).

tors of the whole history concerning them."[121] As this moving passage from Asterius of Amasea's sermons reminds us, vision was believed to contain the power to conjure, constitute, and respond to the presence of the divine. The physical sense of sight was anything but passive in antiquity; it was a form of physical contact between the viewer and the object. For the pilgrim, that gaze extended to the sacred past. The physical sense of sight triggered the "eye of faith," which in turn perceived a past biblical event as a present reality. The tactile and aggressive characteristics of this gaze were grounded in ancient visuality. Sight and touch remained discrete senses, but in late-antique Christian piety their functions converged to create the conditions for a biblical realism. For Paula, or any other pilgrim, to perceive the biblical past with such vividness would have been impossible had she not already shared in the larger culture's inclination to locate touch as the source of vision's power. That haptic function allowed vision to reach into the past and sanctify the present.

Physical vision (and only then spiritual vision) both conjured and engaged this biblical realism, convincing pilgrims that they could indeed gaze more clearly on scripture. Scripture, to these pilgrims, was a lived, visual experience. What happened when that powerful gaze encountered the face of a holy person is the subject of the following chapter.

121. Asterius of Amasea, *Hom.* 9.2 (quoted and trans. in Hunt, *Holy Land Pilgrimage*, 103).

FIVE

How to Read a Face
Pilgrims and Ascetic Physiognomy

Although Anthony of Egypt was regularly besieged by visitors, the silent ones perplexed him most. On one occasion, he asked a frequent visitor why, after repeated visits, the pilgrim requested nothing. "It is enough for me to see you, Father," the man replied.[1] John of Lycopolis, a man who claimed to "possess nothing worth seeing or admiring," was equally baffled by gawking visitors.[2] Other holy men, less patient than Anthony or John, chased away unworthy supplicants, vowing that "no human will see my face!"[3] To many holy men and women, the prospect of becoming a spectacle was deeply unsettling. Yet on the margins of these stories about the fragility of solitude were pilgrims who desired urgently to see, going to extraordinary lengths to gaze on the ascetic's face.

1. *Apophth.*: Anthony 27 (Ward, 7). A sentiment echoed by Eudoxia, who tells Daniel the Stylite that she visits him "to enjoy seeing you face to face and to receive a perfect blessing," *V. Dan. Styl.* 35 (ed. Delehaye, 33.13–15; Baynes/Dawes, 27).
2. *HM* 1.20 (Russell, 55).
3. *Apophth.*: Arsenius 26 (Ward, 13). Cf. *V. Cyr.* (Vivian, 32, cf. 33); *HL* 5 (Alexandra; Meyer, 36–37)

This desire to scrutinize the ascetic body, and particularly the face, is a recurrent theme in the pilgrims' descriptions of their own experiences. Although these descriptions are too sparse to constitute a plausible account of how the holy person actually appeared to the pilgrim, they have the potential to reveal a great deal about how pilgrims perceived. The cumulative effect of these descriptions suggests that travelogues such as the *History of the Monks* and the *Lausiac History* were more than transparent descriptions of past events. They could also serve would-be pilgrims as primers for viewing the ascetic face and body. Taken as both a viewer's guide and a guide to viewing, descriptions of facial appearance provide a valuable point of entry into the viewing habits of pilgrims to holy people. The poetics of bodily description reveal the perceptual constructs, or visuality, inherent in pilgrims' experiences of living saints.[4]

In claiming a link between literary expression and visuality, I take my cue from ancient assumptions about physiognomy, the ability to judge human character from external appearances. Pilgrims' impulses to see and describe the face are best understood by considering the ancients who saw vast interpretive possibilities in the human body. Although physiognomy, both as a method and as a mindset, was never without its critics, it showed remarkable resilience in ancient Mediterranean culture. Well into the late antique period, Christians and pagans claimed that by "reading" individual facial features, they could reach a valid

---

4. On the scrutiny of visual appearance and performative dimensions of ascetic practices, see Patricia Cox Miller, "Desert Asceticism and 'The Body from Nowhere,' " *JECS* 2 (1994): 137–53; Richard Valantasis, "A Theory of the Social Function of Asceticism," in *Asceticism*, ed. Richard Valantasis and Vincent Wimbush (New York: Oxford University Press, 1995), 544–52, esp. 548–49. See also Peter Brown, *The Body and Society: Men, Women, and Sexual Renunciation in Early Christianity* (New York: Columbia University Press, 1988), 221; Geoffrey Galt Harpham, *The Ascetic Imperative in Culture and Criticism* (Chicago: University of Chicago Press, 1987), esp. 25.

assessment of a person's interior states. And these "readings" are embedded in pilgrims' reports.

What began as a hunch soon developed into a formal set of principles and techniques laid out in elaborate physiognomic handbooks. It is this effort at classification that remains closely associated with the word *physiognomy*, which, narrowly defined, stands for a set of prescribed techniques, outlined in various training manuals.[5] The trained physiognomist could consult these manuals, which divided the human body into individual bodily features, and further subdivided each feature into variant sizes and shapes. Each body part represented a sign exposing the person's character, disposition, virtue, and soul.

Such manuals would have been of little use to Christian pilgrims, who wanted more than a field guide to the human face. To pilgrims, the ascetic's face far surpassed the average human face and so could not be reduced to the classifications or meanings suggested by the manuals; most offensive, one suspects, would have been the pagan typologies that drew comparisons with animals! Pilgrims would have to develop another vocabulary by which to decipher and honor the ascetic face.

Manuals that would have been useless to the pilgrims nevertheless remain useful for the modern interpreter of pilgrims' reports. As a repository for cultural attitudes toward physical appearance, physiognomic handbooks offer important insights into ancient pilgrims' desire to scrutinize the ascetic body. Specifically, these handbooks can give the

---

5. The treatises appear in R. Förster, ed., *Scriptores Physiognomonici* (2 vols.; Leipzig: Teubner, 1893). For an overview, including uses of physiognomy in biography and literature, see Elizabeth C. Evans, *Physiognomics in the Ancient World* (Transactions of the American Philosophical Society, n.s. 59/5; Philadelphia: American Philosophical Society, 1969), 5–17. For a valuable gender analysis of physiognomic writing, see Maud W. Gleason, *Making Men: Sophists and Self-Presentation in Ancient Rome* (Princeton: Princeton University Press, 1995), esp. 28–81. On the "logic" of physiognomy, see Tamsyn Barton, *Power and Knowledge: Astronomy, Physiognomics, and Medicine under the Roman Empire* (Ann Arbor: University of Michigan Press, 1994), 95–131.

modern interpreter deeper insights into the verbal portraits that pilgrims made of the ascetics; they supply the formulas and vocabulary for a Christian physiognomy. A closer analysis of these physiognomic assumptions provides the background for an analysis of how Christians adapted and developed a language and literature by which to articulate a meaningful physiognomy for themselves.

In speaking of a Christian physiognomy, this chapter focuses on pilgrims' responses to the facial appearance of ascetics. Monastics developed their own physiognomic enterprise, often exhorting novices on the type of self-fashioning that would result in an "ascetic" appearance.[6] In their vocabulary for ascetic physiognomy, pilgrims put a distinctive face on sanctity, combining techniques of ancient physiognomy with a biblical sensibility. In addition, as a discipline based in visual scrutiny, physiognomy can lead to a deeper understanding of how pilgrims construed the processes and effects of seeing. Because pilgrims rarely commented on the act of seeing,[7] their descriptions of what they saw become important for understanding the viewing *subject* implied in such descriptions. Physiognomy provides a tool by which to uncover these visual processes and the spiritual possibilities for those who engaged in body-reading.

TALES OF "DISTINGUISHING FEATURES"

As late antique saints' lives remind us, seeing a holy person had its rewards. As Theodoret of Cyrrhus described James of Cyrrhestica's open-air asceticism, "He is observed by all comers ... unceasingly under the eyes of spectators."[8] In the *Life of Anthony*, healings, baptisms,

6. For a perceptive treatment of the function of physiognomy in advice to female ascetics, see Teresa M. Shaw, "*Askesis* and the Appearance of Holiness," *JECS* 6 (1998): 485–99.

7. One notable exception: *HM* 1.19 (Russell, 54–55).

8. *HR* 21.5 (Price, 134–35).

and conversions occurred the moment visitors laid eyes on a holy person.[9] Even works with few miracles held similar assumptions about desert monastics; as one bishop described the monks to John Cassian, "Old age and holiness, in bodies now bent over, shines so brightly in their faces that the mere sight of them is able to teach a great deal to those who gaze upon them."[10] That "mere sight" was also behind Palladius's invitation to readers to imagine a face-to-face encounter with the holy people. In his prologue, he urged readers to pay special attention to the physical appearance of ascetics: "Their faces abloom with grey hairs, and the arrangement of their dress . . . and the piety of their language."[11] For him, bodily appearance reveals sanctity. He quotes from Proverbs: "The attire of the man and the gait of his feet and the laughter of his teeth show him for what he is."[12] By these directives, the reader could become a vicarious pilgrim as well as a physiognomist, seeking and scrutinizing physical appearances.

One finds an even keener interest in the facial appearance of monks in the *History of the Monks.* In the first chapter, the face is central to a story about a tribune's wife. Despite various attempts to meet the holy man John, she could not circumvent his long-standing prohibition against female visitors.[13] Only after her husband pleaded to John did he finally agree to meet her, but then only on his own terms: "I shall appear

9. Healings: Athanasius, *V. Ant.* 56. Conversions: ibid., 88.2; *V. Char.* 14. Callinicos, *V. Hypat.* 36.1. Cf. *Apophth.*: Anthony 27.

10. *Conl.* 11.2 (Ramsey, 409). A more sensational "lesson" appears in a story told by Theodoret about a curious monk who watched as a supernatural light was "flashing from the teacher's head and revealing the composition of the letters in the divine oracles" *HR* 3.6 (Price, 39).

11. *HL* prol. 16 (Meyer, 29).

12. Sirach 19:30, quoted in *HL* prol. 16 (Meyer, 29). Cf. John Chrysostom, *Catech.* 4.26.

13. *HM* 1.4–9. Cf. similar tales in *HR* 3.22; Cyril of Scythopolis, *V. Joh. Hesych.* 24 (ed. Schwartz, 219.19–220.4), which mentions a scheme to circumvent the prohibition, a promise of a dream, the dream appearance (but without the reprimand), and the description of the saint's dress and appearance.

to her tonight in a dream, and then she must not still be determined to see my face in the flesh." In that dream John approached her, conferring both a blessing and a reprimand: "Why have you desired to see my face? Am I a prophet or do I stand in the ranks of the just?" The next morning she reported both John's words and his appearance to her husband.

In many respects it is a tidy story: a request is made, then denied, and finally fulfilled, albeit in an unexpected way.[14] More puzzling are the two questions John puts to the woman. Is he denying that he has the face of a prophet? Is he invoking the face of some biblical prophet? It seems odd that all of John's exasperation stems from her desire to see his face. Another curious detail is the fact that she describes John's appearance to her husband, who has already seen John in person. One expects the narrator to mention what was so special about that appearance; but he remains silent on the matter. In the end, the story that has drawn so much attention to the face does not answer its own question: "Why have you desired to see the face?" The face is central to her desire and their encounter; and that face, rather than any specific feature of John's appearance, may be the point.

When Rufinus of Aquileia recounted the story in Latin,[15] he attached even greater importance to the face. In this version, Rufinus adds that the woman was prepared to "endure [as] many dangers as were necessary in order to see his face."[16] And in the vision John urged her "not to go on desiring the bodily face *(faciem corporalem)* of the servants of God in reality."[17] The aftermath of the dream is also described in greater detail: she tells her husband what she saw and heard and details

14. This pattern is reminiscent of the Gospel story of the Syrophoenician/ Canaanite woman (Mk 7:24–30 and Mt 15:21–28, respectively).

15. *PL* 21.392–93. Citations follow the divisions of Schulz-Flügel's edition (PTS 34); translations are from *Lives of the Desert Fathers*, trans. Norman Russell (CS 34; Kalamazoo: Cistercian, 1980), 139–55.

16. Rufinus, *HM* 1.10 (PTS 34:249): "multa namque eam dicebat pertulisse pericula ob hoc tantum, ut faciem eius videret" (Russell, 143).

17. Rufinus, *HM* 1.14 (PTS 34:250).

the man's "dress *(habitum)* and face *(vultum)* and all his distinguishing features *(signa).*"[18] More than the Greek version, this story conveys the effect of the face, but it comes no closer to indicating what is "distinguishing" about John's features.

Several practical and theological explanations may account for Rufinus's decision to emphasize the face and its distinguishing features. Like the waking world, the dream world was filled with impostors and charlatans; perhaps this woman simply needed some form of identification by which to verify that she was indeed visited by John himself. Or perhaps the need to see the "faces of God's servants" may allude to the thorny doctrinal debate about whether one could possibly "see the face of God" or even speak of a God with bodily features.[19] Later in the same chapter, Rufinus adds a speech by John in which the holy man insists that the eyes of the body are incapable of seeing the incorporeal God, who remains perceptible only to the "eye of the heart" *(oculus cordis).*[20] Within this overarching message of incorporeality, Rufinus draws attention to the corporeal aspects of the story. For instance, as John indulges the woman's desire to see the face, he also exhorts her to gaze with the spirit *(spiritu contempleris)* at the monks' deeds and achievements. The tension also carries over to the coda, the woman's post-visionary description of John's distinguishing features, which assures the reader that— the holy man's objections notwithstanding—the face is the source and measure of the miraculous.

One of the distinguishing features of a holy face was the hair. Theodoret reported that Theodosius "wore his hair unkempt and

18. Rufinus, *HM* 1.17 (PTS 34:251). Cf. Russell, 143.

19. On the monks and pilgrims who were engaged in these debates, see Elizabeth A. Clark, *The Origenist Controversy: The Cultural Construction of an Early Christian Debate* (Princeton: Princeton University Press, 1992), 20–25, 33–34, 39–42, 159–93, esp. 184. On the possibility of anti-Origenist revisions to an earlier Greek text, see C. P. Bammel, "Problems of the *Historia Monachorum,*" *JTS* n.s. 47 (1996): 92–104, esp. 99–102.

20. *PL* 21.395–98. Rufinus, *HM* 3.1–34, esp. 20 (PTS 34:255–62, esp. 260).

stretching down to his feet and even further and for this reason had it tied round his waist."[21] Excessively long hair was also a distinguishing feature of saints in later biographies, including Antiochus, an African monk with woolly white hair that "hung down to his loins, and so too did his beard."[22] Likewise, Euthymius's "great beard that reached his stomach" made quite an impression, as it is often mentioned in connection with the monk's "dwarf-like build" and in descriptions of his subsequent dream appearances.[23] The function of the beard as a touchstone of ascetic identity is most starkly pronounced in the tale of Daniel the Stylite, who encountered a grizzled stranger on the road to Palestine. The reader is told only that the stranger was a "very hairy monk (ἔντριχος πάνυ) . . . resembling Saint [Symeon]."[24] The brevity of the description speaks volumes, not only underscoring the identification of hair and spiritual power but also alerting the reader to the stranger's identity long before the protagonist realizes he has met Symeon. Although some Christians warned that excessively long hair could undermine true asceticism,[25] the power of ascetic hair endured in hagiography. For instance, Theodoret reports that the Syrian holy man James of Cyrrhestica had become so accustomed to having his hair "plucked" by visitors that he could no longer feel this depilation.[26] All these episodes drew attention not just to the hair but especially to the face it framed and concealed.

21. *HR* 10.2 (Price, 89); cf. 11.1.

22. *V. Theod. Syc.* 73 (Dawes/Baynes, 137); the portrait also includes details of joining eyebrows and excessively long nails.

23. Cyril of Scythopolis, *V. Euth.* 40 (ed. Schwartz, 57. 20); cf. *V. Euth.* 10 (ed. Schwartz, 20.9–11).

24. *V. Dan. Styl.* 10 (ed. Delehaye, 11. 4; trans. Dawes/Baynes, 12).

25. For example, Jerome, *V. Pauli* 1 (refuting rumors that Paul of Thebes had very long hair); *HM* 8.59 (long hair as conspicuous self-advertisement); Cyril of Scythopolis, *V. Sab.* 22 (ed. Schwartz, 107. 1–7), on the blessing of a beard singed by fire.

26. *HR* 21.9.

To many pilgrims, ascetics' faces were believed to manifest the proofs of the virtuous life. As visitors to John of Lycopolis remark in the *History of the Monks*, "One could see the saint already in his ninetieth year with his body so completely worn out by his *askesis* that even his beard no longer grew on his face."[27] And Palladius's description of Abba Macarius shows a similar scrutiny of the beard and face: he was "slight and without a beard, having hair only about the lips and at the end of the chin, for the asceticism he practiced did not allow hair to sprout on him."[28] In a culture that read flowing beards as trophies of spiritual powers and wisdom,[29] these Christian portraits might appear deflated. Ironically, however, the fact that both authors call attention to the beard—or lack of it—perpetuates the notion of the revelatory beard.[30] Were it simply a matter of conveying the effects of ascetic disciplines, other body parts could just as clearly testify to the damage caused by desert heat, poor diet, or fatigue. Yet, both Palladius and the author of the *History of the Monks* keep the reader's attention on the face as a measure of ascetic success.

To understand the pilgrim's interest in the face, it is important to recall that most pilgrims would have seen little more of the holy person. Visitors to John of Lycopolis or Daniel the Stylite, we are told, had to speak through a small window that would have revealed little of the body behind the wall.[31] Beyond such architectural obstacles was the

---

27. *HM* 1.17 (Russell, 54).

28. *HL* 18.29 (Meyer, 67).

29. H. P. L'Orange, *Apotheosis in Ancient Portraiture* (Cambridge: Harvard University Press, 1947), 30–33, 100, 102, esp. 32, citing Dio Chrysostom, *Orat.* 35.2, 10 ff.; Philostratus, *V. Apoll.* 8.7; Herodotus, *Hist.* 2.36; Lucian, *V. Auctio* 2; id., *Philops.* 29; cf. 32. Cf. Apuleius, *Apol.* 4, and John Englebert and Timothy Long, "Functions of Hair in Apuleius's *Metamorphoses*," *Classical Journal* 68 (1972–73): 236–39 , which offers further literary examples of hair as code for spiritual and mental states.

30. L'Orange, *Apotheosis*, 102.

31. *HM* 1.5; cf. *V. Dan. Styl.* 15.

monastic habit that covered the entire body, except for the face and hands. By the late fourth century, Egyptian monks were adopting a habit that consisted of a cowl as well as a sleeveless tunic, covering the head and shoulders but leaving the forearms exposed.[32] Thus in his meditation on the symbolism of ascetic clothing, Evagrius directed his audience to pay attention to the garment rather than to any skin that might be exposed.[33] The rest of the body is revelatory only insofar as it dons the cowl, belt, scapular, and sheepskin garment, each of which evokes a specific biblical verse, but all of which, together with the staff, constitute a "compendious symbol" of the holy life.[34]

For pilgrims, however, the real symbols of ascetic accomplishment were to be found in the face.[35] Sunken eyes, emaciated cheeks, and thinning hair were badges of honor. Given the all-encompassing monastic habit, the woman's request to see John of Lycopolis's face seems natural. Where else would she find a clearer testimony to his deeds and achievements?

Even for Athanasius, who introduced the spectacle of Anthony's entire body relatively early in the *Life*,[36] the face remained the locus of

32. Joseph Patrich, *Sabas, Leader of Palestinian Monasticism* (Washington, D.C.: Dumbarton Oaks, 1995), 211–14. On the symbolism of garments in hagiographies of male saints, see Lynda Coon, *Sacred Fictions: Holy Women and Hagiography in Late Antiquity* (Philadelphia: University of Pennsylvania Press, 1997), 52–70.

33. Evagrius, *Praktikos* prol. (Bamberger, 12–15), finding symbolic meaning only in the general fact of bare hands.

34. Ibid.; Ps 126:1 (cowl); Jn 5:44 (bare hands); 1 Cor 7:11 (belt); 2 Cor 4:10 (sheepskin); Gen 3:22; cf. Prov 3:18; Rev 22:2, 14, 19 (staff as tree of life). Although Evagrius speaks of the ideal monk rather than of any individual, he regards the habit as externalizing more abstract ideals and virtues, a tendency inherent in physiognomic discourse.

35. For example, *HM* 8.6; 10.9.

36. *V. Ant.* (Gregg, 42): after twenty years' seclusion "his body had maintained its former condition, neither fat from lack of exercise, nor emaciated from fasting and combat with demons, but was just as they had known him prior

lifelong virtues, a visual metonym for a brilliant ascetic career. Describing Anthony's preparation for death, Athanasius highlights this close connection between the facial features and the soul's progress:

> His face had a great and marvelous grace. . . . It was not his height or broad build that distinguished him from the rest, but the stability of character and the purity of the soul. His soul being free of confusion, he held his outer senses also undisturbed, so that from the soul's joy his face was cheerful as well, and from the movements of the body it was possible to sense and perceive the stable condition of the soul, as it is written, *When the heart rejoices, the countenance is cheerful; but when it is in sorrow, the countenance is sad.* (Prov 15:13)[37]

In this description, Athanasius directs the reader's attention to the face, where the hidden soul is best perceived. In contrast to the scene at the fortress, where Athanasius focuses on the hero's overall physique, he reserves his most explicit physical description here for the "cheerful" face, which broadcasts the soul's movements even when the body has become ordinary. Like Palladius, whose prologue called attention to the holy men's faces "abloom with grey hairs," Athanasius uses facial description as a way to show how a pure soul would manifest itself. In the face, writers found a means of rendering virtue visible.

This desire to find the soul revealed in bodily features was not unique to ascetic Christians. In fact, the revelatory body was at the top of the "wish list" for many in the late antique world, as a fable from Lucian's *Hermotimus* suggests. To decide who was the best artist among them, Poseidon, Athena, and Hephaestus entered a competition. Momus was called on to judge their disparate entries. Poseidon made a bull; Athena

---

to his withdrawal." For a perceptive analysis of how this passage reflects Athanasius's theological ideal of the perfect union between body and soul, see David Brakke, *Athanasius and the Politics of Asceticism* (Oxford: Clarendon, 1995), 242.

37. *V. Ant.* 67.4–6 (Gregg, 81); cf. G. J. M. Bartelink, *Athanase d'Alexandrie, Vie d'Antoine* (SC 400; Paris: Cerf, 1994), 313 n.1.

designed a house, and Hephaestus assembled a human being. More art critic than judge, Momus praised Hephaestus for submitting a work in progress, but observed that the man needed "windows in his chest which could be opened to let everyone see his desires and thoughts and if he were lying or telling the truth."[38] Christian pilgrims offered a verbal solution to Momus's desire: their descriptions in effect assembled for the reader sufficient facial details by which to decode and detect a virtuous soul. The connection between facial appearance and soul was considered so strong that Christians eventually provided solely the facial details, leaving the reader to infer the state of the ascetic's soul.

ANCIENT PHYSIOGNOMISTS
AND THEIR CRITICS

By the time Palladius and Athanasius discovered these various "windows" on the soul, physiognomy had been an established practice for many centuries. The notion of a connection between bodily appearance and quality of character can be found as far back as the Homeric epics and hymns. The bodies of heroes and gods were praised as *kalos kagathos*, implying a bond between goodness and beauty, body and soul.[39] That bond, however, was regularly called into question. As the story of Hephaestus's incomplete man suggests, the ancients doubted if the body might resist complete transparency, a way of safeguarding some private sense of the self. In the *Theaetetus*, for instance, Socrates mocks Theodorus's suggestion that Theaetetus's "snub nose and eyes that stick out" provide the basis for any intellectual resemblance

38. Lucian, *Hermotimus* 20 (LCL 6:297–99).

39. For an excellent discussion of archaic Greek views of the body, see Jean-Pierre Vernant, "Mortals and Immortals: The Body of the Divine," in *Mortals and Immortals: Collected Essays*, ed. Froma I. Zeitlin (Princeton: Princeton University Press, 1991), 27–49, esp. 36–37. Jacques André also makes a convincing case for Babylonian precedents for physiognomic analysis (*Traité de physiognomonie: Anonyme latin* [Paris: Belles Lettres, 1981], 9–10).

between the two of them. Tongue in cheek, he bids the young man to draw near: "I want to see for myself what sort of a face I have."[40] Apparently, for Socrates mirrors (and mirror images, in general) are of little worth in the struggle to "know thyself."[41] Face to face with his doppel-gänger, Socrates essentially placed limits on the interpretive possibilities of the human body.[42]

Philosophers' objections to physiognomic scrutiny notwithstanding, the ancients developed methods for classifying physical appearances and judging interior states from them. Some of those techniques were outlined in elaborate checklists detailing specific facial and bodily characteristics and corresponding character types. The earliest surviving guidelines for this practice appear in an anonymous Aristotelian treatise titled *Physiognomonica*. This author described the connection between soul and body thus: "Soul and body, as it seems to me, are affected sympathetically by one another: on the one hand, an alteration of the state of the soul produces an alteration in the form of the body, and contrariwise an alteration in bodily form produces an alteration in the state of the soul."[43] In this sympathetic relation between body and soul, physiognomists were taught to look for visible signs *(semeia)* and then infer their cause in the soul. The signs, they claimed, were to be found all over the body: in ges-

40. *Theaetetus* 144e; cf. 143e (Levett, 261–62).

41. Cf. *P. Oxy.* 31.2603: "A man who has acquired a mirror . . . does not need anyone to inform him or to testify to the character that lies before him," quoted in Dominic Montserrat, *Sex and Society in Graeco-Roman Egypt* (London: Kegan Paul, 1996), 55.

42. On the doppelgänger from a lower class, see Pliny, *Nat. hist.* 7.53 (LCL 2:541).

43. Pseudo-Aristotle, *Physiognomonica*, 808b12–15 (in *The Complete Works of Aristotle*, ed. Jonathan Barnes [2 vols.; Princeton: Princeton University Press, 1984] 1:1242). Cf. Aristotle, *Gen. anim.* 734b, 25–28, on the ensouled face. Cf. also Pliny, who gives a sampling of physiognomic claims, despite his "surprise" that "Aristotle not only believed but also published his belief that our bodies contain premonitory signs of our career" (*Nat. hist.* 11.114.273–76, esp. 273 [LCL 3:605–7]).

tures, facial expressions, hair growth, skin texture, voice, and overall physique. Even the feet spoke of the soul: soft, fleshy feet were thought to betray a soft and "feminine" temperament, whereas delicate and short feet revealed deep-seated malice.[44] As Pliny skeptically remarked, the physiognomist "does not, I imagine, note all these attributes present in one person, but separately, trifling things, as I consider them."[45] What to Pliny was "trifling" detail was, for the physiognomist, all part of a complex hierarchy of signs. For instance, if a man's feet indicated cowardice but the shoulders signaled bravery, the physiognomist would follow a system that held some body parts to be more trustworthy than others. At the top of the hierarchy was the face, the site of a cluster of signs, and home to the most decisive ones, the eyes.[46]

Body language has always been with us: posture, gestures, and facial expressions can convey a range of emotions, moods, and dispositions. If one seeks a more permanent judgment, however, the fleeting emotions behind these expressions make this system of signs too unstable to be of much use to a physiognomist. Physiognomy resisted circumstantial signs, claiming instead to examine essential and unchanging ones. For a stable, essential norm against which to scrutinize personal appearance, they looked to gender, resemblances to animal species, and race; all these traits were thought to leave permanent traces on the human body. Accordingly, ancient physiognomists classified appearances according to their inherent dichotomies: male/female, human/animal, and Greek/barbarian. Through these categories, physiognomists inferred correspondences.

Gendered comparisons presumed that, anatomical sex notwithstanding, every human being could have a combination of "masculine" and

44. *De physiognomonia liber* 72 (André, 103).
45. Pliny, *Nat. hist.* 11.114.274 (LCL 3:605).
46. Pseudo-Aristotle, *Physiognomonica*, 806a20 (Barnes, 1:1239); cf. 814b; *De physiognomonia liber* 20 (André, 66). On significance of the eyes for physiognomic analysis, see Gleason, *Making Men*, 30–34, 55–58; L'Orange, *Apotheosis*, 110, 146 n.22.

"feminine" traits. Thus, a man with "masculine" traits was thought to reveal a mental character that is "violent," "impulsive," "generous," and "savvy." A man with feminine traits, however, revealed a character that is "irascible," "offensive," "envious," "sluggish," "hypocritical," "rash," and "docile."[47] Such classificatory schemes had profound effects on ancient society: they were employed to determine whether one was fit to rule, to marry, or to trade. Whether these inferences are valid is beside the point. They reveal a profound trust in the evidence of the senses. All first impressions, according to this scheme, were to be classified; only then could they be trusted.

The zoological and racial systems employed different bases for comparison[48] while retaining the deep-seated conviction that physical appearances do not lie. Thus, a person whose features bore resemblance to a lion (square visage, deep-set eyes, powerful and sinewy legs) could be assumed to have a soul that is "generous and liberal, proud and ambitious, yet gentle and just."[49] Since swine have small foreheads and were considered stupid, humans with small foreheads must also be stupid. "A small face marks a small soul, as in the cat and the ape: a large face means lethargy, as in asses and cattle."[50] Racial stereotypes also provided the kind of static, essential readings physiognomists desired. Thus a person who had "Egyptian" features was assumed to bear the moral characteristics of the race: "cunning, teachable, rash, and keen on sex."[51]

---

47. *De physiognomonia liber* 3–8, esp. 4 (André, 52–56).

48. Yet even these systems used gendered distinctions to classify species. By this line of thinking, persons who bore resemblances to "masculine" species, such as the lion, boar, or eagle, were ascribed "masculine" character traits and were to be valued over those who bore resemblances to "feminine" species, such as the leopard, deer, hare, or peacock. See *De physiognomonia liber* 8 (André, 56).

49. Pseudo-Aristotle, *Physiognomonica* 809b (Barnes, 1:1244)

50. Pseudo-Aristotle, *Physiognomonica* 811b (Barnes, 1:1246).

51. *De physiognomonia liber* 9 (André, 56); translation from Barton's rhetorical analysis in *Power and Knowledge*, 105.

In all these methods, physiognomists claimed to know causes from effects.[52] As Maud Gleason describes this reasoning process, "What purports to be an inductive science, built up from myriad specific observations, becomes a deductive science based on generalized impressions and preexisting prejudices that are confirmed by observed details."[53] However artificial the inferences may appear to us, the ancients' interest in physiognomic description shows an enormous (if misplaced) trust in visual perception.

Physiognomy remained popular in the Roman period. With the impulse to make unseen realities visible, practitioners promised to reveal the secrets of the face to predict the future. Professional physiognomists were called on to vet prospective disciples, in-laws, and debtors. In the second century, the discipline flourished as physiognomists like Polemo prepared even more elaborate technical digests of facial types.[54] Physiognomy also witnessed a revival of sorts during the fourth century, when one physiognomist drew on earlier treatises to compile an anonymous Latin handbook, *On Physiognomy*. The subject continued to draw new generations of proponents (and critics) even into the modern period.[55]

52. On the logic and implications of ancient physiognomic thought, see Barton, *Power and Knowledge*, 95–132, esp. 104–7; Gleason, *Making Men*, 34–36. See also André, *Traité de physiognomonie*, 7–24.

53. Gleason, *Making Men*, 35.

54. On Polemo, see Gleason, *Making Men*, 28–81, and Leofranc Holford-Strevens, "Aulus Gellius: The Non-Visual Portraitist," in *Portraits: Biographical Representation in the Greek and Latin Literature of the Roman Empire*, ed. M. J. Edwards and Simon Swain (Oxford: Clarendon, 1997), 93–116, esp. 113–16.

55. On the modern legacy of these techniques, see Michael Shortland, "The Power of a Thousand Eyes: Johann Caspar Lavater's Science of Physiognomical Perception," *Criticism* 28 (1986): 379–408, esp. 379–80, with useful bibliography; Barbara M. Stafford, *Body Criticism: Imaging the Unseen in Enlightenment Art and Medicine* (Cambridge: MIT Press, 1991), 84–103; Patrizia Magli, "The Face and the Soul," in *Fragments for a History of the Human Body*, ed. Michel Feher et al. (3 vols.; New York: Zone, 1989), 3:87–127, esp. 90–91.

On Physiognomy shows how deeply entrenched the notion of a readable body had become by the fourth century. Like the authors of the earlier treatises, the Latin author invokes standard anatomical, zoological, and ethnic classification schemes. One important departure, however, lies in the way the author conceptualizes all these inferences as a language with constituent "letters." These letters of physiognomic discourse, he claims, can be combined and recombined to form syllables, words, and eventually entire sentences.[56] Closer to a grammar than a dictionary, this handbook allows for no exceptions, so great is the need for order. The linguistic metaphor also carries the assumption that no single component can reveal its full meaning apart from the other signs. Thus the Latin physiognomist presumes that all judgments are based on a cluster of features rather than on a single trait.[57]

This "deep grammar of the soul"[58] was put to many uses. Physiognomists claimed the ability not only to detect hidden vice but even to foreknow it. The system also provided orators and biographers with a convenient shorthand for praising or maligning characters through coded descriptions of their height, hair, beard, eyes, or attire.[59] Thus emperors were made to look imperial, and criminals had to look criminal. For Pliny, the emperors were to be remembered by their peepers as much as by their deeds: "Augustus had grey eyes like those of horses, the whites being larger than usual in a human being. . . . Claudius Caesar's

---

56. *De physiognomonica liber* 3 (André, 52).

57. On the problem of mixed messages in physiognomy, see *De physiognomonica liber* 10 (André, 58). Cf. Gleason, *Making Men*, 34–35.

58. From Stafford's discussion of the eighteenth-century physiognomist and theologian Johannes Caspar Lavater (*Body Criticism*, 95).

59. Geneva Misener, "Iconistic Portraits," *Classical Philology* 19 (1924): 97–123, esp. 97. Along with Misener's insights, See also Elizabeth C. Evans's enduring studies of ancient physiognomy, esp. "Roman Descriptions of Personal Appearance," *Harvard Studies in Classical Philology* 46 (1935): 43–84, and *Physiognomics in the Ancient World*. One biographer who resisted using physiognomic description was Aulus Gellius; see Holford-Strevens, "Aulus Gellius," 95.

eyes were frequently bloodshot. . . . Gaius had staring eyes. . . . Nero's eyes were dull of sight."[60]

Christian writers also characterized their heroes and villains by providing concise, abbreviated descriptions of personal appearance.[61] The *eikonismos*, as this trope was called, listed distinctive bodily features and markings. Its most practical use was in census reports and in public notices calling for the return of fugitive slaves.[62] Eventually, these brief physical descriptions also appeared in biography and romances as an effective tool for characterization. For instance, the author of the *Acts of Paul* described the apostle Paul as "a man small in size, with a bald head and crooked legs; in good health; with eyebrows that met and a rather prominent nose; full of grace, for sometimes he looked like a man and sometimes he had the face of an angel."[63] Recent attempts to identify the prototype for this description have yielded no conclusive result.[64]

60. Pliny, *Nat. hist.* 11.54.143–44 (LCL 3:521–23). On courtroom use of these techniques, see *Rhet. ad Herennium* 4.47.62–4.49.63. On tropes for describing fugitive slaves, see Montserrat, *Sex and Society*, 56–57.

61. Gilbert Dagron, "Holy Images and Likeness," *DOP* 45 (1991): 23–33.

62. A first-century C.E. census record is preserved from Oxyrhynchus, listing the members of a household along with particular facial details; Pausas is listed "with a scar on his left cheek." The men and women in another household are designated by "a scar on the forehead" or "no identifying mark (ἄσημος)" (*NewDocs* 4 [1987] no. 21, pp. 88, 91.) Fugitive slaves: *P. Oxy.* 51.3616; 51.3617; reprinted in *NewDocs* 8 [1998]: 9–19, esp. 9–10. See Diog. Laertius 4.46–47 (LCL 1:424) on Bion of Borysthenes's slave father, who "had not a face, but a narrative on his face" (ἔχων οὐ πρόσωπον, ἀλλὰ συγγραφὴν ἐπὶ ποῦ προσώπου). On tattooing and branding in antiquity, see C. P. Jones, "*Stigma:* Tattooing and Branding in Graeco-Roman Antiquity," *JRS* 77 (1987): 139–55.

63. *Acts of Paul,* 3 (Wilson, 2:239).

64. Varying explanations of this passage appear in Robert M. Grant, "The Description of Paul in the *Acts of Paul and Thecla*," *VC* 36 (1982): 1–4; Abraham Malherbe, "A Physical Description of Paul," *HTR* 79 (1986): 170–75; Christopher R. Matthews, "Nicephorus Callistus' Physical Description of Peter: An Original Component of the *Acts of Peter?*" *Apocrypha* 7 (1996): 135–45, esp. 140. Rather than seek a one-for-one correspondence, Susan M. Calef proposes that

Putting aside this puzzle, a more modest observation is in order: this unflattering physical description joins an external appearance ("bald head") with a superior, inner character ("full of grace"). Even if it remains doubtful that any physiognomic manual contains the key to these Christian descriptions of bodily appearance, it is clear that this writer perceived a link between bodily appearance and internal states. The links could be ironic, as in the case of this man with "crooked legs" and the "face of an angel"; yet they testified to the keen sense that external and internal were inseparable.[65]

Apocalyptic writers also relied heavily on the *eikonismos* as a way to prepare the reader for the anti-Christ, as this description from the Syriac *Testament of the Lord* suggests: "And these are the signs of him: his head is as a fiery flame; his right eye shot with blood, his left eye blue-black, and he has two pupils. His eye-lashes are white; and his lower lip is large; but his right thigh [is] slender, his feet [are] broad, his great toe is bruised and flat."[66] The signs that make up this description offer readers not only a way to visualize this gruesome enemy but also, more important, a checklist by which to recognize him on the last day. Like physiognomists who claimed to foretell trouble, this description carries the implicit theological message that together face and body reveal the future. The key to salvation, as this description suggests, is the ability to read the facial signs.

---

more attention be paid to the placement and literary function of the description ("Paul 'in the Flesh' in the *Acts of Paul:* Physiognomics and the Search for Parallels," unpublished paper, summarized in *AAR/SBL Annual Meeting Abstracts 1994* [Atlanta: Scholars, 1994], 159).

65. L'Orange observes a juxtaposition of transcendental expressions with unflattering details in portraits of the fourth and fifth centuries (*Apotheosis*, 102–4).

66. *Testament of the Lord*, 11, from *The Testament of the Lord*, trans. James Cooper and Arthur J. McLean (Edinburgh: Clark, 1902), 57–58; quoted in Bernard McGinn, *Antichrist: Two Thousand Years of the Human Fascination with Evil* (San Francisco: HarperSanFrancisco, 1994), 68–74, esp. 68. Although the entire work was redacted during the fifth century, the apocalyptic section (chapters 1–14) may date from the mid-third century.

The salvific force of face-reading could also be applied to one's own features. Monastic leaders often exhorted monks and nuns to be attentive not only to how they might appear to others but also to how they appeared to themselves.[67] This physiognomy of self-assessment appears in Evagrius's advice to virgins: "She who is sad about her blood-shot eyes and the wasting of her flesh will not delight in her pure, passionless soul."[68] His denunciation of vanity should not be misread as a condemnation of self-observation, which was a crucial component in ascetic practice. The advice also points to a deeper connection between physical features and the pure soul. What Evagrius criticizes is not the vanity or attention devoted to those signs but rather the misinterpretation of those signs. If the bloodshot eyes and the pure soul are linked, then *both* signs should inspire delight. This tension between upholding and denying desired physical appearances is not unique to Evagrius. As Teresa Shaw rightly observes, many monastic writers struggled to reconcile the expressive power of external appearance with the conviction that ascetic ideals are ultimately achieved *beyond* the realm of bodily appearance.[69]

In addition to monitoring their own progress, several famous ascetics were said to use their penetrating gaze on others. According to one anecdote, Paul the Simple could "see the state of each one's soul, just as we see their faces."[70] One bishop was remembered for the gift of read-

67. *Apophth.*: Poemen 34 (Ward, 172); for references see Evans, *Physiognomics in the Ancient World*, 78–79.

68. Evagrius, *Sententiae ad virginem*, 51, quoted in Susanna Elm, "Evagrius Ponticus' *Sententiae ad Virginem*," *DOP* 45 (1991): 97–119, esp. 105. Additional examples are discussed in Shaw, "*Askesis* and the Appearance of Holiness," esp. 489–91.

69. Shaw, "*Askesis* and the Appearance of Holiness," 496. "The rhetoric of virginity ... urges conformity to a certain norm of behavior, practices, and choices, while at the same time denying that true virginity is really about such externals."

70. *Apophth.*: Paul the Simple 1 (Ward, 205); cf. Athanasius (*V. Ant.* 67), who cites physiognomic descriptions from Prov 15:13, Gen 31:5, and 1 Sam 16:12 to underscore the sanctity of Anthony's face.

ing faces: he could detect sinners by their black, scorched faces and bloody eyes, and the righteous by their glowing white garments and shining faces.[71] Even demons were powerless to sever this tie between character and outward appearance, as an episode from the *Life of Anthony* makes clear. In one of several temptations, the devil assumed the "visage of a black boy," a disguise that bore the "the likeness of his mind."[72] As Athanasius's phrasing implies, outward appearances may change, but nothing can hide one's true identity from a perceptive physiognomist. Behind all these stories of deception and recognition one finds the physiognomist's faith in the indissoluble relation between sign and signifier, between what is seen and what is hidden but never beyond skilled detection.

This need to establish connections between interior dispositions and facial features may explain why many hagiographers chose to describe the still face, disengaged from its body. Theodoret of Cyrrhus, for instance, captured that still face in his portrayal of Eusebius of Teleda: "We saw his face remain without any change. . . . Likewise his look was not at times grim and cheerful at others, but his eyes always preserved the same orderliness; they were sufficient proof of the calm of his soul."[73] In this example, the subject is at rest, unperturbed by moods or gestures; his external features appear as if immobilized, so that the viewer can discern the stable features of his soul.[74] The static quality of Theodoret's descriptions permits the reader to examine the face and reach a permanent judgment. The face here appears decontextualized so that details from an individual life can be abstracted and recombined,

---

71. Regnault no. 1715 (= J715) in Lucien Regnault, *Les sentences des pères du désert: Série des anonymes* (Spiritualité Orientale 43; Sablé-sur-Sarthe/Bégrolle-en-Mauges: Solesmes/Bellefontaine, 1985), 299–301; cf. *V. Mel.* 34.

72. *V. Ant.* 6 (Gregg, 34); on this topos see Bartelink, *Vie d'Antoine*, 147 n. 2.

73. *HR* 4.10 (Price, 54).

74. Cf. Ammianus Marcellinus, 21.16 (quoted in L'Orange, *Apotheosis*, 125). On this freezing technique in modern physiognomy, see Shortland, "Power of a Thousand Eyes," 392.

forming a curriculum vitae of the ascetic life. By giving his verbal portrait a perfect stillness, Theodoret found a steady plane on which to show virtue achieved, rather than virtue in progress.[75]

To the extent that these descriptions trace (or at least imply) a connection between body and soul, they can illustrate physiognomic assumptions without invoking the technical language of physiognomic handbooks. Palladius never suggests, for instance, that a desert father had the forehead of a pig, lion, or cow. Nor does Athanasius make an issue of Anthony's "Egyptian" face as the basis for inferring his character. Even so, like the pagan physiognomists, these writers were deeply concerned with how one might find the unchanging essence behind the fleeting expressions of the face. To achieve that stillness, pilgrims and hagiographers presented the face as a collage of individual features that could be isolated, examined, and recombined to highlight the salient signs. Given the prevalence of physiognomic thought informing physical descriptions, it seems unlikely that these writers intended to provide what we could consider photographic representations. Instead, the external features were selected as windows onto a soul deep within. The face, or, more specifically, the eye beholding the face, held the key to this repository of ascetic achievement. To understand how Christians transformed that grammar of the soul into a grammar of sanctity, I turn to two facial types, the faces of women and the faces of biblical figures.

WOMEN AND ASCETIC PHYSIOGNOMY

The physical appearance of ascetic women was a problem for late antique Christians. The example from Evagrius reminds us that it was hard to

75. An emphasis also found in ancient statuary depicting philosophers; see Paul Zanker, *The Mask of Socrates: The Image of the Intellectual in Antiquity* (Berkeley: University of California Press, 1995), 124. Cf. Porphyry's descriptions of Plotinus (*V. Plot.* 13; LCL 1: 39): "When he was speaking his intellect visibly lit up his face." Here, however, the state of the soul is only apparent while the sage is in action.

define the appearance of a perfect ascetic woman. As Teresa Shaw has recently noted of treatises on virginity,[76] the ambivalence toward judging female appearance reveals the possibilities and limitations of ascetic physiognomic thought. Building on Shaw's analysis of idealized descriptions, I consider verbal portraits of specific women as they appear in saints' lives and pilgrims' reports. Some of these descriptions depart significantly from the formulas for describing male ascetics. In his *Life of Pelagia of Antioch*, for instance, Jacob recalls his first encounter with Pelagia after she abandoned a life of prostitution to become a monk. Disguised as Pelagius, a renowned male recluse, she successfully hides her female identity from him. Still, his retrospective description reveals a decidedly female body, as he notes how the ravages of asceticism have disfigured the youthful Pelagia: "[She had] become ugly, her pretty eyes had become hollow and cavernous as the result of much fasting and the keeping of vigils. The joints of her holy bones, all fleshless, were visible beneath her skin through emaciation brought on by ascetic practices. Indeed the whole complexion of her body was coarse and dark like sackcloth, as the result of her strenuous penance."[77] Two things may strike the reader here. First, Jacob describes the entire ascetic body, without drawing any connection to her soul.[78] Her ascetic accomplishments are presented in the surfaces of the face, without suggesting what they say about the state of her soul. More unusual is the fact that Pelagia is disguised as a man. Although during this encounter Jacob was under the impression that he stood before a man, as narrator he speaks with the full benefit of hindsight, using the feminine pronoun as a way to anticipate

76. Shaw, "*Askesis* and the Appearance of Holiness," which focuses on Jerome, Athanasius, Basil of Ancyra, Ambrose of Milan, and Eusebius of Emesa.

77. Syr. *Pelagia of Antioch*, 45 (trans. in Susan Ashbrook Harvey and Sebastian Brock, *Holy Women of the Syrian Orient* [Berkeley: University of California Press, 1987], 60).

78. As Dominic Montserrat observes for ancient papyri, descriptions of the entire body are usually reserved for slaves and victims of violence (*Sex and Society*, 56–57). Cf. Gregory of Nyssa, *Ep.* 19.9 (SC 363:248–50).

the discovery of Pelagia's female identity. Although the narrator eventually discovers her true gender, he acknowledges that at the time he was deceived by her disguise. Even when he notes a detail that might give her away, such as her "pretty" eyes, the detail is not included to reveal her gender. One wonders if physiognomy has somehow failed because Jacob fell for the disguise.[79] But that is not the message of this story. Jacob uses physiognomy not as an instrument for unmasking deceptions and disguises but rather to signal the physical traits that reveal a virtuous soul. In this regard, physiognomy has served him well.

There are numerous other examples of physiognomy's power to reveal true ascetic identity, even in circumstances of mistaken gender identity. In one monastic anecdote, when a female ascetic who dressed as a man encountered her estranged husband, he failed to recognize her new, ascetic identity, because she had become as dark as an "Ethiopian."[80] Yet the reader never misses the signs. In both examples, the disguise may conceal the fact that they are women, but the physiognomic descriptions are more concerned with true ascetic identity. Both stories illustrate a common feature of female hagiography: although, in theory, any woman was capable of manly virtue,[81] nevertheless in hagiographic practice it was women dressed as men who most often earned the physiognomist's attention.[82]

79. On physiognomy's power to avoid deceptive appearances, see *De physiognomonia liber* 40 (André, 60).

80. Regnault (no. 1596, 10), *Série des anonymes*, p. 241. The reference to a woman with dark skin may also imply that he mistook his wife for a ghost, recalling a frightening female apparition from *Acts of Peter* 22, cited in John Winkler, "Lollianos and the Desperadoes," *Journal of Hellenic Studies* 100 (1981): 155–81, esp. 160–65.

81. On this topos, see Elizabeth A. Castelli, "Virginity and Its Meaning for Women's Sexuality in Early Christianity," *Journal of Feminist Studies in Religion* 2 (1986): 61–88.

82. Stories of women disguised as men, however, are almost entirely absent from the alphabetical apophthegmata, the exception being the story of a dead

Physiognomic description of disguised women is normally reserved for settings and activities associated with men. Although there were indeed women who actually settled in the farthest deserts or remained itinerant, hagiographers depicted such actions as masculine and thereby transgressive.[83] The hagiographic examples above bear this out: the facial descriptions of Pelagia and the estranged wife occur at the point in the narrative when they are engaged in their most transgressive behaviors, the former living as a recluse in Jerusalem and the latter as a wandering hermit. In Pelagia's story, which is longer, the placement of the facial description is noteworthy. Rather than provide a facial description when we are first introduced to Pelagia, Jacob departs from narrative convention and waits until she is placed in an unusual situation, the hermit's cell. Thus while the hagiographer provides a brief portrait of the elaborately dressed prostitute as she appeared in a public procession,[84] he waits until she has assumed her disguise as Pelagius to provide the reader with a description of her face. This postponement suggests to the reader that women who engage in unusual activities have an unusual appearance.[85] Later hagiographers followed this logic for saints, as in the *Life of Syncletica in the Jordan Desert* (as modern editors have named this anonymous recluse from the sixth century). The narrator recalls how her "face . . . would give off flashing sparks of light" only

amma who is initially mistaken for a man by the monks who discover her corpse. *Apophth.*: Bessarion 4; cf. Susanna Elm, *Virgins of God: The Making of Asceticism in Late Antiquity* (Oxford: Clarendon, 1994), 262, 269–70.

83. Elm, *Virgins of God*, 275–81.

84. *V. Pelag.* 2 (Ward, 67).

85. This technique is not unique to Christian ascetic literature. As Jeanne Fahnestock has observed of heroines in English novels, women who transgress standards of beauty are also likely to have transgressed social expectations. The face, Fahnestock explains, "remains an accurate mirror of the character, for the heroine of irregular features is capable of irregular conduct." ("The Heroine of Irregular Features: Physiognomy and Conventions of Heroine Description," *Victorian Studies* 24 [1981]: 325–50, esp. 330–31).

after "Syncletica" has donned a male hermit's garb.[86] Thus hagiographers reserved the physiognomy of sanctity for women who transcended their femaleness and, in rare cases, such as Syncletica's, their humanity.

These examples invite two further observations about the limits of physiognomic description. First, as used by male hagiographers, it could not testify to the full range of female ascetic experience. Unless the women dressed as men or appeared after death,[87] their appearance went unnoticed. These undisguised women are certainly not absent from the hagiographic record, but their faces are. Physiognomy, then, was a rhetoric reserved for male appearance,[88] a hagiographic tool unprepared to render or read the undisguised female face. Second, the paucity of female facial descriptions reminds us that physiognomic language constructed identity rather than described it. Unlike a photograph, which indiscriminately reproduces all details of physical appearance, physiognomic descriptions selected and reassembled the most telling details.[89]

More than a brief exception to prove the patriarchal nature of physiognomic taxonomies, the glowing female face shows how some ancient Christian writers stretched and experimented with the physiognomic vocabulary they inherited. This distinctively biblical physiognomy merits closer attention.

86. *De Syncletica in deserto Iordanis* 14 (Vivian, 51). Cf. Gregory of Nyssa's descriptions of his sister's glowing body and her "Godlike face" (θεοειδὲς ... πρόσωπον) after death (*V. Macrinae* 32.8–12; 34.27–28; cf. 15.15–19).

87. *Mir. Thec.* 14 (Dagron, 327–29); Regnault, no. 1715 (= J 715), in *Série des anonymes*, 299–301.

88. As Maud Gleason has observed of the use of physiognomy in sophistic rhetoric (*Making Men*, 58–81, esp. 58–60), it was first and foremost a discourse among men, a coded language by which orators defined and gauged masculinity. If Gleason is correct, then it becomes easier to understand why Christians who adopted physiognomic conventions employed them to praise only women who disguised themselves as males.

89. An observation made by Dagron, "Holy Images and Likeness," 25; cf. Magli, "The Face and the Soul," 91.

GLOWING FACES

Two biblical facial types in particular captured the pilgrims' imagination: the face of patriarchs (especially Moses) and those of the angels. A description of Arsenius captures the mix-and-match technique by which these were invoked: his appearance "was angelic, like that of Jacob. His body was graceful and slender, his long beard reached down to his waist. Through much weeping his eyelashes had fallen out."[90] Here the author has combined three types of signs: the biblical referent (angel, Jacob), the youthful body (graceful, slender), and the aging body (long beard, no eyelashes). Neither denying the debilitating effects of ascetic practice nor succumbing to them completely, the description includes a reversal of this process, suggesting a body no longer subject to decay.

Some descriptions completely biblicize the face, as in that of Pambo, who "received the image of the glory of Adam when his face shone like lightning and he was like a king sitting on his throne." As if to suggest that these traits are not unique to Pambo, the author mentions that "it was the same with Abba Silvanus and Abba Sisoes."[91] The *History of the Monks* also ascribes a luminous face to Abba Or: "He looked just like an angel. He was about ninety years old and had a brilliant white beard down to his chest. And his face was so radiant that the sight of him alone filled one with awe."[92] Another desert father, Theon, had "the

90. *Apophth.*: Arsenius 42 (Ward, 19).

91. *Apophth.*: Pambo 12 (Ward, 197).

92. *HM* 2.1 (Ward, 63; trans. modified). Angelic images are frequent in the *HM*; see *Historia monachorum*, ed. and trans. André-Jean Festugière, (SH 53; Brussels: Bollandistes, 1971), 29 n.3. Other angelic faces appear in *Apophth.*: Silvanus 23 (Ward, 224). The apophthegmata (alphabetic collection) report that God glorified the fourth-century monk Pambo "so that one could not gaze steadfastly at his face *[prosopon]* because of the glory which his face possessed" (*Apophth.*: Pambo 1; Ward, 196, modified). The luminous face is a common theme in Theodoret (*HR* 3.6; 7.4; 21.9). For additional examples see Violet

face of an angel giving joy to his visitors by his gaze and abounding with much grace."[93] And Paul the Simple was said to have a "shining face and white body."[94] Angelic faces became a shorthand for any monk who lived in perfect imitation of angels: they beheld God, sang his praises, prayed continuously, and transcended the frail human body.[95] The glowing face evoked a broader set of associations. Radiance and light were typically thought to be features of divinized bodies, not just in ancient Greek culture but also for ascetics.[96] Rather than present a body broken by ascetic practice, the pilgrims could use references to light and angels to show asceticism's highest achievement, the reversal of the body's decay and its transformation into the glorified body of the resurrection.

The message of these multiple references to angelic bodies and faces is more difficult to understand. With references to light so abundant in the *History of the Monks*, one discovers what the art historian H. P. L'Orange described as a "stereotyped mask of majesty,"[97] dispelling individual traits. Yet, is the Egyptian desert necessarily robbed of meaning by this "mask"? The cumulative effect of these angelic references

MacDermot, *The Cult of the Seer in the Ancient Middle East* (Berkeley: University of California Press, 1971), 753 §§ 35, 37; Graham Gould, *The Desert Fathers on Monastic Community* (Oxford: Clarendon Press, 1993), 181–82.

93. *HM* 6.2; *Apophth.*: Pambo 12. Compare *HM* 7.1 (Russell, 69): "Even the sight of [Elias] was very impressive."

94. *Apophth.*: Paul the Simple 1 (Ward, 205).

95. For example, *Apophth.*: Macarios of Alexandria 3; cf. Regnault, no. 1618 (=N618) in *Série des anonymes*, 263. On this topos, see [K.] Suso Frank, ΑΓΓΕΛΙΚΟΣ ΒΙΟΣ: *Begriffsanalytische und begriffsgeschichtliche Untersuchung zum "engelgleichen Leben" im frühen Mönchtum* (Beiträge zur Geschichte des alten Mönchtums und des Benediktinerordens 26; Munster: Aschendorff, 1964). For additional references, see Pierre Miquel, "Monachisme," *DS* 10:1554.

96. Miller, "Desert Asceticism," 141–42. Cf. Apuleius, *Met.* 11.24; L'Orange, *Apotheosis*, 95–96; Vernant, "Mortals and Immortals," 44–45.

97. L'Orange, *Apotheosis*, 118.

conveys a great deal. The fact that the author of the *History of the Monks* comments explicitly on that angelic radiance precisely when describing a large gathering of nameless monks suggests that the angelic life is corporate. The author describes the five hundred or so brothers gathered around Apollo as "looking like a real army of angels, drawn up in perfect order, robed in white."[98] Such monks are paradigmatic in their manifestation of the biblical past, rendered here in ways that would have satisfied the rhetorician who wrote the *Ad Herennium:* for the use of biblicizing physical detail achieves a more brilliant description of the ascetics, or, in the words of the rhetorician, "more vivid, when expressing everything so lucidly [lit., before the eyes, *ante oculos ponit*] that [it] can . . . be touched by the hand."[99]

As literary tropes, these descriptions tell us little about the actual appearance of the ascetic, but they do reveal an underlying habit of viewing, or "perceptual construct," a sensory guide to seeing the ascetic body apart from any constraints of time or space.[100] All these references to the faces of patriarchs and angels suggest that the face was no longer considered the locus of personal identity, where eye, chin, and forehead provided any number of windows onto the individual's past and present. In these monastic examples, the face had become the canvas of biblical identity, so that Pambo, Silvanus, and Sisoes were synonymous and indistinguishable behind the glare of their shining faces. And by the sixth century, when Cyril of Scythopolis described Euthymius as being so bright that he resembled a beacon, sending out miraculous rays,[101] the luminous monk had become too bright to show himself. As Hip-

---

98. *HM* 8.19 (Russell, 73). Cf. Regnault, no. 1487 (= N487), in *Série des anonymes*, 165, about a monk keeping as his goal an uninterrupted immersion in the biblical past.

99. *Rhet. ad Herennium* 4.49.62 (LCL [Cicero] 1:385).

100. The term is borrowed from Miller, "Desert Asceticism," 137.

101. *V. Euth.* 22 (ed. Schwartz, 35.1–3; Price, 30); cf. *V. Sab.* 7 (ed. Schwartz, 91.1; Price, 99).

polyte Delehaye astutely observes, the "custom of accumulating on a single head all the glories of preceding heroes" erodes the individual on whom they are conferred, "such that the hero entirely loses his true physiognomy and emerges in disguise."[102]

The erosion of individual portraiture through biblical typology is hardly new to students of hagiography.[103] More striking is what takes the place of personal identity: a biblical typology crafted through details of physical appearance, a biblicized physiognomy. What Delehaye referred to as a "disguise" in pilgrims' writings amounts to a Christianized phys-iognomic system. Showing little concern for elaborate schemes of gen-der, animal characteristics, or ethnicity, Christians collapsed all these schemes into a biblical one. The final (and briefest) chapter of the *History of the Monks* bears out this development: "We also visited another John in Diolcos, who was the father of hermitages. He, too, was endowed with much grace. He looked like Abraham and had a beard like Aaron's. He had performed many miracles and cures, and was especially successful at healing people afflicted with paralysis and gout."[104] One might describe

102. *The Legends of the Saints* (trans. V. M. Crawford; London: University of Notre Dame, 1961), 19.

103. For example, Bernard Flusin, *Miracle et histoire dans l'œuvre de Cyrille de Scythopolis* (Paris: Études Augustiniennes, 1983), esp. 85, 102; Susan Ashbrook Harvey, "Women in Early Byzantine Hagiography: Reversing the Story," in *"That Gentle Strength": Historical Perspectives on Women in Christianity*, ed. Lynda L. Coon, Katherine J. Haldane, and Elisabeth W. Sommer (Charlottesville: University Press of Virginia, 1990), 36–59; Derek Krueger, "Typological Figu-ration in Theodoret of Cyrrhus's *Religious History* and the Art of Postbiblical Narrative," *JECS* 5 (1997): 393–419. See also the work of Marc Van Uytfanghe, who claims that the hagiographer "actualizes" the Bible more than its subject, esp. *Stylisation biblique et condition humaine dans l'hagiographie mérovingienne [600–750]* (Brussels: Koninklijke Akademie voor Wetenschappen, Letteren en schone Kunsten van België, 1987), esp. part 2.

104. *HM* 26. All references to John's face are missing from Rufinus's Latin adaptation (*PL* 21.460 = Rufinus, *HM* 33 [PTS 34:384]).

this chapter as a miniature verbal portrait. Yet on closer examination, it lacks any descriptive force. There is the effect of resemblance, but without any indication of the basis for the resemblance; the reader is never told what specifically about John's appearance suggests a resemblance to Abraham or Aaron. We are dealing with a description that is no description at all.[105] To this author, the fact of resemblance is what mattered most, sending the message that resembling biblical exemplars and performing miracles are intimately bound. In this chapter, then, the reader is told not how to recognize John but rather how John acquired his miraculous powers to heal paralysis and gout: through a resemblance to Abraham and Aaron, he appropriated the biblical past.

Just as icons eclipse the identity of the subject, so too these facial descriptions removed the individuals behind those faces. These verbal portraits give the sense of a historical individual but stop short of presenting a personal portrait. As Gilbert Dagron observes, "The writer or the painter brings his model to the threshold of individuality, but it is up to the reader to do the rest."[106] Individuality is approximated but never fully achieved in these descriptions, which remake individual identity into biblical and paradisiac prototypes. The *eikonismos* simulated an experience that allowed the reader to perceive Abraham, Aaron, Moses, or an angel in the face of a holy person.

When integrated into travel writing, physiognomic description functioned as another tool by which to fragment and selectively reassemble pilgrims' experiences. By moving from one facial feature to the next, the writer broke up his subject into parts through which the audience could visualize the ascetic, a technique resembling the advice in late antique

105. To some degree it can be seen as the verbal antecedent of the silhouette, a diagnostic device favored by Enlightenment physiognomists. Much as a silhouette freezes and abstracts the human personality, admitting "neither motion, nor light, nor volume, nor features," so the description of John presents only a shadow of the person (Stafford, *Body Criticism*, 97–98, esp. 100).

106. Dagron, "Holy Images and Likeness," 26.

progymnastic exercises for describing persons in constituent parts.[107] Just as travel writers extracted monuments from their historical and social contexts, pilgrims extracted and isolated faces from their immediate spatial and temporal situations with the help of physiognomic description. The face, like the monument, could evoke both what is and what was, in large part because physiognomic perception froze and stabilized the face. Just as monuments provided a way to order and control the evidence of the senses, so physiognomic description ordered the visual experience of meeting holy people. All these descriptions, whether seen in the context of travel writing or physiognomic description, imply a habit of viewing.

THE EYE OF FAITH AND THE LEGIBLE FACE

We return to the eye, the starting place of physiognomic investigation as well as the arbiter of conflicting signs, as many manuals claimed.[108] Cicero reminded orators that the "eyes are the dominant feature of the face," the first place an audience looks. He advised orators to maintain "constant management of the eyes . . . for fear of slipping into looks that are in bad taste or into some distortion."[109] The physiognomist, too, had to manage the eye so that it could attain a correct reading of what was invisible to the uninitiated. In this regard, it is possible to speak of a

107. On the rhetorical advice to visualize persons by proceeding in parts from head to toe, see Aphthonius, *Prog.* 12 (37.9–11 Rabe); Nicolaus of Myra, *Prog.* (69.12–17, Felten), cited in Michael Roberts, *The Jeweled Style: Poetry and Poetics in Late Antiquity* (Ithaca: Cornell University Press, 1989), 42 n. 17. Cf. Quintilian, *Inst. orat.* 9.2.40 (on presenting the subject in parts rather than as a whole to achieve more vivid visualization).

108. *De physiognomonia liber* 10 (André, 58), in which twenty-four of the seventy chapters devoted to the body's "signs" address the eyes (ibid., 10–80, esp. 10, 20–43 [André, 66–84]); cf. Gleason, *Making Men*, 30, 34.

109. Cicero, *De orat.* 3.59.222–23 (LCL 2:177–79).

physiognomic gaze, a mode of perception that isolates and reorganizes the evidence of the senses.[110] That gaze, however, is only implicit in ancient discussions of physiognomics; they include little explicit instruction on how to train the eye.

Ancient physiognomists regarded the eyes as objects to be scrutinized rather than as the instruments of scrutiny.[111] The format of the handbooks bears out this priority, offering a checklist of physiognomic signs rather than a treatise on viewing. Details were organized to facilitate the cultivation of a memory for specific signs and their rank among other signs.[112] Yet, as any ancient trained in the arts of memory would admit, the cultivation of memory was a matter of the eye. That memory, according to the fourth-century *On Physiognomy*, was to be cultivated through the lingering gaze, and the novice was advised to watch patiently for genuine signs *(naturalia)* to emerge, avoiding fleeting *(temporalibus)* or false appearances.[113]

Even if the pagan handbooks paid scant attention to how the physiognomist saw, pilgrims to the living were mindful of it. They may not have invoked the "eye of faith" as much as pilgrims to holy places did. Yet they described their visual experiences in sufficient detail to convey

110. Shortland, "Power of a Thousand Eyes," 388.

111. An interesting contrast is the importance of the physiognomist's eye in treatises from the Enlightenment. During the eighteenth century Johann Caspar Lavater insisted that "all men who have eyes have talents to become physiognomists" (*Essays on Physiognomy*, 62, quoted in Shortland, "Power of a Thousand Eyes," 390). One had to cultivate a "third eye," one that would do what the untrained eyes cannot: isolate, magnify, and discern the contours of facial and bodily parts (Shortland, "Power of a Thousand Eyes," 391–92, 397; cf. Stafford, *Body Criticism*, 84). The hermeneutic implications are explored by Carsten Zelle, "Soul Semiology: On Lavater's Physiognomic Principles," in *The Faces of Physiognomy: Interdisciplinary Approaches to Johann Caspar Lavater*, ed. Ellis Shookman (Columbia, S.C.: Camden, 1993), esp. 52–53.

112. *De physiognomonia liber* 11 (André, 58–59).

113. Ibid. (André, 59–60).

the value they placed on the visual processes that shaped their perceptions. As two modes of visual scrutiny, the pilgrim's eye of faith and the
physiognomist's gaze shared much. Like pilgrims' reports, physiognomic description can create a sense of order out of confusion. Both
travel writers and physiognomists aimed to equip readers with a sense of
control and insight. With that control came the assurance that a body
says what it means. To these travelers, physiognomy provided the language of last resort, allowing their eyes to read the soul's inscriptions on
the body.[114]

Similar to the "eye of faith" awakened at the holy places, the form of
vision developed by pilgrims to the living was both lingering and tactile.
Just as the physiognomist pierced the surfaces of external appearances
to gain insight into the deepest recesses of the soul, so the eye of faith
looked through signs to perceive another, more genuine reality. For
Paula, that reality was biblical. After seeing Golgotha and Bethlehem,
the next (and last) occasion when Paula visualized a biblical figure was
when she visited monks in Egypt. "In each holy man," Jerome reports,
"she believed she was seeing Christ."[115] Elsewhere, Jerome described a
similar gaze, when he spoke of how the apostles looked on Jesus of
Nazareth: "With more penetrating eyes, [they] beheld not merely what
appeared, but what was hidden away in the body."[116] Both examples
suggest a lingering gaze, capable of looking through and beyond exter-

114. Confidence in this pure language of the body was most enthusiastically
endorsed by Lavater when he wrote, "Even now, every hand, every finger, every
muscle is a meaningful language for eyes that prejudice and ignorance have not
blinded to nature, which is nothing but expression, nothing but physiognomy,
but visual presentation of the invisible, nothing but revelation of the language
of truth" (*Aussichten*, 110–11; translated in Zelle, "Soul Semiology," 53). For a
fascinating discussion of Lavater's theological justification for physiognomy, see
Stafford, *Body Criticism*, 91–93.

115. *Ep.* 108.14 (NPNF 2.6.202).

116. Jerome, *Hom.* 61 (FC 57: 32–33).

nal appearances to find "hidden" realities. These physiognomic descriptions suggest that the face is not only legible but transparent, revealing the secrets stored in the body.[117]

Likewise, the face of the male ascetic constituted the meeting ground of the biblical past and the pilgrim's present. With a parallax vision capable of perceiving both ascetic achievement and biblical presence, the pilgrim could gaze at and through the face, a textured window onto the biblical past. By using facial descriptions that assimilated holy persons into biblical figures, pilgrims destabilized or even displaced individual identity altogether; but this was a small price to pay for the stable, visual experience of discovering the face of a biblical patriarch. Physiognomic scrutiny constituted the biblical hero by disassembling the ascetic face in order to conjure a biblical one in its place. Put in temporal terms, the pilgrim dismantled a biographic present as a way to enter a biblical past.

This collapsing of time is what sets apart Christian uses of physiognomy from their pagan counterparts. Although the mechanics of the physiognomic gaze are similar in the pagan manuals and the Christian travelogues, the hidden realities remain distinct. Pagans used physiognomic analysis to cast a suspicious gaze into the future and detect hidden vice: Should I trust this man with my money? Does he have a criminal disposition? Christian pilgrims were less interested in reading faces to detect misers, liars, or gluttons; they hoped instead to discover biblical patriarchs, prophets, and angels. What the travelogues suggest, then, is that pilgrims gazed on holy people for a glimpse into a sacred past, rather than into the future. In physiognomic rhetoric, pilgrims found a nimble vehicle for glorification, rather than a "technology of suspicion."[118]

117. Cf. J.-M. Fontanier, "Sur une image hiéronymienne: Le visage sidéral de Jésus," *Revue des sciences philosophiques et théologiques* 75 (1991): 251–56.

118. The phrase is borrowed from Gleason, *Making Men*, 55.

For pilgrims to the living, the eye of faith was physiognomic in nature. By seeing faces as well as seeing through them, pilgrims to holy people also engaged in a type of biblical realism. It detected resemblances as a way to form a bridge to the biblical past. The pilgrim saw the external appearance, which provided the *semeia*, which would engage a more piercing vision. In other words, one gazed *at* external features in order to gaze *through* them. Whether visualizing biblical events or coming face to face with the shining face of an angel, pilgrims transcended temporal barriers. Seeing the face of the desert saints allowed pilgrims to participate in the biblical past and scriptures in new ways. As a mode of seeing, then, the "eye of faith" allowed pilgrims to the living to interpret bodily appearance, using the assumptions of ancient physiognomy, to serve their need for a biblical realism. As a driving force of their pilgrimages, this technique gave rise to a visual piety that combined physiognomic scrutiny with the tactile gaze of extramissionist optics; the result was analogous to the type of biblical realism encountered at the holy places.

More important, this Christianized physiognomy lent itself particularly well to a practice that sought out sanctity in living, moving destinations, such as the holy person. With physiognomy, pilgrims had the means to freeze and isolate the biblical face. Whether that lips on that face scolded or dismissed the pilgrim was beside the point. What was important was the way physiognomic description could still that face long enough to allow the perception of biblical realities. This physiognomic rhetoric, with its biblicizing tendency, performs a function similar to that of the Brazilian storytelling encountered by Candace Slater while studying a local saint.[119] Unlike the pilgrims' stories, Slater observed, stories told by the residents of the saint's town included many concrete details about the saint's actions, shade of eyes, gait, tone of

119. *Trail of Miracles: Stories from a Pilgrimage in Northeast Brazil* (Berkeley: University of California Press, 1986), esp. 117–48.

voice, and gestures, all of which conferred a "physical as well as moral presence" on this figure.[120] To similar ends, late antique pilgrims employed physiognomic description to give a physical presence to the biblical reality they experienced. The verbal portraits, then, were "products of and for visualization,"[121] a biblicized physiognomy pilgrims devised to make the Bible visible, and not just audible, in the desert.[122] By drawing on physiognomy to describe their visits, pilgrims to the living found a language for portable sanctity. If the sacred destination stared back, the pilgrim had the physiognomic eye to circumvent that stare and see the soul within. One no longer needed to stand at the site of the crucifixion to see Christ or on Mount Sinai to see Moses. Instead, the pilgrim could come face to face with these biblical exemplars by gazing intently at the face of a holy monk.

120. Ibid., 123–24.
121. The phrase is David L. Haberman's (*Journey through the Twelve Forests: An Encounter with Krishna* [New York: Oxford, 1994], xiii). For a stimulating analysis of John Chrysostom's use of verbal portraits, see Margaret M. Mitchell, "The Archetypal Image: John Chrysostom's Portraits of Paul," *Journal of Religion* 75 (1995): 15–43, esp. 19–28.
122. Cf. the perceptive analysis of orality in desert hermeneutics by Douglas Burton-Christie, *The Word in the Desert: Scripture and the Quest for Holiness in Early Christian Monasticism* (New York: Oxford University Press, 1993).

SIX

Pilgrims to the Living
and the Memory of the Eyes

As one grows familiar with the *History of the Monks* and the *Lausiac History*, it is easy to forget that for lay Christians in late antiquity, monks and nuns were indeed strange. The authors of these works navigated between the exotic and the familiar, using travel writing and physiognomic techniques to construct and control the reader's perceptions. The brief notice, in particular, maintained a firm grip on the reader's attention, directing it to the biblical quality of these perceptions. As a framing device, the brief notice edited and reshaped the perception of monastic life. Within those tightly controlling narrative devices, the authors and audiences presupposed a particular mode of vision, the eye of faith, with which pilgrims and audiences claimed to see external details but also to pierce them in order to conjure the biblical realities that were believed to rest just beneath the surface of ascetic appearance. Through this mode of vision, the biblical past irrupted into the pilgrim's present.

The subtle interplay between biblical realism, monasticism, and the eye of faith is not unique to pilgrimage. In this final chapter, I explore the affinities between pilgrims' assumptions about vision and the visual experiences related to other aspects of piety in late antiquity through a selective investigation of Christian attitudes toward the veneration of relics and the cult of icons. Although either one of these subjects merits several book-length studies, I limit my remarks to the conception of the beholder inherent in these devotions, leaving aside particular images, architecture, or ornamentation related to those practices.[1]

Whether on pilgrimage to places or to people, Christians accented the visual as a way to integrate the contradictions of their experiences. In describing monks as familiar patriarchs, prophets, and apostles, pilgrims extended the biblical vocabulary to monastic settings and to the desert generally. Through these travelogues, audiences witnessed not only the world of monasticism but also the world of the Bible itself. In short, travel writing and physiognomy made the biblical past accessible.

Instrumental in that accessibility was the brief notice, which provided "concrete vehicles for conception," to borrow the words of David Haberman.[2] As Haberman observes for Braj, a circuit of holy places relating to Krishna, storytelling serves as "a language by means of which a previously inaccessible world is evoked and realized."[3] The same applies to Christian pilgrims to the living, who framed their subjects as outside individual and regional history in order to "evoke," or draw out, the biblical past. The short notices of the saints in these travelogues lent themselves well to this process of abstraction, reconstitution, and "externalization."[4] List-like descriptions reduced the monastic life to the elements of the biblical image: a telling beard, a reminiscent charism, a biblical landscape. Unlike John Chrysostom, who addressed his audience of new converts with monks present in the room, the pilgrims felt no compulsion to remind the readers what to "overlook;" instead they were free to omit the types of details the preacher had to confront. If the ties between city and desert compli-

---

1. For a rich synthesis of material and literary evidence relating to shrines, see now Cynthia Hahn, "Seeing and Believing: The Construction of Sanctity in Early-Medieval Saints' Shrines," *Speculum* 72 (1997): 1079–1106.

2. David Haberman, *Journey through the Twelve Forests: An Encounter with Krishna* (New York: Oxford University Press, 1994), 53.

3. Ibid.

4. Ibid., 54.

cated the picture, then such details were muted.[5] If the body in motion disrupted the biblical image, then the writer focused on the face at rest. Rendering the Bible visible meant freezing, isolating, and then highlighting the biblical image perceived within. Only then might the audience see Moses, Jacob, Aaron, or angels.

Miracles and typology were two other means for rendering the Bible visible to readers of the travelogues. In tales about miraculous feedings, healings, and the abundance of nature, travel writers gave a quantity and substance, a concreteness, to this biblicizing effect. Abraham's looks, Aaron's beard, or Jacob's shining appearance put a face on that biblical past. And wherever the pilgrim-authors claimed that the monks continued the work of Jesus and the apostles, the authors biblicized the present.

Underlying these efforts is the conviction that the biblical past would become visible only to those who were capable of both seeing and responding to the sacred presence they beheld. The "eye of faith," as Christians referred to this interactive visuality, was tactile as well as visual, not just in the sense of contact but even of engagement. As the literary critic Gabriel Josipovici once said, "By touching, I think, we experience a sense of our own implication in a history longer and broader than our personal one: I am—and it is—and touch can somehow affirm that truth."[6] For the same reasons that Josipovici values touch, that is to say, for its ability to lead him into the past, late antique pilgrims cherished sight. By implicating them in the biblical past, sight manifested the reality of Abraham, Moses, and Jesus in the monastics they encountered.[7] Yet without the tactile aspect of vision, pilgrims such as Paula would never have been able to persuade audiences that the sacred past could be seen in the dank air of a cave.

5. For an insightful treatment of this selectiveness, see James E. Goehring, "The Encroaching Desert: Literary Production and Ascetic Space in Early Christian Egypt," *JECS* 1 (1993): 281–96.

6. Gabriel Josipovici, *Touch* (New Haven: Yale University Press, 1996), 70.

7. The prologues and epilogues to these travelogues set the short-term journey in a much broader context of sacred history. Typically the time of Jesus

In the pilgrims' texts, vision provided a vehicle to the past. Their lingering gaze scoured the cracks and crevices of the present for a means to enter and thereby bear witness to that past. Unlike theologians who warned against deceptive perceptions,[8] pilgrims trusted the eyes of the body. Far from dimming the eyes of faith, the eyes of the body, as pilgrims described them, were believed to open and engage the eyes of faith. In this respect, pilgrims drew from physiognomic thought and optics to elongate the visual ray of extramissionist theories. Whereas optics imagined a ray that stopped at the surface of its object, pilgrims believed the ray touched the surface of the object and then continued to illuminate the biblical reality within. The "hand" of that tactile gaze reached behind the surface appearance and drew the eternal face into a temporal one. That aggressive vision, capable of integrating the biblical past into the meditative present, is also to be found in other types of veneration. By evoking some of these affinities, we may notice the outlines of a larger ritual context for late antique pilgrimage. I examine a few examples from relic veneration and the cult of icons with the aim of identifying how the processes and the effect of vision defined the religious experiences involved.

In late antiquity several devotional practices assumed an increasingly sensory and particularly a visual dimension. The Eucharist, relics, and eventually icons became conduits for divine presence precisely because of the visual experiences they elicited in the beholder. As diverse as these ritual objects of bread, bone, and image might have appeared, the practices surrounding them shared a common conception of vision and the beholder. This commonality suggests that one can go beyond loose affinities to speak of a "visual piety," by which I mean Christian practices in which a lingering gaze conjures a sacred presence.

---

or even of the patriarchs is the stated beginning for the entire narrative. See for example, *HM* prol. 4, epil. 2; *HL* prol. 6.

8. For instance, Ambrose of Milan: "We cannot comprehend such heavenly truth with hands or eyes or ears, because what is seen is temporal, but what is not seen is eternal" (*De bono mortis,* 3.10 [FC 65:77]).

That lingering gaze was central to fourth-century eucharistic practices.[9] As Cyril of Jerusalem describes the ritual, the chanter invited communicants to "taste and see that the Lord is good."[10] No sooner had he invoked these two senses than Cyril warned the communicant to mistrust the physical sense of taste. Instead he showed how to sanctify and prepare the eye to receive this full, divine presence. The new converts were instructed to take the eucharistic wine and touch their "eyes and brow and the other sense organs" with it.[11] As Cyril understood the Eucharist, the eye was privileged as the organ that senses the whole divine presence from its parts. With the wine still fresh on the eye, the catechumen consumed the bread, an act that Cyril claimed would make the "face of the soul shine."[12] All this was in preparation for the soul's vision of God, an experience akin to the eye's all-encompassing and singular perception.[13] In the Eucharist, as Cyril explained it, not only is the physical eye sanctified through ritual gestures, but those very acts prepare the eye of faith to see divine realities, with an immediacy that is the unique property of physical vision.

John Chrysostom also invoked the connection between seeing and biblical realism in his description of the Eucharist. In *On the Priesthood* he described how the priest must be "pure as if he were standing in heaven itself."[14] The immediacy of that divine perception, according to John, was rooted in visual experience. He exhorted the congregants, "When you see the Lord sacrificed and lying before you, and the High Priest standing over the sacrifice and praying, and all who partake being

9. For an insightful discussion of the sensory implications of the Eucharist see Geir Hellemo, *Adventus Domini: Eschatological Thought in Fourth-Century Apses and Catecheses* (Leiden: Brill, 1989), 183–84, 188–94.

10. Cyril of Jerusalem, *Cat. Myst.* 5.21 (FC 64:203; cf. Ps 34:9).

11. Cyril of Jerusalem, *Cat. Myst.* 5.22 (FC 64:203).

12. Cyril of Jerusalem, *Cat. Myst.* 4.9 (FC 64:186; cf. Ps. 104.15).

13. Cyril of Jerusalem, *Cat.* 6.2 (FC 61:148–49); Hellemo, *Adventus Domini*, 191–92.

14. John Chrysostom, *De sacerdotio*, III.4 (Neville, 70).

tinctured with that precious blood, can you think that you are still among men and still standing on earth? Are you not at once driven to heaven?"[15] As these two bishops understood the eucharistic rituals, the goal was to integrate visual experience, biblical realism, and the participation of the beholder. When the eyes or vision came in contact with a small drop of wine or a broken piece of bread, the entire salvific drama was thought to fill up the space and encompass the viewer.

Christian discussions of relics also point to a visual piety that attached tremendous power to the beholder. A relic has no intrinsic meaning or existence. If detached from its worshipping community, it is void of power or significance: even Jerome conceded to his opponent Vigilantius that a relic is indeed "a bit of powder wrapped in a costly cloth."[16] But Jerome also knew that the eyes of the devout could bring that bit of powder to life. For the onlookers who welcomed the prophet Samuel's relics as they were translated to Chalcedon, it was "as if they beheld a living prophet in their midst."[17] Implied in this remark is that any wholeness attributed to the object is an effect of the beholder's eye. Visual perception constitutes that reality of wholeness.

Gregory of Nyssa described at greater length the role of the beholder in generating this presence in a sermon honoring the martyr Theodore: "Those who behold [the relics] embrace them as though the actual body, applying all their senses, eyes, mouth, and ears; then they pour forth tears for his piety and suffering, and bring forward their supplications to the martyr as though he were present and complete."[18]

15. Ibid.

16. Jerome, *C. Vigilant.* 5 (NPNF 2.6.419).

17. Ibid. On the *adventus* ceremony see Kenneth G. Holum and Gary Vikan, "The Trier Ivory, *Adventus* Ceremonial, and the Relics of St. Stephen," *DOP* 33 (1979): 115–33, esp. 116–20. On the Roman imperial antecedents for the practice, see Sabine G. MacCormack, *Art and Ceremony in Late Antiquity* (Berkeley: University of California Press, 1981), 17–61.

18. *PG* 46.740ab; translated in E. D. Hunt, *Holy Land Pilgrimage in the Later Roman Empire (A.D. 312–460)* (Oxford: Clarendon, 1982), 133.

Here it is the senses, and not strictly the relic, that provide the "tool for conjuring up the physical presence of the saint."[19]

In other cases, the sense of sight acted alone to conjure and contemplate the saint's presence from a fragment. In a letter accompanying a fragment of the Cross, Paulinus of Nola emphasized the power of the eye to define the object of veneration: "Let not your faith shrink because the eyes of the body behold evidence so small; let it look with the inner eye on the whole power of the cross in this tiny segment. Once you think that you behold the wood on which our Salvation, the Lord of majesty, was hanged with nails whilst the world trembled, you, too, must tremble, but you must also rejoice."[20] In this passage, vision constitutes and responds to the presence of the divine, restoring the presence of the whole Cross out of a tiny fragment. That generative power of vision is readily apparent in the way Paulinus fills out the image. The eye here has recreated the entire biblical event, furnishing Christ, the nails, the witnesses, and their reaction to the sight. Fragmentation may have diminished the size of the Cross, but the eye can mend those breaks. Likewise, the passing of time may have separated the devotee from the event of the Crucifixion, but vision overcomes that temporal fragmentation.[21] Seeing the sliver of wood makes it possible to imitate the witnesses to the event and thereby participate in the event itself.[22]

19. Ernst Kitzinger, "The Cult of Images before Iconoclasm," *DOP* 8 (1954): 83–150, esp. 116.

20. *Ep.* 31.1 (Walsh, 126).

21. On the function of the relic and the *passio* for integrating past, present, and future, see Peter Brown, *The Cult of the Saints: Its Rise and Function in Latin Christianity* (Chicago: University of Chicago Press, 1981), 78–82. Patricia Cox Miller has recently noted the paradox of fragments that "remained miraculously whole despite being constantly broken up into fragments" (" 'Differential Networks': Relics and Other Fragments in Late Antiquity," *JECS* 6 [1998]: 113–38, esp. 122).

22. Cf. Hunt (*Holy Land Pilgrimage*, 132), who comments on the passage: "Paulinus' interpretation here amounts to a reproduction, through the portable

In one of the most extensive discussions of relics in late antique literature, the bishop Victricius of Rouen, a friend of Paulinus, reiterated the
power of vision in the act of veneration. When gazing at a relic, Victricius explained, one sees blood and ashes with the eyes of the body; only
then do the eyes of the heart open, allowing the viewer to recognize the
presence of the saint in a small fragment.[23] Here again, physical seeing
is the first step to reconstituting wholeness from a fragment.

That conjuring power of vision is also inherent in the veneration of
images as understood by the eighth-century theologian John of Damascus. As a defender of images, John felt compelled to defend all forms of
visual piety, whether icons, holy places, or relics. Incarnational theology
is central to his program because it marks a moment in time when God
made himself visible. "I boldly draw an image of the invisible God, not
as invisible, but as having become visible for our sakes by partaking of
flesh and blood."[24] As a result of that event, believers see God in new
ways. "Before" and "after" here represent two modes of seeing. As John
explained this bifurcated visuality: "I gaze upon the image of God, as
Jacob did, but in a different way. For he only saw with spiritual sight
what was promised to come in the future, while the memory of Him
who became visible in the flesh is burned into my soul."[25] According to
John, this comprehensive and continuous revelation resulted in the
incarnate God suffusing the universe with many types of images or representations of himself.

---

medium of the relics, of the immediate and visual reaction by the pilgrims at the
holy places *in situ*."

23. *De laude sanctorum*, 10 (*PL* 20.452; Herval, 134–36). "Cur igitur
reliquias appellamus? Quia rerum imagines et signa sunt verba. Subjicitur oculis
cruor et limus. Sed nos nunc totum in parte dicendo non corporalium luminum
obices sed cordis oculos aperimus?"

24. *De imag.* 1.4 (Anderson, 16); cf. 3.17: "All images reveal and make perceptible those things which are hidden."

25. Ibid., 1.22 (Anderson, 30).

The notion that many things can represent God and thus reveal God is illustrated in John's discussion of what he calls "relative worship," that is, worship of people and things who bear the divine image but are not divine in and of themselves. Holy people and holy places belong to this category. God dwells in holy people because they have become "likenesses" of God. And holy places merit worship because they are also "receptacles of divine power."[26] What unites these forms of relative worship is not their discrete forms but rather the notion that the worshiper "approach[es] God" through them.[27]

Words, people, pictures, and objects are worthy of veneration, John insists, because they produce visible reminders of God. In this respect, they share equivalent functions. Although Christians venerate different forms, each form has the function of making the divine visible. The equivalence in effect secures John's position. Doing away with images will not dispel the idea that God remains visible in other forms. "Either refuse to worship any matter, or stop your innovations."[28] On what grounds can John equate such diverse types of "matter"? What made it possible for him to assume that a drawing, an object, a person, and a word have equivalent functions? His entire argument is grounded in the eye, an eye capable of knowing the incarnate God and the visible Bible. By this reasoning, scripture itself is an image that makes the divine present to the senses.

These eighth-century debates over images called into question what pilgrims had puzzled over for centuries prior to this controversy: What makes the divine visible? And can the senses satisfy the desire to perceive God? For iconophiles, such as John of Damascus, a theory of the beholder was crucial to the defense of sacred images. More important

---

26. Ibid., 3.33–34: θείας ἐνεργείας δοχεῖα. I thank Robert Wilken for bringing this passage to my attention.

27. Ibid., 3.33 (Anderson, 85).

28. Ibid., 1.22; cf. (Anderson, 36).

for our purposes is the realization that long before John and others articulated this theory of the beholder, pilgrims to the living were engaging in visual practices with the same goals: to render and perceive divine presence. The fourth- and fifth-century texts about physical and spiritual journeys suggest that far from introducing a new debate over the power of vision, the painted icon reopened a debate that had its origins in the visual practices of pilgrims in earlier centuries. Icon veneration was neither the first form of visual piety nor the last. The icon painter concretized what the pilgrim-authors sought to create with words: a static, decontextualized figure through which to perceive the presence of the divine.[29]

John's eloquent defense of images was composed centuries after Paula, Palladius, and Theodoret had visited saints in the desert. But he relied on an understanding of vision to be found in the devotion of pilgrims who came centuries before him. Unlike iconoclasts, who insisted on privileging the written word over images as the authentic means for knowing God, both late antique pilgrims and eighth-century iconophiles could confer equal status on the written word and images.[30] To pilgrims and iconophiles, scripture was not bound to any particular physical object, whether a book or an image. Rather, it was a lived experience that was both visible and visual. Separated by centuries, both forms of visual piety put the beholder at the center of all sacred encounters, conferring greater significance on the act of seeing than on the object seen. Thus in privileging vision as a vehicle by which to enter and participate in the biblical past, pilgrims set a vital precedent for the cult of icons.

29. On this equivalence between word and image, see Gilbert Dagron, "Holy Images and Likeness," *DOP* 45 (1991): 23–33.

30. For a stimulating discussion of the cultural and theological context of Byzantine iconoclasm, see Averil Cameron, "The Language of Images: The Rise of Icons and Christian Representation," in *The Church and the Arts*, ed. Diana Wood (Studies in Church History; Oxford: Blackwell, 1992), 1–42, esp. 29.

The idea that the pilgrim's destination contained the scattered image of the divine presence was a potent one. It infused the fragments of pilgrims' writings, informed their descriptions, and privileged vision as the sensory mode by which to reintegrate those moments of recognition. Pilgrims engaged the eyes of faith in a participatory devotion, one that linked them to the biblical past. This sensory piety shaped the ways Christians defined their physical and spiritual journeys as well as their responses to holy people, living and dead. By this tactile and conjuring eye of faith, pilgrims articulated a theology of vision that would find its fullest expression in the cult of icons. In a hymn to the holy man Julian Saba, Ephrem the Syrian captures best the role of vision in gathering a scattered divine presence:

> I have seen you scattered;
> > I have seen you recollected.
> > Both you and your brothers
> > > are depicted in our Lord.[31]

Like this poet, the pilgrims learned how to see living saints. Through the travelogues, they found a biblical past scattered in the living saints they encountered; and with the lingering gaze of the eye of faith, they found a way to "recollect" those sacred moments.

---

31. Edmund Beck, *Des heiligen Ephraem des Syrers Hymnen auf Abraham Kidunaya und Julianos Saba* (CSCO 322 & 323; Louvain: Peeters, 1972), 322.43, III.3, translated in Sidney Griffith, "Julian Saba, 'Father of the Monks' of Syria," *JECS* 2 (1994): 185–216, esp. 205.

SELECT BIBLIOGRAPHY

PRIMARY SOURCES

For individual saints' lives not in major collections (e.g., Cyril of Scythopolis, *Vitae*) see under *Vita* ———.

Achilles Tatius. *Leucippe et Clitophon*. LCL. Translated by S. Gaselee. Rev. ed. Cambridge: Harvard University Press, 1969.

Ambrose of Milan. *De bono mortis*. Translated in Michael P. McHugh, *Saint Ambrose: Seven Exegetical Works*. FC 65. Washington, D.C.: Catholic University of America Press, 1972.

Antonius Diogenes. *The Wonders beyond Thule*. Summarized in Photius, *Bibliotheca*, 166, edited by R. Henry. Paris: Budé, 1960. Translated by Gerald N. Sandy in *Collected Ancient Greek Novels*, edited by B. P. Reardon, 775–82. Berkeley: University of California Press, 1989.

Apocalypse of Paul. See *Visio Pauli*.

Apophthegmata patrum. Greek alphabetical collection: *PG* 65, cols. 72–440. Translated in Benedicta Ward, *The Sayings of the Desert Fathers: The Alphabetical Collection*. CS 59. Kalamazoo: Cistercian, 1975. Other collections: (1) *Les apophtegmes des pères: Collection systématique (chapîtres I–IX)*. Edited by

Jean-Claude Guy. SC 387. Paris: Cerf, 1993. (2) *Les sentences des pères du désert: Série des anonymes.* Edited by Lucien Regnault. Spiritualité orientale 43. Sablé-sur-Sarthe/Bégrolle-en-Mauges: Solesmes/Bellefontaine, 1985.

Apuleius. *Metamorphoses (Asinus Aureus).* LCL. 2 vols. Translated by J. Arthur Hanson. Cambridge: Harvard University Press, 1989.

Aristotle. LCL. 23 vols. Translated by Harold P. Cook et al. Cambridge: Harvard University Press, 1926–62.

———. *The Complete Works of Aristotle. The Revised Oxford Translation.* 2 vols. Translated and edited by Jonathan Barnes. Princeton: Princeton University Press, 1984.

———. *De sensu and De memoria.* Edited and translated by G. R. T. Ross. Cambridge: Cambridge University Press, 1906.

Asterius of Amasea. *Homiliae.* Text: *Asterius of Amasea. Homilies I–XIV.* Edited by C. Datema. Leiden: Brill, 1970.

Athanasius. *Contra gentes.* Text and trans.: Contra Gentes *and* De Incarnatione *by Athanasius.* Edited and translated by Robert W. Thomson. Oxford: Clarendon, 1971.

———. *De incarnatione Verbi Dei.* Text: *Sur l'incarnation du Verbe.* Edited by Charles Kannengiesser. SC 199. Paris: Cerf, 1973. Translated in *St. Athanasius on the Incarnation.* Crestwood, N.Y.: Saint Vladimir's Seminary Press, 1989.

———. *Lettre à des vierges qui étaient allées prier à Jérusalem.* Edited and translated by J. Lebon in "Athanasiana Syriaca: Une lettre attribuée à saint Athanase d'Alexandrie." *Le Muséon* 41 (1928): 169–215. Translated in David Brakke, *Athanasius and the Politics of Asceticism.* Oxford: Clarendon, 1995, 292–302.

———. *Vita Antonii.* See *Vita Antonii.*

Basil of Caesarea. *Epistulae.* Text: *Saint Basile, Lettres.* 3 vols. Edited by Yves Courtonne. Paris: Belles Lettres, 1957–66. Translated by Roy J. Deferrari in *St. Basil: Letters.* 4 vols. LCL. Cambridge: Harvard University Press, 1961–62.

Betz, Hans Dieter, ed. *The Greek Magical Papyri in Translation, Including the Demotic Spells.* 2d ed. Chicago: University of Chicago Press, 1992.

Bordeaux Pilgrim. See *Itinerarium Burdigalense.*

Callinicos. *Vita Hypatii.* See *Vita Hypatii.*

Cassian, John. *Conlationes.* Text: *Jean Cassien: Les conférences.* 3 vols. Edited by
 E. Pichery. SC 42, 54, 64. Paris: Cerf, 1953, 1958, 1959. Translated by Boniface
 Ramsey in *John Cassian: The Conferences.* ACW 57. New York: Paulist, 1997.

Cyril of Jerusalem. *Catecheses.* Text: *Cyrilli opera.* 2 vols. Edited by Joseph Rupp.
 1860. Translated by Leo P. McCauley and Anthony A. Stephenson in *The
 Works of Saint Cyril of Jerusalem.* 2 vols. FC 61, 64. Washington, D.C.:
 Catholic University of America Press, 1969, 1970.

———. *Catéchèses mystagogiques.* Text: *Cyrille de Jérusalem: Catéchèses mystagogiques.* Edited by Auguste Piédagnel and translated by Pierre Paris. SC 126
 bis. Paris: Cerf, 1988. Translated by Leo P. McCauley and Anthony A.
 Stephenson in *The Works of Saint Cyril of Jerusalem.* 2 vols. FC 64. Washington, D.C.: Catholic University of America Press, 1970.

Cyril of Scythopolis. *Vita Euthymii.* Text: *Kyrillos von Skythopolis.* Edited by
 Eduard Schwartz. TU 49.2. Leipzig: Hinrichs, 1939. Translated by R. M.
 Price in *Cyril of Scythopolis: The Lives of the Monks of Palestine.* CS 114. Kala-
 mazoo: Cistercian, 1991.

Diodorus Siculus. 10 vols. Translated by C. H. Oldfather. LCL. Cambridge:
 Harvard University Press, 1935.

Egeria. See *Itinerarium Egeriae.*

Ephrem. *Sermo de Domino nostro.* Text: *Des Heiligen Ephraem des Syrers* Sermo de
 Domino nostro. Edited by E. Beck. CSCO 270–71. Louvain, 1966. Translated by Edward B. Mathews Jr. and Joseph P. Amar in *St. Ephrem the Syrian:
 Selected Prose Works,* FC 91:273–332. Washington, D.C.: Catholic University of America Press, 1994.

Eunapius. *Vitae sophistarum.* Text and trans.: *Philostratus and Eunapius: Lives of
 the Sophists.* Translated by Wilmer C. Wright. LCL. Cambridge: Harvard
 University Press, 1921.

Evagrius of Pontus. *Practicus.* Text: *Évagre le Pontique: Traité pratique, ou le
 moine.* 2 vols. Edited by Antoine Guillaumont and Claire Guillaumont. SC
 170–71. Paris: Cerf, 1971. Translated by John E. Bamberger in *Evagrius Ponticus:* Praktikos *and* Chapters on Prayer. CS 4. Kalamazoo: Cistercian, 1981.

———. *Ep. ad Melaniam.* Translated by M. Parmentier in "Evagrius of Pontus' 'Letter to Melania' I." *Bijdragen, tijdschrift voor filosofie en theologie* 46 (1985): 2–38.

Expositio totius mundi et gentium. Edited and translated by Jean Rougé. SC 124.
 Paris: Cerf, 1966.

Gregory of Nazianzus. *Orationes.* Text: *Grégoire de Nazianze: Discours 27–31, discours théologiques.* Edited by P. Gallay. SC 250. Paris: Cerf, 1974. Translated in Lionel Wickham and Frederick Williams, *Faith Gives Fullness to Reasoning: The Five Theological Orations of Gregory Nazianzen.* Commentary by Frederick W. Norris. Leiden: Brill, 1991.

Gregory of Nyssa. *Epistulae.* Text: *Grégoire de Nysse, Lettres.* Edited by Pierre Maraval. SC 363. Paris: Cerf, 1990. Translated by William Moore and Henry Austin Wilson in *Select Writings and Letters of Gregory, Bishop of Nyssa.* NPNF, 2d series. Grand Rapids: Eerdmans, 1988. Vol. 5.

Gregory of Nyssa. *Vita Moysis.* See *Vita Moysis.*

———. *In Cantica Canticorum.* Text: *Gregorii Nysseni in Canticum Canticorum.* Edited by Werner Jaeger and Hermann Langerbeck. Gregorii Nysseni Opera, 6. Leiden: Brill, 1960. Translated by Casimir McCambley in *Saint Gregory of Nyssa: Commentary on the Song of Songs.* Brookline, Mass.: Hellenic College Press, 1987.

———. *Vita Macrinae.* See *Vita Macrinae.*

Historia monachorum in Aegypto. Greek text: *Historia monachorum in Aegypto.* Edited by André-Jean Festugière. SH 34 (1961, repr. with French translation, SH 53 [1971]). Translated by Norman Russell in *Lives of the Desert Fathers.* CS 34. Kalamazoo: Cistercian, 1980. Latin text: *Tyrannius Rufinus, Historia monachorum sive De vita sanctorum patrum.* Edited by Eva Schulz-Flügel. PTS 34. Berlin: De Gruyter, 1990.

Itinerarium Burdigalense. Text: *Itineraria et alia geographica.* Edited by P. Geyer and O. Cuntz. CCSL 175–76. Turnhout: Brepols, 1965. 175.1–26. Standard page numbers are those of P. Wesseling, *Vetera romanorum itinera.* Amsterdam, 1735. Translated by extracts in John Wilkinson. *Egeria's Travels to the Holy Land,* 153–63. Rev. ed. Jerusalem: Ariel. Warminster: Aris & Phillips, 1981.

Itinerarium Egeriae. Text: *Itineraria et alia geographica.* Edited by P. Geyer and O. Cuntz. CCSL 175–76. Turnhout: Brepols, 1965. *Égérie, journal de voyage.* Edited and translated by Pierre Maraval. SC 296. Paris: Cerf, 1982. Translated by John Wilkinson in *Egeria's Travels to the Holy Land.* Rev. ed. Jerusalem: Ariel.Warminster: Aris & Phillips, 1981.

Jerome. *Epistulae.* Text: *Saint Jérôme, Lettres.* 8 vols. Edited and translated by Jérôme Labourt. Paris: Belles Lettres, 1949–63. Translated by W. H. Freemantle in *St. Jerome: Letters and Select Works.* NPNF, 2d series. Grand Rapids: Eerdmans, 1989. Vol. 6.

————. *Homiliae*. Translated by Marie Liguori Ewald in *The Homilies of Saint Jerome*. 2 vols. FC 48, 57. Washington, D.C.: Catholic University of America Press, 1966.

————. *Vita Pauli*. See *Vita Pauli*.

John Chrysostom. *In Iohannem homiliae*. Text: *PG* 59, cols. 23–482. Translated by Thomas Aquinas Goggin in *Saint John Chrysostom: Commentary on Saint John the Apostle and Evangelist*. 2 vols. FC 33, 41. New York: Fathers of the Church, 1957, 1960.

————. *Catecheses*. Edited by Antoine Wenger in *Huit catéchèses baptismales inédites*. SC 50. Paris: Cerf, 1957. Translated by Paul W. Harkins in *St. John Chrysostom: Baptismal Instructions*, 8.4. ACW 31. New York: Newman, 1963.

John Moschus. *Pratum spirituale*. Text: *PG* 87, cols. 2851–3112. Translated by John Wortley in *The Spiritual Meadow of John Moschos*. CS 139. Kalamazoo: Cistercian, 1992.

John of Damascus. *Contra imaginum calumniatores orationes tres*. Text: *Die Schriften des Johannes von Damaskos* vol. 3. Edited by Bonifatius Kotter. PTS 17. Berlin: De Gruyter, 1975. Translated by David Anderson in *St. John of Damascus: On the Divine Images, Three Apologies against Those Who Attack the Divine Images*. Crestwood: Saint Vladimir's Seminary Press, 1980.

Lactantius. *De opificio dei*. Translated by Mary Francis McDonald in *Lactantius: The Minor Works*. FC 54. Washington, D.C.: Catholic University of America Press, 1965.

Leontius Neapolis. *Life of Symeon the Holy Fool*. Text: *Das Leben des heiligen Narren Symeon von Leontios von Neapolis*. Edited by Lennart Rydén. Uppsala: Almquist and Wiksell, 1963. Translated by Derek Krueger in *Symeon the Holy Fool*. Berkeley: University of California Press, 1996, 131–71.

Lucian. *Verae Historiae*. Translated by A. M. Harmon in *Lucian I*. LCL. Cambridge: Harvard University Press, 1913, repr. 1990, 247–357.

————. *Hermotimus*. Translated by K. Kilburn in *Lucian VI*. LCL. Cambridge: Harvard University Press, 1959, 259–415.

Nemesius of Emesa. *De natura hominis*. Text: *PG* 40, cols. 514–817. Translated by W. Telfer in *Cyril of Jerusalem and Nemesius of Emesa*. Library of Christian Classics 4. Philadelphia: Westminster, 1955.

Nicholas of Sion. *The Life of Saint Nicholas of Sion*. Edited and translated by Ihor Ševčenko and Nancy Patterson Ševčenko. Brookline, Mass.: Hellenic College Press, 1984.

Palaephatus. *De incredibilis.* 1902 Teubner text, repr. in *Peri apistōn* with translation by Jacob Stern. Wauconda, Ill.: Bolchazy-Carducci, 1996.

Palladius. *Historia Lausiaca.* Text: *The Lausiac History of Palladius.* 2 vols. Edited by Cuthbert Butler. Texts and Studies 6. Cambridge: Cambridge University Press, 1904. Translated in R. T. Meyer, *Palladius: The Lausiac History.* ACW 34. New York: Newman, 1964.

———. *De gentibus Indiae et Bragmanibus.* Edited by Wilhelm Berghoff. Meisenheim am Glan: Anton Hain, 1967.

Paphnutius. *Vita Onnophrius.* Text: *Coptic Texts,* IV: *Coptic Martyrdoms.* Edited by E. A. Wallis Budge. London, 1914, repr. New York: AMS, 1977, 205–24. Translated in Tim Vivian, *Histories of the Monks of Upper Egypt and the Life of Onnophrius.* CS 140. Kalamazoo: Cistercian, 1993.

Paulinus of Nola. *Epistulae.* Edited by G. de Hartel. CSEL 29–30 (1894). Translated in P. G. Walsh, *Letters of St. Paulinus of Nola.* 2 vols. ACW 35–36. Westminster, Md.: Newman, 1966–67.

Philostratus, *V. Apollonii Tyanae.* LCL. 2 volumes. Translated by F. C. Conybeare. London: Heinemann, 1912.

Phlegon of Tralles. *Miracula.* Text: In *Paradoxographorum Graecorum reliquiae.* Edited by Alexander Giannini. 169–219. Milan: Istituto Editoriale Italiano, 1965. Translated by William Hansen in *Phlegon of Tralles'* Book of Marvels. Exeter: University of Exeter Press, 1996.

De physiognomonia liber. Text and trans.: *Traité de physiognomonie: Anonyme latin.* Edited by Jacques André. Paris: Belles Lettres, 1981.

Piacenza Pilgrim. See *Pseudo-Antonini Placentini itinerarium.*

Plato. *Timaeus.* Text and trans.: *Plato.* Vol. 7. Translated by R. G. Bury. LCL. Cambridge: Harvard University Press, 1952.

———. *Theaetetus.* Text and trans.: *The* Theaetetus *of Plato.* Edited and translated by Myles Burnyeat and M. J. Levett. Indianapolis: Hackett, 1990.

Pliny. *Naturalia historia.* LCL. 10 vols. Translated by H. Rackham. Cambridge: Harvard University Press, 1952.

Plutarch, *V. Thes.* In *Plutarch's Lives.* 11 vols. Translated by Bernadotte Perrin. LCL. Cambridge: Harvard University Press, 1914. 1:1–87.

Pseudo-Antonini Placentini itinerarium. Text: *Itineraria et alia geographica.* Edited by P. Geyer and O. Cuntz. CCSL 175–76. Turnhout: Brepols, 1965. Translated in John Wilkinson, *Jerusalem Pilgrims before the Crusades.* Warminster: Aris & Phillips, 1977, 79–89.

Pseudo-Aristotle. *Physiognomica*. In *Scriptores Physiognomonici*, 2 vols. Edited by R. Förster. Leipzig: Teubner, 1893. Vol. 1. Translated in Jonathan Barnes, ed., *The Complete Works of Aristotle: The Revised Oxford Translation*. 2 vols. Princeton: Princeton University Press, 1984. 1:1237–50.

Pseudo-Basil. *De hominis structura*. Text: *Basile de Césarée. Sur l'origine de l'homme: Hom. X et XI de l'Hexaéméron*. Edited and translated by Alexis Smets and Michel Van Esbroeck. SC 160. Paris: Cerf, 1970.

Pseudo-Dionysius. Text: *Corpus Dionysiacum*. Edited by Beate Suchla, Gunter Heil, and A. M. Ritter. PTS 33, 36. Berlin: DeGruyter, 1990–1991. Also in *La hiérachie céleste*. Edited by R. Roques, G. Heil, and M. Gaudillac. SC 58 bis. Paris: Cerf, 1970. Translated in Colm Luibheid and Paul Rorem, *Pseudo-Dionysius: The Complete Works*. CWS. New York: Paulist, 1987.

Pseudo-Lactantius. *De passione Domini*. Text: CSEL 27 (1893): 148–51. Edited by Samuel Brandt. Translation: ANF 7:327–28.

Pseudo-Macarius. *Homiliae*. Text: *Die 50 geistlichen Homilien des Makarios*. Edited and translated by Hermann Dörries, Erich Klostermann, and Matthias Kroeger. PTS 6. Berlin: De Gruyter, 1964. Translated in George A. Maloney, *Pseudo-Macarius: The Fifty Spiritual Homilies and the Great Letter*. CWS. New York: Paulist, 1992.

Pseudo-Shenoute. *On Christian Behaviour*. Edited by K. H. Kuhn. CSCO, 206–7/ Scriptores Coptici, 29–30. Louvain: CSCO, 1960.

Rufinus. *Historia monachorum*. See *Historia monachorum* (Latin text).

Sulpicius Severus. *Dialogues*. Translated by Alexander Roberts. NPNF 2.11.

De Syncletica in deserto Iordanis. Text: *Analecta Bollandiana* 100 (1982): 305–17. Edited by Bernard Flusin and J. Paramelle.

Theodore of Mopsuestia. *Catechetical Homilies*. In *The Commentary on the Nicene Creed* and *The Commentary on the Lord's Prayer and the Sacraments of Baptism and Eucharist*. Edited and translated by A. Mingana. Woodbrooke Studies 5 and 6. Cambridge: W. Heffer & Sons, 1932–33.

Theodoret of Cyrrhus. *Historia religiosa*. Text: *Théodoret de Cyr: Histoire des moines de Syrie*. Edited and translated by Pierre Canivet and Alice Leroy-Molinghen. SC 234, 257. Paris: Cerf, 1977, 1979. Translated in R. M. Price, *History of the Monks of Syria*. CS 88. Kalamazoo: Cistercian, 1985.

Victricius of Rouen. *De laude sanctorum*. Text: PL 20.452. Repr. with French translation in René Herval, *Origines chrétiennes de la IIe Lyonnaise gallo-romaine à la Normandie ducale (IVe–XIe siècles)*. Rouen: Maugard. Paris: Picard, 1966.

Visio Pauli. Text: *Eschatologie et au-delà: Recherches sur* L'apocalypse de Paul. Edited by Claude Carozzi. Aix-en-Provence: Publications de l'Université de Provence, 1994. Translation based on M. R. James edition (1893), in *The Apocryphal New Testament*, edited by J. K. Elliott, 616–44. Oxford: Clarendon, 1993.

Vita Antonii by Athanasius. Text: *Athanase d'Alexandrie: Vie d'Antoine.* Edited by G. J. M. Bartelink. SC 400. Paris: Cerf, 1994. Translated in Robert C. Gregg, *Athanasius: The Life of Anthony.* CWS. New York: Paulist, 1980.

Vita Charitonis. Text: G. Garitte, "La vie prémétaphrastique de S. Chariton." *Bulletin de l'institut historique belge de Rome* 21 (1941): 5–46. Translated in Leah di Segni, *"The Life of Chariton."* In *Ascetic Behavior in Greco-Roman Antiquity: A Sourcebook.* Edited by Vincent Wimbush. Minneapolis: Fortress, 1990, 393–421.

Vita Cyri. Text: *Coptic Texts*, vol. 4, *Coptic Martyrdoms.* Edited by E. A. Wallis Budge. London: British Museum, 1914. Reprinted New York: AMS, 1977, 128–36. Excerpts translated in Tim Vivian, "The Story of Abba Pambo," in *Journeying into God: Seven Early Monastic Lives.* Minneapolis: Fortress, 1996.

Vita Danielis stylitae (Vita antiquior). Text: *Les Saints stylites.* Edited by Hippolyte Delehaye. SH 14. Brussels: Société des Bollandistes, 1923, 1–94. Translated in Elizabeth A. Dawes and N. Baynes, *Three Byzantine Saints.* Crestwood, N.Y.: Saint Vladimir's Seminary Press, 1977, 7–71.

Vita Hypatii by Callinicos. Text and trans.: *Callinicos: Vie d'Hypatios.* Edited and translated by G. J. M. Bartelink. SC 177. Paris: Cerf, 1971.

Vita Macrinae by Gregory of Nyssa. Text: *Grégoire de Nysse: Vie de sainte Macrine.* Edited and translated by Pierre Maraval. SC 178. Paris: Cerf, 1971.

Vita Melaniae Iunioris by Gerontius. Text: *Vie de Sainte Mélanie.* Edited by Denys Gorce. SC 90. Paris: Cerf, 1962. Translated in Elizabeth A. Clark, *The Life of Melania the Younger.* Studies in Women and Religion 14. New York: Edwin Mellen, 1984.

Vita Moysis by Gregory of Nyssa. Text: *Gregorii Nysseni: De vita Moysis.* Edited by Herbert Musurillo. Gregorii Nysseni Opera, vol. 7, part 1. Leiden: Brill, 1964. Translated in Abraham J. Malherbe and Everett Ferguson, *Gregory of Nyssa: The Life of Moses.* CWS. New York: Paulist, 1978.

Vita Pachomii. Text: *Sancti Pachomii vitae graecae.* Edited by F. Halkin. SH 19 (1932). Translated in Armand Veilleux, *Pachomian Koinonia: The Lives, Rules and Other Writings of Saint Pachomius and His Disciples*, vol. 1, *The Life of Saint*

Pachomius and His Disciples. 3 vols. CS 45–47. Kalamazoo: Cistercian, 1980–1982.

Vita Pauli. Text: H. Hurter in W. Oldfather et al., *Studies in the Text Tradition of St. Jerome's* Vitae Patrum. Urbana: University of Illinois Press, 1943. Translated by Paul B. Harvey Jr., "Jerome, *Life of Paul, The First Hermit.*" In *Ascetic Behavior in Greco-Roman Antiquity: A Sourcebook.* Edited by Vincent Wimbush. Minneapolis: Fortress, 1990, 357–69.

Vita Pelagiae. Texts and trans.: *Pélagie la Pénitente: Métamorphoses d'une légende,* vol. 1, *Les textes et leur histoire.* 2 vols. Edited and translated by Pierre Petitmengin et al. Paris: Études Augustiniennes, 1981. Latin: translated in Benedicta Ward, *Harlots of the Desert: A Study of Repentance in Early Monastic Sources.* CS 106. Kalamazoo: Cistercian, 1987. Also in Helen Waddell, *The Desert Fathers.* London, 1936. Repr. Ann Arbor: University of Michigan Press, 1957. Syriac: translated in Sebastian P. Brock and Susan Ashbrook Harvey, *Holy Women of the Syrian Orient.* Berkeley: University of California Press, 1987.

Vita Simeonis stylitae. Translated in Robert Doran, *The Lives of Simeon Stylites.* CS 112. Kalamazoo: Cistercian, 1992.

Vita Syncleticae. Text: *PG* 1488–1557. Translated in Elizabeth A. Castelli. "Pseudo-Athanasius, *The Life and Activity of the Holy and Blessed Teacher Syncletica.*" In *Ascetic Behavior in Greco-Roman Antiquity: A Sourcebook,* edited by Vincent Wimbush, 265–311. Minneapolis: Fortress, 1990.

Vita Theodori Syceatae. Translated in Elizabeth A. Dawes and N. Baynes, *Three Byzantine Saints.* Crestwood, N.Y.: Saint Vladmir's Seminary Press, 1977.

SECONDARY WORKS

Achtemeier, Paul J. "Jesus and the Disciples as Miracle Workers in the Apocryphal New Testament." In *Aspects of Religious Propaganda in Judaism and Early Christianity,* edited by Elisabeth Schüssler Fiorenza, 149–86. Notre Dame: University of Notre Dame Press, 1976.

Allison, Dale C. "The Eye is the Lamp of the Body (Matthew 6.22–23=Luke 11.34–36)." *New Testament Studies* 33 (1987): 61–83.

Amat, Jacqueline. *Songes et visions: L'au-delà dans la littérature latine tardive.* Paris: Études Augustiniennes, 1985.

Aziz, Barbara Nimri. "Personal Dimensions of the Sacred Journey: What Pilgrims Say." *Religious Studies* 23 (1987): 247–61.

Bagnall, Roger. *Egypt in Late Antiquity*. Princeton: Princeton University Press, 1993.

Baldovin, John F. *The Urban Character of Christian Worship: The Origins, Development, and Meaning of Stational Liturgy*. Orientalia Christiana Analecta 228. Rome: Pont. Institutum Studiorum Orientalium, 1987.

Bammel, C. P. "Problems of the *Historia Monachorum*." *JTS* n.s. 47 (1996): 92–104.

Bartelink, G. J. M. *Quelques observations sur ΠΑΡΡΗΣΙΑ dans la littérature paléochrétienne*. Graecitas et latinitas christianorum primaeva, Supplementa 3. Nijmegen: Dekker & Van de Vegt, 1970.

Barton, Carlin. *The Sorrows of the Ancient Romans: The Gladiator and the Monster*. Princeton: Princeton University Press, 1993.

Barton, Tamsyn. *Power and Knowledge: Astronomy, Physiognomics, and Medicine under the Roman Empire*. Ann Arbor: University of Michigan Press, 1994.

Bartsch, Shadi. *Decoding the Ancient Novel: The Reader and the Role of Pictorial Description in Heliodorus and Achilles Tatius*. Princeton: Princeton University Press, 1989.

Beare, John I. *Greek Theories of Elementary Cognition: From Alcmaeon to Aristotle*. Oxford: Clarendon, 1906.

Betz, Hans Dieter. "Matthew vi.22f and Ancient Greek Theories of Vision." In *Text and Interpretation: Studies in the New Testament Presented to Matthew Black*, edited by Ernest Best and R. M. Wilson, 43–56. Cambridge: Cambridge University Press, 1979.

Bishop, Peter. *The Myth of Shangri-La: Tibet, Travel Writing, and the Western Creation of Sacred Landscape*. Berkeley: University of California Press, 1989.

Borgeaud, Philippe. "The Open Entrance to the Closed Palace of the King: The Greek Labyrinth in Context." *History of Religions* 14 (1975): 1–27.

Brakke, David. *Athanasius and the Politics of Asceticism*. Oxford: Clarendon, 1995.

Bridel, Philippe. "La dialectique de l'isolement et de l'ouverture dans les monastères kelliotes: Espaces réservés—espaces d'accueil." In *Le site monastique copte des Kellia: Sources historiques et explorations archéologiques*. Geneva: Mission suisse d'archéologie copte, 1986.

Brightman, Robert S. "Apophatic Theology and Divine Infinity in St. Gregory of Nyssa." *Greek Orthodox Theological Review* 18 (1973): 97–114.

Brock, Sebastian. "Clothing Metaphors as a Means of Theological Expression in Syriac Tradition." In *Typus, Symbol, Allegorie bei den österlichen Vätern und ihren Parallelen im Mittelalter,* edited by M. Schmidt, 11–40. Regensburg: Friedrich Pustet, 1982.

Brown, Peter. *The Making of Late Antiquity.* Cambridge: Harvard University Press, 1978.

———. "The Rise and Function of the Holy Man in Late Antiquity." *JRS* 61 (1971): 80–101. Repr. in id., *Society and the Holy in Late Antiquity,* 103–52. Berkeley: University of California Press, 1982.

———. "The Saint as Exemplar in Late Antiquity." In *Saints and Virtues,* edited by John Stratton Hawley, 3–14. Berkeley: University of California Press, 1987.

———. *The Body and Society: Men, Women and Sexual Renunciation in Early Christianity.* New York: Columbia University Press, 1988.

———. *The Rise of Western Christendom: Triumph and Diversity,* A.D. 200–1000. Oxford: Blackwell, 1996.

Buck, D. F. "The Structure of the Lausiac History." *Byzantion* 46 (1976): 292–307.

Bunge, Gabriel. "Palladiana I: Introduction aux fragments coptes de *L'histoire lausiaque,* " *Studia Monastica* 32 (1990): 79–129.

Burridge, Richard A. *What Are the Gospels? A Comparison with Graeco-Roman Biography.* Society for New Testament Studies Monograph Series 70. Cambridge: Cambridge University Press, 1991.

Burton-Christie, Douglas E. " 'Practice Makes Perfect': Interpretation of Scripture in the *Apophthegmata Patrum.*" *SP* 20 (1989): 213–18.

———. *The Word in the Desert: Scripture and the Quest for Holiness in Early Christian Monasticism.* New York: Oxford University Press, 1993.

Calef, Susan M. "Paul 'in the Flesh' in the *Acts of Paul:* Physiognomics and the Search for Parallels." Unpublished paper, summarized in *AAR/SBL Abstracts 1994,* 159. Atlanta: Scholars, 1994.

Cameron, Averil. *Christianity and the Rhetoric of Empire: The Development of Christian Discourse.* Sather Classical Lectures 55. Berkeley: University of California Press, 1991.

———. "The Language of Images: The Rise of Icons and Christian Representation." In *The Church and the Arts,* edited by Diana Wood, 1–42. Studies in Church History. Oxford: Blackwell, 1992.

Campbell, Mary B. *The Witness and the Other World: Exotic European Travel Writing, 400–1600*. Ithaca: Cornell University Press, 1988.

———. " 'The Object of One's Gaze': Landscape, Writing, and Early Medieval Pilgrimage." In *Discovering New Worlds: Essays on Medieval Exploration and Imagination*, edited by Scott D. Westrem, 3–15. New York: Garland, 1991.

Canévet, Mariette. "Sens spirituel." In *DS* 14:598–617.

Canivet, Pierre. *Le monachisme syrien selon Théodoret de Cyr*. Théologie historique 42. Paris: Beauchesne, 1977.

Canter, H. V. "Personal Appearance in the Biography of the Roman Emperors." *Studies in Philology* 25 (1928): 385–99.

Cardman, Francine. "The Rhetoric of Holy Places: Palestine in the Fourth Century." *SP* 17.1 (1982): 18–25.

Carozzi, Claude. *Eschatologie et au-delà: Recherches sur L'apocalypse de Paul*. Aix-en-Provence: Publications de l'Université de Provence, 1994.

———. *Le voyage de l'âme dans l'au-delà dans la littérature latine, Ve–XIIIe siècle*. Paris: Boccard, 1994.

Carruthers, Mary J. *The Book of Memory: A Study of Memory in Medieval Culture*. Cambridge Studies in Medieval Culture 10. Cambridge: Cambridge University Press, 1990.

———. *The Craft of Thought: Meditation, Rhetoric, and the Making of Images, 400–1200*. Cambridge: Cambridge University Press, 1998.

Casey, R. "The Apocalypse of Paul." *JTS* 34 (1933): 1–32.

Castelli, Elizabeth A. "Virginity and Its Meaning for Women's Sexuality in Early Christianity." *Journal of Feminist Studies in Religion* 2 (1986): 61–88.

Chadwick, Henry. "John Moschus and His Friend Sophronius the Sophist." *JTS* 25 n.s. (1974): 41–74.

Chadwick, Owen. *John Cassian*. 2d ed. Cambridge: Cambridge University Press, 1968.

Chidester, David. *Word and Light: Seeing, Hearing, and Religious Discourse*. Urbana: University of Illinois Press, 1992.

Chitty, Derwas J. *The Desert a City: An Introduction to the Study of Egyptian and Palestinian Monasticism under the Christian Empire*. Crestwood, N.Y.: Saint Vladimir's Seminary Press, 1966.

Clark, Elizabeth A. *Ascetic Piety and Women's Faith: Essays on Late Ancient Christianity*. Studies in Women and Religion 20. Lewiston, N.Y.: Mellen, 1986.

———. *The Origenist Controversy: The Cultural Construction of an Early Christian Debate*. Princeton: Princeton University Press, 1992.

———. "Holy Women, Holy Words: Early Christian Women, Social History, and the 'Linguistic Turn.'" *JECS* 6 (1998): 413–30.

Classen, Constance. "Sweet Color, Fragrant Song: Sensory Models of the Andes and the Amazon." In *Worlds of Sense: Exploring the Senses in History and across Culture*. New York: Routledge, 1993.

Coleiro, E. "St. Jerome's Lives of the Hermits," *VC* 11 (1957): 161–78.

Coleman, Janet. *Ancient and Medieval Memories: Studies in the Reconstruction of the Past*. Cambridge: Cambridge University Press, 1992.

Collins, John J. and Michael Fishbane, eds. *Death, Ecstasy, and Other Worldly Journeys*. Albany: State University of New York Press, 1995.

Culler, Jonathan. "The Semiotics of Tourism." American Journal of Semiotics 1 (1981): 127–42. Repr. in id., *Framing the Sign: Criticism and Its Institutions*. Norman: University of Oklahoma Press, 1988.

Dagron, Gilbert. "Le culte des images dans le monde byzantin." In *Histoire vécue du peuple chrétien*, edited by Jean Delumeau. 1:133–60. Toulouse: Privat, 1979.

———. "Image de bête et image de Dieu: La physiognomonie animale dans la tradition grecque et ses avatars byzantins." In *Poikilia: Études offertes à Jean-Pierre Vernant*, 69–80. Paris: Éditions de l'École des Hautes Études en Sciences Sociales, 1987.

———. "Holy Images and Likeness." *DOP* 45 (1991): 23–33.

Daniélou, Jean. *Platonisme et théologie mystique: Essai sur la doctrine spirituelle de Saint Grégoire de Nysse*. Paris: Aubier, 1944.

———. "Terre et paradis chez les Pères de l'Église." *Eranos Jahrbuch* 22 (1953): 433–72.

———. *From Shadows to Reality: Studies in the Biblical Typology of the Fathers*. Westminster, Md.: Newman, 1960.

———. "Saint Grégoire de Nysse dans l'histoire du monachisme." In *Théologie de la vie monastique: Études sur la tradition patristique*, 131–41. Théologie 49. Aubier: Montaigne, 1961.

Davidson, J. "The Gaze in Polybius's *Histories*." *JRS* 81 (1991): 10–24.

Delehaye, Hippolyte. *L'ancienne hagiographie byzantine: Les sources, les premiers modèles, la formation des genres*. Edited by B. Joassart and X. Lequeux. SH 73. Brussels: Société des Bollandistes, 1991.

Deonna, Waldemar. *Le symbolisme de l'oeil*. Paris: Boccard, 1965.

Déroche, V. "Quelques interrogations à propos de la *Vie de Saint Syméon le Jeune*." *Eranos* 94 (1996): 63–83.

Desreumaux, Alain, and Francis Schmidt, eds. *Moïse géographe: Recherches sur les représentations juives et chrétiennes de l'espace*. Paris: Vrin, 1988.

Dickie, Matthew. "The Fathers of the Church and the Evil Eye." In *Byzantine Magic*, edited by Henry Maguire, 9–34. Cambridge: Harvard University Press, 1995.

Dillon, Matthew. *Pilgrims and Pilgrimage in Ancient Greece*. New York: Routledge, 1997.

Douglass, Laurie. "A New Look at the *Itinerarium Burdigalense*." *JECS* 4 (1996): 313–34.

Dundes, Alan, ed. *The Evil Eye: A Casebook*. Madison: University of Wisconsin Press, 1992.

Dupront, Alphonse. *Du sacré: Croisades et pèlerinages, images et langages*. Bibliothèque des histoires. Paris: Gallimard, 1987.

Eade, John, and Michael J. Sallnow, eds. *Contesting the Sacred: The Anthropology of Christian Pilgrimage*. London: Routledge, 1991.

Eck, Diana. *Darśan: Seeing the Divine Image in India*. 2d rev. ed. Chambersburg, Penna.: Anima, 1985.

Elliott, Alison Goddard. *Roads to Paradise: Reading the Lives of the Early Saints*. Hanover: University Press of New England, 1987.

Elm, Susanna. "Perceptions of Jerusalem Pilgrimage as Reflected in Two Early Sources on Female Pilgrimage (Third and Fourth Centuries, A.D.)." *SP* 20 (1987): 219–23.

———. "Evagrius Ponticus' *Sententiae ad Virginem*." *DOP* 45 (1991): 97–119.

———. *Virgins of God: The Making of Asceticism in Late Antiquity*. Oxford: Clarendon, 1994.

Elsner, John (Jaś). "From the Pyramids to Pausanias and Piglet: Monuments, Travel, and Writing." In *Art and Text in Ancient Greek Culture*, edited by Simon Goldhill and Robin Osborne, 225–54. Cambridge: Cambridge University Press, 1994.

———. *Art and the Roman Viewer: The Transformation of Art from the Pagan World to Christianity*. Cambridge: Cambridge University Press, 1995.

Evans, Elizabeth Cornelia. "Roman Descriptions of Personal Appearance." *Harvard Studies in Classical Philology* 46 (1935): 43–84.

———. "The Study of Physiognomy in the Second Century A.D." *Transactions of the American Philological Association* 72 (1941): 96–108.

———. "Literary Portraiture in Ancient Epic." *Harvard Studies in Classical Philology* 58–59 (1948): 189–217.

———. *Physiognomics in the Ancient World.* Transactions of the American Philosophical Society, n.s. 59/5. Philadelphia: American Philosophical Society, 1969.

Evelyn-White, H. G. *The Monasteries of Wadi 'n Natrûn.* 3 vols. New York: Metropolitan Museum of Art, 1933.

Fahnestock, Jeanne. "The Heroine of Irregular Features: Physiognomy and Conventions of Heroine Description." *Victorian Studies* 24 (1981): 325–50.

Falk, Nancy. "To Gaze on the Sacred Traces." *History of Religions* 16 (1977): 281–93.

Feldherr, Andrew. *Spectacle and Society in Livy's* History. Berkeley: University of California Press, 1998.

Ferguson, Everett. "Progress in Perfection: Gregory of Nyssa's *Vita Moysis.*" *SP* 14 (1976): 307–14.

Ferguson, John. *Utopias of the Classical World.* Ithaca: Cornell University Press, 1975.

Festugière, André-Jean. *Antioche païenne et chrétienne: Libanius, Chrysostome, et les moines de Syrie.* Paris: Boccard, 1959.

———. "Lieux communs littéraires et thèmes de folk-lore dans l'hagiographie primitive." *Wiener Studien* 73 (1960): 123–52.

———. *Les moines d'orient.* 4 vols. Paris: Cerf, 1961–65.

Flusin, Bernard. *Miracle et histoire dans l'œuvre de Cyrille de Scythopolis.* Paris: Études Augustiniennes, 1983.

Fontanier, J.-M. "Sur une image hiéronymienne: Le visage sidéral de Jésus." *Revue des sciences philosophiques et théologiques* 75 (1991): 251–56.

Fraigneau-Julien, B. *Les sens spirituels et la vision de Dieu selon Syméon le Nouveau Théologien.* Paris: Beauchesne, 1985.

Frank, [K.] Suso. *ΑΓΓΕΛΙΚΟΣ ΒΙΟΣ: Begriffsanalytische und begriffsgeschichtliche Untersuchung zum "engelgleichen Leben" im frühen Mönchtum.* Beiträge zur Geschichte des alten Mönchtums und des Benediktinerordens 26. Munster: Aschendorff, 1964.

Frankfurter, David. *Religion in Roman Egypt: Assimilation and Resistance.* Princeton: Princeton University Press, 1998.

Freedberg, David. *The Power of Images: Studies in the History and Theory of Response*. Chicago: University of Chicago Press, 1989.

Fuhrmann, Manfred. "Die Mönchgeschichten des Hieronymus: Formexperimente in erzählender Literatur." In *Christianisme et formes littéraires de l'antiquité tardive en Occident*, edited by Manfred Fuhrmann, 41–100. Entretiens Fondation Hardt, 23. Geneva: Vandoeuvres, 1977.

Fürst, J. "Untersuchungen zur Ephemeris des Diktys von Kreta." *Philologus* 61 (1902): 377–440, 593–622.

Gabba, Emilio. "True History and False History in Classical Antiquity." *JRS* 71 (1981): 50–62.

Gerhart, Mary. "Generic Studies: Their Renewed Importance in Religious and Literary Interpretation." *JAAR* 45 (1977): 309–25.

Gero, Stephen. "Hypatius of Ephesus on the Cult of Images." In *Christianity, Judaism and Other Greco-Roman Cults: Studies for Morton Smith at Sixty*, edited by Jacob Neusner, 2:208–16. Brill: Leiden, 1975.

Gleason, Maud. "The Semiotics of Gender: Physiognomy and Self-Fashioning in the Second Century C.E." In *Before Sexuality*, edited by David Halperin, John Winkler, and Froma Zeitlin, 389–415. Princeton: Princeton University Press, 1990.

———. *Making Men: Sophists and Self-Presentation in Ancient Rome*. Princeton: Princeton University Press, 1995.

Goehring, James E. "New Frontiers in Pachomian Studies." In *The Roots of Egyptian Christianity*, edited by James E. Goehring and Birger Pearson, 236–57. Studies in Antiquity and Christianity. Philadelphia: Fortress, 1986.

———. "The World Engaged: The Social and Economic World of Early Egyptian Monasticism." In *Studies in Antiquity and Christianity: Essays in Honor of James M. Robinson*, edited by Jack Sanders, James E. Goehring, and Charles Hedrick. Sonoma: Polebridge, 1990.

———. "The Origins of Monasticism." In *Eusebius, Christianity, and Judaism*, edited by Harold W. Attridge and Gohei Hata, 235–55. Leiden: Brill, 1992.

———. "The Encroaching Desert: Literary Production and Ascetic Space in Christian Egypt." *JECS* 1 (1993): 281–96.

———. "Withdrawing from the Desert: Pachomius and the Development of Village Monasticism in Upper Egypt." *HTR* 89 (1996): 267–85.

———. *Ascetics, Society, and the Desert: Studies in Early Egyptian Monasticism.* Harrisburg, Penna.: Trinity Press International, 1999. (Includes reprinted essays listed above.)

Gorce, Denys. "Die Gastfreundlichkeit des altchristichen Einsiedler und Mönche." *Jahrbuch für Antike und Christentum* 15 (1972): 66–91.

Gould, Graham. "A Note on the *Apophthegmata Patrum.*" *JTS* n.s. 37 (1986): 133–38.

———. *The Desert Fathers on Monastic Community.* Oxford: Clarendon, 1993.

Grabar, André. *Martyrium: Recherches sur le culte des reliques et l'art chrétien antique.* 2 vols. Paris, 1946. Repr. London: Variorum, 1972.

Grant, Robert M. "The Description of Paul in the *Acts of Paul and Thecla.*" *VC* 36 (1982): 1–4.

Griffith, Sidney. "Julian Saba, 'Father of the Monks' of Syria." *JECS* 2 (1994): 185–216.

Guillaumont, Antoine. "Le dépaysement comme forme d'ascèse dans le monachisme ancien." *École Pratique des Hautes Études, Ve section: Sciences religieuses, Annuaire* 76 (1968): 31–58. Repr in id., *Aux origines du monachisme chrétien,* 89–116.

———. "La conception du désert chez les moines d'Égypte." In id., *Revue de l'histoire des religions* 188 (1975): 3–21. Repr. in id., *Aux origines du monachisme chrétien,* 67–88.

———. *Aux origines du monachisme chrétien: Pour une phénomenologie du monachisme.* Spiritualité orientale, 30. Bégrolles-en-Mauges: Abbaye de Bellefontaine, 1979.

Guy, Jean-Claude. "Remarques sur le texte des *Apophthegmata Patrum.*" *RSR* 43 (1955): 252–58.

Hägg, Tomas. *The Novel in Antiquity.* Berkeley: University of California Press, 1983.

Hahm, David E. "Early Hellenistic Theories of Vision and the Perception of Color." In *Studies in Perception: Interrelations in the History of Philosophy and Science,* edited by Peter K. Machamer and Robert G. Turnbull, 60–95. Columbus: Ohio State University Press, 1978.

Hahn, Cynthia. "Seeing and Believing: The Construction of Sanctity in Early-Medieval Saints' Shrines." *Speculum* 72 (1997): 1079–1106.

Harpham, Geoffrey Galt. *The Ascetic Imperative in Culture and Criticism.* Chicago: University of Chicago Press, 1987.

Hartog, François. *The Mirror of Herodotus: The Representation of the Other in the Writing of History*, translated by Janet Lloyd. Berkeley: University of California Press, 1988.

———. *Mémoire d'Ulysse: Récits sur la frontière en Grèce ancienne.* Paris: Gallimard, 1996.

Harvey, Susan Ashbrook. "The Sense of a Stylite: Perspectives on Simeon the Elder." *VC* 42 (1988): 376–94.

———. *Asceticism and Society in Crisis: John of Ephesus and the* Lives of the Eastern Saints. Berkeley: University of California Press, 1990.

———. "Women in Early Byzantine Hagiography: Reversing the Story." In *"That Gentle Strength": Historical Perspectives on Women in Christianity*, edited by Lynda L. Coon, Katherine J. Haldane, and Elisabeth W. Sommer, 36–59. Charlottesville: University Press of Virginia, 1990.

———. "St. Ephrem on the Scent of Salvation." *JTS* n.s. 49 (1998): 109–28.

Hausherr, I. *Les leçons d'un contemplatif: Le traité de l'oraison d'Évagre le Pontique.* Paris: Beauchesne, 1960.

Hellemo, Geir. *Adventus Domini: Eschatological Thought in Fourth-Century Apses and Catecheses.* Leiden: Brill, 1989.

Helms, Mary W. *Ulysses' Sail: An Ethnographic Odyssey of Power, Knowledge, and Geographical Distance.* Princeton: Princeton University Press, 1988.

Higgins, Iain Macleod. *Writing East: The "Travels" of Sir John Mandeville.* Philadelphia: University of Pennsylvania Press, 1997.

Himmelfarb, Martha. *Tours of Hell: An Apocalyptic Form in Jewish and Christian Literature.* Philadelphia: Fortress Press, 1983.

———. *Ascent to Heaven in Jewish and Christian Apocalypses.* New York: Oxford University Press, 1993.

Hirschfeld, Yizhar. *The Judean Desert Monasteries in the Byzantine Period.* New Haven: Yale University Press, 1992.

Holford-Strevens, Leofranc. "Aulus Gellius: The Non-visual Portraitist." In *Portraits: Biographical Representation in the Greek and Latin Literature of the Roman Empire*, edited by M. J. Edwards and Simon Swain, 93–116. Oxford: Clarendon, 1997.

Holum, Kenneth G., and Gary Vikan. "The Trier Ivory, *Adventus* Ceremonial, and the Relics of St. Stephen." *DOP* 33 (1979): 115–33.

Howes, David, ed. *The Varieties of Sensory Experience: A Sourcebook in the Anthropology of the Senses.* Toronto: University of Toronto Press, 1991.

Howes, David, and Constance Classen. "Sounding Sensory Profiles." In *The Varieties of Sensory Experience: A Sourcebook in the Anthropology of the Senses*, edited by David Howes. Toronto: University of Toronto Press, 1991.

Hunt, E. D. *Holy Land Pilgrimage in the Later Roman Empire (A.D. 312–460)*. Oxford: Clarendon, 1982.

———. "Travel, Tourism, and Piety in the Roman Empire: A Context for the Beginnings of Christian Pilgrimage." *Échos du monde classique* 28 (1984): 391–417.

Immerwahr, Henry R. " 'Ergon': History as a Monument in Herodotus and Thucydides." *American Journal of Philology* 81 (1960): 261–90.

Jaeger, Mary. *Livy's Written Rome*. Ann Arbor: University of Michigan Press, 1997.

James, Liz, and Ruth Webb. "'To Understand Ultimate Things and Enter Secret Places': Ekphrasis and Art in Byzantium." *Art History* 14 (1991): 1–17.

Kazhdan, Alexander, and Henry Maguire. "Byzantine Hagiographical Texts as Sources on Art." *DOP* 45 (1991): 1–22.

Kech, Herbert. *Hagiographie als christliche Unterhaltungsliteratur: Studien zum Phänomen des erbaulichen Anhand der Mönchsviten des hl. Hieronymus*. Göppinger Arbeiten zur Germanistik 225. Göppingen: Alfred Kümmerle, 1977.

Kelly, J. N. D. *Jerome: His Life, Writings, and Controversies*. New York: Harper and Row, 1975.

Kennedy, George A. "Historical Survey of Rhetoric." In *Handbook of Classical Rhetoric in the Hellenistic Period, 330 B.C.–A.D. 400*, edited by Stanley E. Porter, 3–41. Leiden: Brill, 1997.

Kitzinger, Ernst. "The Cult of Images before Iconoclasm." *DOP* 8 (1954): 83–150.

Kötting, Bernhard. *Peregrinatio Religiosa: Wallfahrten in der Antike und das Pilgerwesen in der alten Kirche*. Regensburg: Westphalia, 1950.

———. "Wallfahrten zu lebenden Personen im Altertum." In *Wallfahrt kennt keine Grenzen*, ed. L. Kriss-Rettenbeck and G. Mohler, 226–34. Munich/Zurich: Schell & Steiner, 1984.

———. "Gregory von Nyssas Wallfahrtskritik." *SP* 5 = TU 80 (1962): 360–67. Reprinted in Bernhard Kötting, *Ecclesia peregrinans: Das Gottesvolk unterwegs (Gesammelte Aufsätze)*. 2 vols. Münsterische Beiträge zur Theologie 54/2. Munster: Aschendorff, 1988.

Krueger, Derek. "Typological Figuration in Theodoret of Cyrrhus's *Religious History* and the Art of Postbiblical Narrative." *JECS* 5 (1997): 393–419.

Kühnel, Bianca. *From the Earthly to the Heavenly Jerusalem: Representations of the Holy City in Christian Art of the First Millennium.* Römische Quartalschrift für christliche Altertumskunde und Kirchengeschichte Supp. 42. Rome: Herder, 1987.

Lane Fox, Robin. *Pagans and Christians.* New York: Knopf, 1987.

Lattimore, Richmond. *Themes in Greek and Latin Epitaphs.* Urbana: University of Illinois Press, 1962.

LeGoff, Jacques. "The Medieval West and the Indian Ocean: An Oneiric Horizon." In *Time, Work, and Culture in the Middle Ages,* trans. Arthur Goldhammer, 189–200. Chicago: University of Chicago Press, 1980.

Leyerle, Blake. "John Chrysostom on the Gaze." *JECS* 1 (1993): 159–74.

———. "Landscape as Cartography in Early Christian Pilgrimage Narratives." *JAAR* 64 (1996): 119–43.

Limberis, Vasiliki. "The Eyes Infected by Evil: Basil of Caesarea's Homily *On Envy.*" *HTR* 84 (1991): 163–84.

Lindberg, David C. *Theories of Vision from al-Kindi to Kepler.* Chicago: University of Chicago Press, 1976.

L'Orange, H. P. *Apotheosis in Ancient Portraiture.* Instituttet for Sammenlingnende Kulturforskning. Oslo: H. Aschehour, 1947. Cambridge: Harvard University Press, 1947.

Loraux, Nicole. *The Experiences of Tiresias: The Feminine and the Greek Man,* translated by Paula Wissing. Princeton: Princeton University Press, 1995.

MacCannell, Dean. *The Tourist: A New Theory of the Leisure Class.* New York: Schocken, 1976.

MacCormack, Sabine G. *Art and Ceremony in Late Antiquity.* Berkeley: University of California Press, 1981.

MacDermot, Violet. *The Cult of the Seer in the Ancient Middle East.* Berkeley: University of California Press, 1971.

MacMullen, Ramsay. "The Preacher's Audience (A.D. 350–400.)" *JTS* n.s. 40 (1989): 503–11.

Magli, Patrizia. "The Face and the Soul." In *Fragments for a History of the Human Body,* edited by Michel Feher et al., 3:87–127. 3 vols. New York: Zone, 1989.

Maguire, Eunice Dauterman, Henry P. Maguire, et al. *Art and Holy Powers in the Early Christian House.* Illinois Byzantine Studies 2. Urbana: University of Illinois Press, 1989.

Maguire, Henry. "The Art of Comparing in Byzantium." *Art Bulletin* 70 (1988): 88–103.

———. "Garments Pleasing to God: The Significance of Domestic Textile Designs in the Early Byzantine Period." *DOP* 44 (1990): 215–24.

———, ed. *Byzantine Magic.* Cambridge: Harvard University Press, 1995.

Makoweicka, Elzbieta. "Monastic Pilgrimage Centre at Kellia in Egypt." In *JAC Suppl.* 20. 2:1002–15.

Malamut, Élisabeth. *Sur la route des saints byzantins.* Paris: CNRS Editions, 1993.

Malherbe, Abraham. "A Physical Description of Paul." *HTR* 79 (1986): 170–75.

Maloney, Clarence, ed. *The Evil Eye.* New York: Columbia University Press, 1976.

Mango, Cyril, ed. *The Art of the Byzantine Empire, 312–1453.* Sources and Documents in the History of Art. Englewood Cliffs, N.J.: Prentice-Hall, 1972.

Maraval, Pierre. "Fonction pédagogique de la littérature hagiographique d'un lieu de pèlerinage: L'exemple des *Miracles de Cyr et Jean*." In *Hagiographie, culture, et sociétés (IVe–IX e siècle)*, 383–97. Paris: Études Augustiniennes, 1981.

———. "Le temps du pèlerin (IVe–VIIe siècles)." In *Le temps chrétien de la fin de l'antiquité au Moyen Age (IIIe–XIIIe siècles)*, edited by Jean-Marie Leroux, 479–85. Paris: CNRS, 1984.

———. "La Bible des pèlerins d'Orient." In *Le monde grec ancien et la Bible*, edited by Claude Mondésert, 387–97. Paris: Beauchesne, 1984. Revised and translated version appears as "The Bible as a Guide for Early Christian Pilgrims to the Holy Land," in *The Bible in Greek Christian Antiquity*, edited and translated by Paul M. Blowers, 375–88. Notre Dame: University of Notre Dame Press, 1997.

———. *Lieux saints et pèlerinages d'Orient: Histoire et géographie des origines à la conquête arabe.* Paris: Cerf, 1985.

———. "Égérie et Grégoire de Nysse: Pèlerins aux lieux saints de Palestine." In *Atti del convegno internazionale sulla* Peregrinatio Egeriae, 315–31. Arezzo: Accademia Petrarca di lettere arti e scienze, 1987.

———. "La lettre 3 de Grégoire de Nysse dans le débat christologique." *Revue des sciences religieuses* 61 (1987): 74–89.

————. "Saint Jérôme et le pèlerinage aux lieux saints de Palestine." In *Jérôme entre l'Occident et l'Orient (Actes du colloque de Chantilly, 1986)*, edited by Yves-Marie Duval, 345–53. Paris: Études Augustiniennes, 1988.

————. "L'attitude des Pères du IVe siècle devant les lieux saints et les pèlerinages." *Irénikon* 65 (1992): 5–23.

————. "Les itinéraires de pèlerinage en Orient (entre le 4e et le 7e S.)." In *JAC* Suppl. 20. 1:291–300.

————. "The Bible as a Guide for Early Christian Pilgrims to the Holy Land." In *The Bible in Greek Christian Antiquity*, edited and translated by Paul M. Blowers, 375–88. Notre Dame: University of Notre Dame Press, 1997.

Marincola, John. *Authority and Tradition in Ancient Historiography*. Cambridge: Cambridge University Press, 1997.

Markus, Robert A. *The End of Ancient Christianity*. Cambridge: Cambridge University Press, 1990.

————. "How on Earth Could Places Become Holy? Origins of the Christian Idea of Holy Places." *JECS* 2 (1994): 257–71.

Matthews, Christopher R. "Nicephorus Callistus' Physical Description of Peter: An Original Component of the *Acts of Peter?*" *Apocrypha* 7 (1996): 135–45.

McGinn, Bernard. *The Presence of God: A History of Western Christian Mysticism*, vol. 1, *The Foundations of Mysticism: Origins to the Fifth Century*. 4 vols. New York: Crossroad, 1991.

————. *Anti-Christ: Two Thousand Years of the Human Fascination with Evil*. San Francisco: HarperSanFrancisco, 1994.

Metcalf, Barbara D. "The Pilgrimage Remembered: South Asian Accounts of the *Hajj*. " In *Muslim Travelers: Pilgrimage, Migration, and the Religious Imagination*, edited by Dale F. Eickelman and James Piscatori, 85–107. Berkeley: University of California Press, 1990.

Miles, Gary B. *Livy: Reconstructing Early Rome*. Ithaca: Cornell University Press, 1995.

Miles, Margaret R. "Vision: The Eye of the Body and the Eye of the Mind in Saint Augustine's *De trinitate* and *Confessions*." *Journal of Religion* 63 (1983): 125–42.

————. *Image as Insight: Visual Understanding in Western Christianity and Secular Culture*. Boston: Beacon, 1985.

―――. *Practicing Christianity: Critical Perspectives for an Embodied Spirituality.* New York: Crossroad, 1988.

(Miller), Patricia Cox. *Biography in Late Antiquity: A Quest for the Holy Man.* Berkeley: University of California Press, 1983.

Miller, Patricia Cox. "Desert Asceticism and 'The Body from Nowhere' " *JECS* 2 (1994): 137–53.

―――. "Jerome's Centaur: A Hyper-icon of the Desert." *JECS* 4 (1996): 209–33.

―――. " 'Differential Networks': Relics and Other Fragments in Late Antiquity." *JECS* 6 (1998): 113–38.

Misener, Geneva. "Iconistic Portraits." *Classical Philology* 19 (1924): 97–123.

Mohrmann, Christine. "Égérie et le monachisme." In *Corona Gratiarum: Miscellanea Patristica Historica et Liturgica Eligio Dekkers O.S.B. XII Lustra Complenti Oblata.* 1:163–80. Bruges: Nijhoff, 1975.

Morinis, Alan, ed. *Sacred Journeys: The Anthropology of Pilgrimage.* Westport, Conn.: Greenwood, 1992.

Morse, Ruth. *Truth and Convention in the Middle Ages: Rhetoric, Representation, and Reality.* Cambridge: Cambridge University Press, 1991.

Natalucci, Nicoletta. "Egeria ed il monachesimo femminile." *Benedictina* 35 (1988): 37–52.

Ousterhout, Robert, ed. *The Blessings of Pilgrimage.* Illinois Byzantine Studies 1. Urbana: University of Illinois Press, 1990.

Patlagean, Evelyne. "À Byzance: Ancienne hagiographie et histoire sociale." *Annales: e.s.c.* 23 (1968): 106–26. Translated as "Ancient Byzantine Hagiography and Social History" in *Saints and their Cults: Studies in Religious Sociology, Folklore and History,* edited by Stephen Wilson, 101–21. Cambridge: Cambridge University Press, 1983.

Patrich, Joseph. *Sabas, Leader of Palestinian Monasticism.* Washington, D.C.: Dumbarton Oaks, 1995.

Pearson, Birger A., and James E. Goehring, eds. *The Roots of Egyptian Christianity.* Philadelphia: Fortress, 1986.

Pervo, Richard. *Profit with Delight: The Literary Genre of the Acts of the Apostles.* Philadelphia: Fortress, 1987.

Pietrella, E. "I pellegrinaggi ai Luoghi Santi e il culto dei martiri in Gregorio di Nissa." *Augustinianum* 21 (1981): 135–51.

Piovanelli, Pierluigi. "Les origines de *L'apocalypse de Paul* reconsidérées." *Apocrypha* 4 (1993): 25–64.

Pratt, Mary Louise. *Imperial Eyes: Travel Writing and Transculturation*. New York: Routledge, 1992.

Rahner, K. "Le début d'une doctrine des cinq sens spirituels chez Origène." *Revue d'ascétique et de mystique* 13 (1932): 113–45.

Rapp, Claudia. "Storytelling as Spiritual Communication in Early Greek Hagiography: The Use of *Diegesis*." *JECS* 6 (1998): 431–48.

Regnault, Lucien. *Les pères du désert à travers leurs apophtegmes*. Sablé-sur-Sarthe, Solesmes, 1987.

———. *La vie quotidienne des pères du désert en Égypte au IVe siècle*. Paris: Hachette, 1990.

Roldanus, J. *Le Christ et l'homme dans la théologie d'Athanase*. Leiden: Brill, 1968.

Romm, James S. *The Edges of the Earth in Ancient Thought: Geography, Exploration, and Fiction*. Princeton: Princeton University Press, 1992.

———. "Novels beyond Thule: Antonius Diogenes, Rabelais, Cervantes." In *The Search for the Ancient Novel*, edited by James Tatum, 101–16. Baltimore: Johns Hopkins University Press, 1994.

Roncoroni, Angelo. "Sul De passione Domini Pseudolattanziano." *VC* 29 (1975): 208–21.

Rorem, Paul. "The Uplifting Spirituality of Pseudo-Dionysius." In *Christian Spirituality*, vol. 1, *Origins to the Twelfth Century*, edited by Bernard McGinn and John Meyendorff, 1132–51. New York: Crossroad, 1989.

———. *Pseudo-Dionysius: A Commentary on the Texts and an Introduction to Their Influence*. New York: Oxford University Press, 1993.

Rousseau, Philip. *Ascetics, Authority, and the Church in the Age of Jerome and Cassian*. Oxford: Oxford University Press, 1978.

———. *Pachomius: The Making of a Community in Fourth-Century Egypt*. Berkeley: University of California Press, 1985.

Rubenson, Samuel. *The Letters of St. Antony: Origenist Theology, Monastic Tradition, and the Making of a Saint*. Bibliotheca Historico-Ecclesiastica Lundensis 24. Lund, Sweden: Lund University Press, 1990.

Ruppert, Peter. *Reader in a Strange Land: The Activity of Reading Literary Utopias*. Athens: University of Georgia Press, 1986.

Said, Edward. *Orientalism*. New York: Pantheon, 1978.

Satran, David. *Biblical Prophets in Byzantine Palestine: Reassessing the* Lives of the Prophets. Leiden: Brill, 1995.

Saulnier, Christine. "La vie monastique en Terre Sainte auprès des Lieux de Pèlerinages (IVe s.)." *Miscellanea Historiae Ecclesiasticae* 6, section 1: *Les transformations dans la société chrétienne au IVe siècle*, 223–48. Bibliothèque de la revue d'histoire ecclésiastique 67. Brussels, 1983.

Schulz-Flügel, Eva. "The Function of the *Apophthegmata* in *Vitae* and *Itineraria.*" In *SP* 18, *Papers of the 1983 Oxford Patristics Conference*, edited by Elizabeth A. Livingstone, 2:281–91. Kalamazoo: Cistercian, 1989.

Shaw, Teresa M. "*Askesis* and the Appearance of Holiness." *JECS* 6 (1998): 485–99.

Shortland, Michael. "The Power of a Thousand Eyes: Johann Caspar Lavater's Science of Physiognomical Perception." *Criticism* 28 (1986): 379–408.

Silverstein, Theodore. *Visio Sancti Pauli*. Studies and Documents 4. London: Christophers, 1935.

Simon, Gérard. *Le regard, l'être, et l'apparence dans l'optique de l'antiquité*. Paris: Seuil, 1988.

Sivan, Hagith. "Who Was Egeria? Piety and Pilgrimage in the Age of Gratian." *HTR* 81 (1988): 59–72.

———. "Pilgrimage, Monasticism, and the Emergence of Christian Palestine in the Fourth Century." In *The Blessings of Pilgrimage*, edited by Robert Ousterhout, 54–65. Urbana: University of Illinois Press, 1990.

Slater, Candace. *Trail of Miracles: Stories from a Pilgrimage in Northeast Brazil*. Berkeley: University of California Press, 1986.

Smelik, K. A. D., and E. A. Hemelrijk. " 'Who Knows Not What Monsters Demented Egypt Worships?': Opinions on Egyptian Animal Worship in Antiquity as Part of the Conception of Egypt." In *Aufstieg und Niedergang der römischen Welt*, edited by H. Temporini and W. Haase, ser. 2, vol. 17, part 4, 1853–2337. Berlin: DeGruyter, 1984.

Smith, Jonathan Z. *To Take Place: Toward Theory in Ritual*. Chicago: University of Chicago Press, 1987.

Stafford, Barbara M. *Body Criticism: Imaging the Unseen in Enlightenment Art and Medicine*. Cambridge: MIT Press, 1991.

Stanbury, Sarah. *Seeing the* Gawain-*Poet: Description and the Act of Perception*. Philadelphia: University of Pennsylvania Press, 1991.

Stancliffe, Clare. *St. Martin and His Hagiographer.* Oxford: Clarendon, 1983.

Starowieyski, M. "Bibliographia Egeriana." *Augustinianum* 19 (1977): 297–318.

Stewart, Columba. *Cassian the Monk.* New York: Oxford University Press, 1998.

Stratton, George Malcolm. *Theophrastus and the Greek Physiological Psychology before Aristotle.* London: George Allen & Unwin, 1917.

Synnott, Anthony. "Puzzling over the Senses: From Plato to Marx." In *The Varieties of Sensory Experience: A Sourcebook in the Anthropology of the Senses,* edited by David Howes. Toronto: University of Toronto Press, 1991.

Tatum, James, ed. *The Search for the Ancient Novel.* Baltimore: Johns Hopkins University Press, 1994.

Théologie de la vie monastique: Études sur la tradition patristique. Théologie 49. Aubier: Montaigne, 1961.

Thümmel, Hans Georg. *Die Frühgeschichte der ostkirchlichen Bilderlehre: Texte und Untersuchungen zur Zeit vor dem Bilderstreit.* TU 139. Berlin: Akademie Verlag, 1992.

Trapp, M. B. "Plato's *Phaedrus* in Second-Century Greek Literature." In *Antonine Literature,* edited by D. A. Russell, 141–73. Oxford: Clarendon, 1990.

Turner, Victor, and Edith Turner. *Image and Pilgrimage in Christian Culture.* New York: Columbia University Press, 1978.

Valantasis, Richard. "A Theory of the Social Function of Asceticism." In *Asceticism,* edited by Richard Valantasis and Vincent Wimbush, 544–52. New York: Oxford University Press, 1995.

Van Uytfanghe, Marc. "L'empreinte biblique sur la plus ancienne hagiographie occidentale." In *Le monde latin antique et la Bible,* edited by Jacques Fontaine and Charles Pietri, 565–611. Paris: Beauchesne, 1985.

———. *Stylisation biblique et condition humaine dans l'hagiographie mérovingienne (600–750).* Brussels: Koninklijke academie voor Wetenschappen, Letteren en schone Kunsten van België, 1987.

Vasaly, Ann. *Representations: Images of the World in Ciceronian Oratory.* Berkeley: University of California Press, 1993.

Vermeer, G. F. M., *Observations sur le vocabulaire du pèlerinage chez Égérie et chez Antonin de Plaisance.* Latinitas Christianorum primaeva, 19. Nimègue, 1965.

Vernant, Jean-Pierre. *Mortals and Immortals: Collected Essays,* edited by Froma I. Zeitlin. Princeton University Press, 1991.

Vikan, Gary. *Byzantine Pilgrimage Art.* Washington, D.C.: Dumbarton Oaks, 1982.

———. "Art, Medicine, and Magic in Early Byzantium." *DOP* 38 (1984): 65–86.

———. "Pilgrims in Magi's Clothing: The Impact of Mimesis on Early Byzantine Pilgrimage Art." In *The Blessings of Pilgrimage,* edited by Robert Ousterhout, 97–107. Urbana: University of Illinois Press, 1990.

Walker, P. W. L. *Holy City, Holy Places? Christian Attitudes to Jerusalem and the Holy Land in the Fourth Century.* Oxford: Clarendon, 1990.

Walters, C. C. *Monastic Archaeology in Egypt.* Warminster: Aris & Phillips, 1974.

Ward, Benedicta, "Introduction." In *The Lives of the Desert Fathers: The Historia Monachorum in Aegypto,* translated by Norman Russell. CS 34. Kalamazoo: Cistercian, 1980.

———. "Signs and Wonders: Miracles in the Desert Tradition." *SP* 18, 539–42. Oxford and New York: Pergamon Press, 1982. Repr. in Benedicta Ward, *Signs and Wonders: Saints, Miracles, and Prayers from the Fourth Century to the Fourteenth.* Hampshire: Variorum, 1992.

Weitzmann, Kurt. "*Loca Sancta* and the Representational Arts of Palestine." *DOP* 28 (1974): 31–55.

Wilken, Robert L. *The Land Called Holy: Palestine in Christian History and Thought.* New Haven: Yale University Press, 1992.

Wilkinson, John. "L'apport de Saint Jérôme à la topographie." *Revue biblique* 81 (1974): 245–57.

———, ed. *Jerusalem Pilgrims before the Crusades.* Warminster: Aris & Phillips, 1977.

Winkler, John. "Lollianos and the Desperadoes." *Journal of Hellenic Studies* 100 (1981): 155–81.

———. *Auctor & Actor: A Narratological Reading of Apuleius's* Golden Ass. Berkeley: University of California Press, 1985.

Wipszycka, Ewa. "Aspects économiques de la vie aux Kellia." In *Le site monastique des Kellia: Sources historiques et explorations archéologiques.* Geneva: Mission suisse d'archéologie copte, 1986, 117–44. Reprinted in Ewa Wipszycka, *Études sur le christianisme dans l'Egypte de l'Antiquité.* Studia Ephemeridis Augustinianum vol. 52, 332–62. Rome: Institutum Patristicum Augustinianum, 1996.

Young, Frances M. *From Nicaea to Chalcedon: A Guide to the Literature and Its Background.* Philadelphia: Fortress, 1983.

Zanker, G. "*Enargeia* in the Ancient Criticism of Poetry." *Rheinisches Museum für Philologie* 124 (1981): 297–311.

Zanker, Paul. *The Mask of Socrates: The Image of the Intellectual in Antiquity.* Berkeley: University of California Press, 1995.

Zelle, Carsten. "Soul Semiology: On Lavater's Physiognomic Principles." In *The Faces of Physiognomy: Interdisciplinary Approaches to Johann Caspar Lavater,* edited by Ellis Shookman. Columbia, S.C.: Camden, 1993.

INDEX

Text: 10/15 Janson
Display: Janson
Composition: Impressions Book & Journal Services, Inc.
Printing and binding: Haddon Craftsmen
Index: Barbara Cohen